HEARTS IN TRANSCENDENCE

HUMAN CONSCIOUSNESS LIBERATED

A LEXANDER D E F OE

authorHOUSE®

AuthorHouse™
1663 Liberty Drive
Bloomington, IN 47403
www.authorhouse.com
Phone: 1-800-839-8640

This book is a work of non-fiction. Unless otherwise noted, the author and the publisher make no explicit guarantees as to the accuracy of the information contained in this book and in some cases, names of people and places have been altered to protect their privacy.

Published by AuthorHouse 01/14/2015

ISBN: 978-1-4969-6008-5 (sc)
ISBN: 978-1-4969-5991-1 (e)

Library of Congress Control Number: 2014922503

Any people depicted in stock imagery provided by Thinkstock are models, and such images are being used for illustrative purposes only.
Certain stock imagery © Thinkstock.

This book is printed on acid-free paper.

Because of the dynamic nature of the Internet, any web addresses or links contained in this book may have changed since publication and may no longer be valid. The views expressed in this work are solely those of the author and do not necessarily reflect the views of the publisher, and the publisher hereby disclaims any responsibility for them.

"Sitting down with 'Hearts in Transcendence' is like engaging in a fireside chat with a kind, loving friend, delving into deeper self and our most intimate existential queries and angst. I especially appreciate Alexander's warm, welcoming tone that encourages the tight and broken parts within to let go in the compassionate recognition of the trials of human suffering."

– Jana Dixon, author of 'Biology of Kundalini' and 'Inner Arts 1 – Practicum'

"'Hearts in Transcendence' is a truly inspiring look at higher states of consciousness and their practical benefits ... It is filled with practical exercises about how to open our mind and heart to experience what it means to be truly alive and human. Highly recommended!"

– Dean Shrock, Ph.D., author of 'Doctor's Orders: Go Fishing' and 'Why Love Heals'

"I thoroughly enjoyed 'Hearts in Transcendence.' Alexander has created a superbly well-written book on transcendental consciousness states. I highly suggest this book to anyone who seeks to uncover their highest potential and experience self-transcendence."

– Steve G. Jones, Ed.D., Clinical Hypnotherapist

TABLE OF CONTENTS

Acknowledgments ix

Premise xi

Introduction: Capturing Moments of Transcendence 1

Chapter 1: The Mind Illusion...13
  Rise of a Thinking Culture..23
  The Heart's Promise 26
  Lesser Magic 33
  Eavesdrop on Life's Secrets 39

Chapter 2: Sublimated Consciousness......................................47
  Detox from the Mind Illusion 50
  Between Realities 57
  Escape From Plato's Cave..66
  Raise Anima's Creative Fire 77

Chapter 3: The Reimagined Self...85
  Language and Power 87
  Building Selves 103
  This Meaningless World 110

Chapter 4: Reclaiming Disavowed Emotions..........................115
  Lost Parts of Ourselves...122
  Embrace Raw Emotion...130
  Congruence 137
  Reignite the Flame 141

Chapter 5: Transformational Mind States............................149
  Cultivation of Inner Power 153
  Peak Meditation Experiences......................................162
  Conscious and Unconscious Union 175

Chapter 6: Relational Depth 185
  Deeper Connections..189
  Creative Potential 198
  Construct-Free Consciousness....................................207
  New Realities..210

Chapter 7: Ultimate Freedom 219
    Motionless Shape 225
    The Final Revolution 237
    Living Outside of Ourselves 247

Chapter 8: Our Higher Mind Potential....................................259
    Subtle Minds: Metaphors 263
    Extended Mind Capabilities 273
    Transcendence 281

Appendices 289
    Appendix A: Double Standard Skepticism 291
    Appendix B: The Transpersonal Dream............................301
    Appendix C: Toolkit...305
    Appendix D: Notes...317

ACKNOWLEDGMENTS

This book is dedicated to those who have searched for a deeper purpose in life, having persisted to find meaningful answers in a world that often fails to ask the right questions.

I would like to thank my dearest mother for her encouragement when I was forming the earliest ideas for this book. I would also like to express my appreciation for my one and only, Izabel, for her support during the writing process. Much gratitude is also due to all those who took part in the discussions centered on the vast range of topics this book delves into. In particular, I am forever grateful to my close friends who stimulated numerous conversations and reflections on the nature of consciousness, transcendence, and human potential. These discussions inspired me to see this project through to completion.

PREMISE

Moments of expanded human consciousness have captivated the hearts and minds of philosophers throughout millennia. Despite how we might see the world through certain philosophies and scientific theories about the nature of consciousness, there is something alluring about the direct experience of self-consciousness. Experiences in which we transcend the personal self and connect with broader states of awareness are therefore well worth exploring. There comes a point in human experience in which the reliance on external theories, whether philosophical or scientific, becomes redundant. At such a point, the direct unfiltered experience of life is paramount – it is here that we endeavor to expand our consciousness threshold from a practical, approachable stance.

Before the Age of Reason, profound states of self-transcendence were associated with religious experiences of divination. In modern times, such states tend to be studied within psychological science. Yet, aside from examining the theories and models behind consciousness, it's critical that we learn to make sense of transcendence as it pertains to us in a direct fashion. In this book, I endeavor to take a refreshing approach to consciousness, a hands-on perspective, if you will. I introduce several explorations and self-awareness techniques that encourage readers to arrive at new practical understandings in their own lives.

Philosophical frameworks, no matter how well thought out and articulate, can also serve as barriers to direct conscious experience, leading us into an intellectualization of consciousness. For example, the attainment of higher states in theological accounts tends to be considered in terms of particular rituals, lessons, and dogmas, rather than through direct spiritual experience. This divide between doctrine and experience can be noted in most religions, and more often than not, this divide separates us from the heart of spiritual experience.

Threads of distinction between higher and lower (or broad and narrow) experiences of consciousness run through most religious and ontological theories. In all religions, we can look to a central doctrine, and then we can also discover the direct experience of spiritual transcendence from which that doctrine was born. In science, like religion, we also have definitions of consciousness: Altered and baseline, normal and abnormal, healthy and pathological, and so forth. These definitions, again, refer to a mere theoretical understanding. For each definition, there is also a corresponding firsthand experience.

Such definitions have echoed through the epochs, and at the heart of each one remains the lingering question of self. How does human conscious experience translate into the procedural construction of an individual self, a distinct identity, a personality-level existence? Scientists and religious leaders alike have struggled with the question of self-consciousness through the ages, resorting to their respective devices – observation and faith. Yet, at the heart of it, human beings can encounter and experience a soul essence at the personal level, a consciousness that appears to be ever-present. There is a certain sacredness of experience here that is accessible to all, and this is well worth engaging with. All encounters with consciousness are, in a manner, encounters with transcendence, as our consciousness is never fixed nor stagnant. It is never definable to a singular instant, it is ever-flowing, ever-evolving. It is rather the intellectual mind that attempts to define consciousness to certain parameters or limits.

Once we recognize our conscious experience for what it is, the canvas of life itself takes on quite a different appearance. In fact, people who report self-transcendence experiences tend to talk about a drastic change in their worldview. A broader experience of self-consciousness comes about. Some refer to a newfound awareness, an Awareness (with a capital 'A'), as Igor Kufayev put it. This awareness is the recognition of the broader-self, the all-self.

Rather than consolidating theories of consciousness in this book, I would like to instead encourage you to reflect on your personal experience of self-consciousness. What is the nature of consciousness? In this book I'm not going to ask you about what a local religious leader tells you regarding this question, or the answer that a neuroscience professor might provide. Instead, I am going to ask you to take a more courageous approach: To look within your own heart for the answers. The personal experiences that led me to write this book were not grounded in religion nor science, but rather in practical observation on the nature of existence and self, and thus, I would like to encourage you to take a similar empirical approach here.

One day, after learning a basic meditation technique, I commenced a simple practice of sitting in a quiet place for a few minutes a day. I embraced the experience of just being. For a moment, I stopped interacting with my thoughts, my emotions, and even with my body. I focused instead on the essential experience of what it is to just be. After a time, I would notice that the darkness behind my closed eyelids would begin to expand, it expanded further and further outward, and in doing so, this darkness began to transform into a three-dimensional blackness that traversed the distance in all directions.

As my practice advanced, I began to perceive colors, images, and what I could best describe as short motion pictures, appear in my mind's eye. These visual impressions were not related to active thought, as I was not thinking about anything when these visions arose. Later, I discovered that these impressions corresponded to direct experiences with the unconscious and super-conscious mind. I found that when I quieted myself within, I could see more, I could connect with more conscious experience beneath the surface. I had a canvas of sorts for interacting with the conscious and unconscious mind – a bridge between worlds – and this, I found absolutely fascinating. These experiences convinced me, beyond a doubt, about how much hidden potential is awaiting to be discovered just below the surface of our constructed identities.

After a period of exploring the world of meditation and esoteric practices, it dawned on me that most people live their lives believing that their threshold of conscious experience is somehow immutable. Most wake each morning and find that the same sense of 'I' is always there (to borrow William James' notion of the continual stream of consciousness). In my practice, I discovered that the experience of 'I' is much more fluid than it is made out to be, and certain factors create the illusion of a fixed consciousness threshold. The true nature of the self, who you are, is much broader than the cognitive definitions and personality factors you may have come to accept about yourself over the years.

Meditation practices such as the technique I adopted can be best harnessed when we learn how to use the power of focus to direct our awareness – this unlocks the secrets that determine our self-experience. In meditation, we take our focus from our thoughts and then decide upon a new focus, and we can indeed choose from an entire spectrum of conscious, unconscious, and super-conscious potential to place our attention on. The problem here is that most novice meditators do not recognize the vastness of this potential at first. This grand spectrum features broad potentialities, worlds much vaster than our conceptions of them.

The following quote, which has been attributed to the Buddha, is useful in our discussion so far: "The thought manifests as the word; the word manifests as the deed; the deed develops into habit; and habit hardens into character." Consider what would happen if we reversed this quote for a moment. One's character begins to change when one's habits begin to change, and these habits change as a result of new behaviors that come about from a new focus that takes form. It all starts with focus, doesn't it? In following this, the grand consciousness spectrum can be experienced firsthand. Our connection to higher states of consciousness can be, in part, determined by how we decide to focus our awareness.

So, the premise I'd like to propose here is that consciousness has an intimate link with our self-experience in this world. There is little sense theorizing about consciousness, we must rather experience, expand, and understand ourselves on a deeper level in order to grasp our broader conscious potential. Shamans and esoteric philosophers have understood the importance of self-transcendence throughout the ages, and historical documents have alluded to countless encounters with higher states of consciousness in which a person transcends the boundaries of their constructed self (their intellectualized self-concept). Yet, in our modern culture, most of us unquestioningly accept our normal range of emotional and spiritual awareness as a baseline for self-experience. In doing so, we often forget that one of the intrinsic qualities of consciousness is to expand, transform, and discover new experiences. This runs counter to how we process the world on a cognitive level, instead clinging to the familiar, the safe, and the predictable: Experiences that promise repetition.

It is only in the last few decades that scholars have begun to consider human consciousness on a spectrum leading to self-realization and psycho-spiritual maturation. Researchers have now begun to discover that the expansion of our consciousness threshold corresponds with our personal development, quality of life, and spiritual connectedness. Rhea White, founder of the 'Exceptional Human Experience Network,' instigated a major change in attitudes toward the study of altered states. White suggested that a number of altered consciousness experiences are in fact exceptional human experiences (EHEs). She argued that EHEs have tremendous potential for spiritual growth and emotional maturity. I support this idea strongly, and I believe that it is important to recognize the potential of exceptional, or transcendental, states of human experience more broadly in our world. It's also crucial that we remember that altered states do not just come about due to neurological damage or errors in cognitive-perceptual processing. Rather, exceptional states of consciousness often arise when engaging with the human experience at a deeper level, and quite often show us a new means of engaging with life, and with ourselves, and with others.

Over time, insights and lessons learned from transcendent states can be integrated into our self-experience. A good example of this is that of near-death experiences (NDEs), which often involve a glimpse of self-transcendence. Bruce Greyson, Professor of Psychiatry and Neurobehavioral Sciences at the University of Virginia, found that NDEs which occur as a result of suicide can inhibit future suicidal tendencies, as these experiences have such an immensely powerful impact upon a person's self-concept. Some people who have NDEs find that their perspective about life and death transforms, as they experience their consciousness beyond the temporary death of the corporeal body.

Yet, such profound experiences are seldom cultivated, and in most cases people either believe these experiences to be delusions or spontaneous states of spiritual enlightenment. Few test the experience firsthand and attempt cultivating it in a methodical fashion. For example, most religions appear to have been born from of a mental conceptualization of real, tangible experience with higher consciousness. Yet, rather than cultivating these states and teaching their practical significance, most doctrines appear to enforce the idea that transcendence is impossible, other than with the aid of spiritual guru, master, priest, or other initiated person.

The cultivation of transcendental states is not just possible, but also practical. Take this example. A spiritual guru's experience of expanded consciousness might appear quite normalized indeed, if we consider that the guru has meditated for the previous two decades. On the other hand, from the vantage point of an outsider who has had perhaps just a handful of deep meditation experiences, this guru's normalized state of consciousness might appear quite extraordinary, powerful, and moving. From the outsider's perspective, it's much too tempting to adopt an attitude of praising the guru as an enlightened being, rather than asking the following question instead: How did the guru achieve this state, and how could I achieve a similar threshold of conscious experience?

The above example raises another question: Are transcendent experiences unique occurrences, or can we experience moments of transcendence in even the most mundane of situations? In this book, I suggest that we are responsible for furthering our conscious development, and there is no sense waiting for a special external experience, spiritual occurrence, or divine initiation. The potential to explore and expand our consciousness spectrum arises within. Thus, in this book I propose that it is important to become aware of, and remove, the inner obstacles to deeper conscious experience, rather than attempting to instigate transcendental states via external means. Once we remove the obstacles to Self-recognition (capitalized here to highlight the contrast between the ego-self and the higher self – the concept of the ultimate Self referred to in Hinduism), broader states of conscious experience become accessible and we no longer need to search for them.

You might recall a parent or mentor that you looked up to as a child who inspired you on your life journey, perhaps a teacher or a close friend who told you something along the lines of "you can achieve anything that you put your mind to." For most, words of inspiration and encouragement are rare sparks in an otherwise difficult reality, a reality riddled with insurmountable expectations and judgments from others. Many of us have stumbled through cobwebs of other people's beliefs, judgments, and expectations, consequently becoming misdirected and temporarily taken off course from pursuing our true life mission – disconnected from our souls. The constructed self that is driven by expectation and judgment is out-of-sync with the deeper experience of soul within, the True Self.

In that sense, it is important to return to the basic experiences of consciousness: Core happiness, raw emotional connections with others, and a deeper sense of inner freedom. Often the most basic and core experiences in life are the most powerful. These pursuits touch the conscious soul, rather than catering to the constructed self. Unfortunately, as we become adults, we move from a state of direct conscious experience into a state of intellectualized-consciousness. From our intellectualized framework of life, we never focus on the experience of life for the sake of living, experiencing and connecting with others, but we rather focus on worries, plans, fears, expectations and demands that take us out of peak states into a constricted fear-driven states. Those worries serve our limited existence in the material realm, rather than nourishing our ever-expansive soul.

Therefore, as part of this book's overall process, I will critique our commonly held beliefs about societal roles, gender stereotypes, work expectations, relationship dynamics, and daily routines that limit our conscious self-expression. In this manner, transcendental consciousness states have the role of helping us to transcend the confines of our outdated, self-limiting, and non-useful worldviews and behaviors. This involves removing the mask of the constructed self in order to expand one's consciousness to encompass broader experiences.

To provide an example of this process, let's consider the conditions most conducive to states of self-transcendence. Transcendence experiences most often occur in moments during which we forget about how we know ourselves in terms of the personality-self, and instead experience life in the totality of the present moment, without preconception. Not surprisingly, it is during moments such as these that we flourish in life. Consider, for instance, the first date of your very first relationship. Consider your first day of starting a new job or a new business. Each time we pursue something new, our creativity and excitement about life raises to a peak level. Events such as these give us a glimpse into the nature of transcendental consciousness states. During these experiences we leave behind, temporarily, the baggage of 'me,' and we capture a glimpse of what it feels like to be reborn. Such experiences liberate us from the mundane routines of our baseline mode of living, if even for a moment.

Transcendent experiences also lead us to question the nature of self. Who am I? What are the limitations and potentials of my conscious experience? To commence our quest, we must first begin to ask these big questions about human consciousness, the nature of self, and the nature of the soul. David Chalmers' hard problem of consciousness challenges us to go a bit further than a material definition that explains how basic processes such as cognitive processing and concentration appear to work. We must rather consider whether a materialistic definition of consciousness can explain more profound experiences, such as how we come to experience the smell of a rose, the taste of a strawberry, or the touch of a lover.

Some theorists have challenged the notion that consciousness arises in the brain altogether, suggesting that consciousness comes first, and material existence follows. Such an explanation seems to help account for mind-over-matter phenomena, anomalous phenomena that would otherwise appear inexplicable if we were to take the position that consciousness is born and dies in the human brain. This perspective is also relevant to questions of life after death. Most importantly, understanding the nature of consciousness goes right to the heart of what it means to be alive and human.

In 2005, researcher Susan Blackmore presented at the 'Skeptics Society Brain, Mind, and Consciousness Conference.' During the presentation, Blackmore argued that we cannot know for certain whether we are conscious or not. How can we know for sure that we are conscious beings? It is important to ask such questions in order to avoid living our lives in an unconscious manner, unquestioning. Else, we fail to engage with life, and consequently, with our true nature; we drift through life, as zombies, our potential unrealized. In the process of asking questions about the nature of personal consciousness, we recognize that we can engage with and expand our conscious experience to new frontiers.

Hence, perhaps a simpler question to start with is one of conscious engagement in life. What is the purpose of cultivating exceptional states of human consciousness? This is a question that researchers in the domain of positive psychology have brought into mainstream focus over the last decade. Do we live our lives at an optimal level of conscious engagement? Is our society functioning at the pinnacle of collective human potential? In my early twenties I came to realize that, in fact, most people are not living their full potential, nor are they even aware of their heart's true intention. For me, discovering a sense of inner purpose appeared far more important than any generic marker of success that is often used in our world such as financial, scholarly or athletic success. I believed then, and continue to believe, that true self-mastery, true success, arises from knowing ourselves, from looking within and becoming conscious of our true nature and purpose.

In my psychology classes, I sometimes prompt students to ask themselves the following question: "What do I really want in life, sincerely, from the bottom of my heart, regardless of whatever anyone else might have to say about it?" At least a few students are often surprised by the question, and remark that no-one has ever sincerely asked them, or that they had never thought to ask themselves. Have you ever felt a passion from the depths of your heart toward life, or a particular person, or activity that you were involved in? When did you last experience this? It is so important to embrace moments in which we feel completely in-sync with our souls, and to cultivate these states of consciousness. It is in these states that we connect with the deepest parts of ourselves and learn how to expand the boundaries of self.

To provide one example of this, during my clinical placements as a counsellor I discovered that people tend to limit the amount of happiness in their lives via their assumptions and expectations in life. These assumptions about their own potential, about other people's intentions, and about the world at large disallow them an authentic encounter with their true self, their essential conscious experience. In fact, such a large number of people seem to disavow their essential experience and replace it with a cognitive marker, an intellectual framework for life. Most people's preconceptions about life, about love, about death, about religion, and so forth, tend to be quite specific, and often inaccurate. Even their understanding of self, of the determinants behind their personality, tends to be based in flawed assumptions. Few people pause and question who they really are, at the soul-level, at the heart-level.

Who are you, really, beyond the mask of the constructed self? What is it that drives you, beneath the surface? What is it that animates you? What is it that engages you in the here-and-now? Aren't these questions central to understanding the limits and potentials of our consciousness?

Exploring such questions brings us closer to experiencing a purposeful and enriching life, a life in which our consciousness is engaged and most active. Instead of drifting through the dreams of others, we wake up, engage, and become more alert and connected with the world. From this stance, we can discover the more practical implications of working with consciousness states. We can learn to cultivate more "peak states of consciousness," as Grant McFetridge and Wes Gietz put it. These moments of clarity about ourselves, and about life, grant us a unique chance to expand our consciousness threshold to new boundaries. And, as a direct result, our sensory acuity becomes crystalized, and our inner world becomes enlivened. 'Follow your bliss' might seem a trivial cliché to insert here, but now that we consider it, modern research has confirmed the hidden wisdom in these words, highlighting just how important it is to discover our authentic driving force in life.

William James suggested that human consciousness can be considered in terms of a stream in perpetual flow. When we experience such moments of unadulterated flow and pure connectedness, it becomes clear that we have a much greater reign over our experience of consciousness than we might at first believe. As I will explore throughout this book, when we depend upon our analytical faculties out of proportion with our hearts, we tend to experience our consciousness in a disjointed manner, out-of-flow. Yet, at the core, our conscious experience of life is not supposed to be disjointed. Its natural course is one of perpetual flow and movement, unfoldment, and creative growth. This is observable in all natural phenomena.

Individuals who maintain a state of continual flow are more inclined to engage with the moment, with life as-it-is, rather than their conceptualization of it. When in-flow, projects seem to come along perfectly and come together seamlessly. For a writer, the words may just flow from her mind onto the page with little effort. The meaning behind the words comes together too, and the writing requires little revision to perfect. For a basketball player, he may shoot a basketball right into the hoop several times in a row – but it wasn't concentration or planning that helped him make such a strategic play, rather it was being in-flow, being in the 'zone' of the game.

The notion of flow is thus essential in our consideration of transcendent and exceptional states of human consciousness. If we do not consistently seek to engage our awareness in that which is occurring inside and outside of our frame of self, then we miss out on some of the most enriching and meaningful moments in life. Yet, when we do make the effort to engage and move into flow, something quite magical happens. A state of deep-seated mindfulness and awareness comes about, and this mindfulness can articulate into a state of self-transcendence and direct soul-experience. This is a state of meta-mind, so to speak. We transcend the fabric of personality-self and, almost paradoxically, make contact with a place beyond ourselves. Here the boundaries between personal (local) and cosmic (non-local) consciousness begin to blur.

These peak moments of transcendence are sometimes difficult to put into words. Take for instance a deeply moving experience of true love. The power of love can mend a broken heart. It can inspire us to move mountains and to create new worlds. Volumes can be written of it, and yet it is difficult to put a clear-cut description on a singular concept such as love. Isn't it? Perhaps the reason is that the actual essence of true love cannot be contained. It is not subject to description nor fixed meaning. It is transcendental. It moves us, but we can never capture it nor contain it. Many human experiences are transcendental in nature just as this. These experiences show us a glimpse of something beyond, something inconceivable to the intellectual mind, and yet something greater than ourselves that can be experienced and felt within our hearts.

I believe that most people at some point in their lives have experienced a moment of transcendence, in which they have stepped outside of their personality-self to witness an extraordinary connectedness, emotional depth, and engagement with life. However, most forget about such peak experiences in passing, rather than cultivating them and working toward them. Although these experiences may arise in states of flow, when we are doing something that we love, or during mystical and spiritual practices, this is not always the case. It is possible to also experience moments of transcendence in everyday life, in our relationships, in our work, and so forth. This relates to the central tenet presented in this book. Not only can moments of transcendence be brought about consciously, but connecting with ourselves at a deeper level is easier than we might at first believe. So, before we jump right into this book's main content, let's consider, what are transcendental experiences? And, how can we go about placing moments of transcendence on the spectrum of human consciousness?

Moments of transcendence occur when we experience a depth of profound clarity in life, a clarity that comes from a place beyond the constructed self. You may recall a moment in your life when your awareness spontaneously expanded to encompass the environment around you, as you became aware of all of the sights, sounds, and sensations at a much more heightened sensory level than you ever had experienced before. Or, you might have once experienced a rich emotional connection that somehow seemed more meaningful, deeper than regular and mundane emotional states. You may have experienced a state of peace and stillness that rose from within and expanded to ecstatic proportions. Each of the above can be considered examples of self-transcendence, and each relates to a state of consciousness that touches a place of pure being, a place that exceeds what we have come to define as personal awareness.

Consider four of the common qualities of transcendental experiences below. Although a large number of transcendental experiences include mystical aspects such as encountering visions or glimpses of divine wisdom, these are not the defining characteristics of self-transcendence. At their most basic level, moments of transcendence show us that there is more to life than our limited mental framework of experiencing the world.

Though no account of transcendence is equivalent to another, states of transcendence tend to have a number of common qualities reported among individuals:

1) A temporary loss of our mental commentary or life-script: We forget how we ought to act for a moment and find that an inner intelligence and spontaneity takes over.

2) Spontaneously having feelings that transcend the regular spectrum of emotions: Spontaneously feeling a powerful state of love, or happiness just being alive. Often, these spontaneous emotions and feelings have no trigger or cause. These feelings just arise for the sake of experience, which can be contrast with traditional emotional reactions which are triggered by life events or cognitions.

3) The suffering associated with previous emotional and physical pain (such as trauma or chronic pain) spontaneously disappears for a moment, as though someone had just lifted the entire world from our shoulders, leaving us as light as a feather.

4) Mental definitions and barriers begin to blur, as race, gender, age, religion, politics and other classifications no longer hold a prerequisite for developing a meaningful connection with other human beings.

Thousands of anecdotes attest to other qualities and attributes that differ from the four common features mentioned above, however the above are intended to give readers a glimpse of some of the more common features reported.

I should also note that each of the above qualities tends to be felt completely with one's entire being, rather than merely known intellectually. Transcendental experiences, when they do occur, tend to feel like a rare gem among the mundane tedium of life. These states consume our entire attention, our entire consciousness. However these states of consciousness are more common than most of us would believe. In fact, these experiences are natural aspects of the human condition – an inherent birth-right, so to speak, an unfoldment of conscious potential. Transcendental states do not reflect a superhuman or extra-human state of being. Rather, these experiences help us reconnect with our essential nature beneath the surface.

The process of exploring transcendent states unfolds at each dimension of human experience: 1) Mental, 2) emotional, and 3) spiritual.

Consider, mental potential, for instance: During experiences of transcendence, the mind engages with the external environment at a much deeper level than what we retain and perceive with our surface-level awareness. These deeper levels of mind-engagement are both accessible and approachable. Trance-work, hypnosis, and meditation techniques lend testament to just how precisely our unconscious minds can assimilate and recollect very fine details about our external environment and inner world. As we lower our threshold of awareness, access to this acute information becomes seamless.

Consider, emotional potential: Human beings are capable of expressing infinite love and compassion. This is evident through examples of countless historical figures noted for their altruism, as well as spontaneous acts of kindness we can encounter all around us when we look for them. Emotions like envy, greed, irritation and fear retain very little energy when contrast with the insurmountably more powerful emotions that reflect our true nature, such as states of joy, love, peace, and bliss. The latter move us into congruence with our souls, while negative emotions appear to limit our conscious experience instead. As we let go of surface-level ill-will toward others, a powerful feeling of compassion and peace arises from within – a deep love and acceptance of others and ourselves.

Consider, spiritual potential: Transcendental experiences are often characterized by a deeper state of connectedness to our inner Self. Mystic and author Robert Bruce referred to this connection as a re-awakening to one's "higher aspect." Transcendental states of consciousness often cause us to re-evaluate our religious and philosophical beliefs by showing us the experiential value of living for the sake of living, rather than thinking about and ruminating on the process of living (contemplating how we should live, could live, ought to live, and so forth and so on).

The experience of raw consciousness appears to be very innocent and direct, free from mental filters or intellectual musings. We can intellectualize consciousness until we are bored to death, and yet never know what it truly is to be conscious, that is, until we take the path inward. This is precisely the process Gnostic Master Samael Aun Weor referred to when he suggested that the one who meditates seeks more than just inner peace, "what he seeks is information." When we seek knowledge and wisdom with our spiritual sight (looking inward) we pursue gnosis (inner knowledge). This knowledge cannot be intellectualized with the scientific method, it can only be known via direct experience, direct witnessing, and personal evidence. Thus, during transcendence states, people often experience a state of no-mind, subsequently they cannot explain their experiences intellectually, but emotionally and spiritually these states can account for some the most powerful aspects of a person's life.

Moments of transcendence can also appear inexplicable because the content of these experiences challenges our assumptions about the laws of physics and the boundaries of human potential. For example, accounts of psi (anomalous phenomena) in which a person experiences transcendence of their physical abilities are reported around the world. An example of psi is the demonstration of telepathic communication with another person, using mind reading, rather than verbal or written communication. To a skeptical reader, these accounts seem ridiculous, ludicrous, and tantamount to charlatanism. But there is some truth to the hidden abilities of the mind that we can cultivate during moments of transcendence. Even simple acts such as unimaginable courage, creativity, or kindness, can come about from such states, and more complex and heatedly debated abilities of the mind are also commonly reported as a component of transcendent states.

So, with that in mind, let's jump right in to our exploration of transcendence. Before I finish the premise of this book, I would like to make a brief note here about the format that I have decided to adopt in this book. If you have no interest in reading about the general structure used in this book, then go ahead and skip to the Introduction. I won't mind. It is, after all, your book to read. So, I do hope that you feel comfortable in deciding which order to read this book in, weaving into useful sections while negating those you would prefer to revisit later. The most important factor I had in mind when writing this book is that you, as the reader, are able to experience firsthand some of the consciousness states and experiences that I have written about. The remainder is an afterthought.

It is worth mentioning that transcendental consciousness states have struggled with finding a comfortable place in scientific literature, and it is common to note that altered and spiritual states of consciousness are discussed in popular psychological discourse more often than in the scientific disciplines. This is unusual, as some of the most prominent psychologists, including Abraham Maslow and William James, alluded to transcendence as the penultimate goal of the human being (second only to total spiritual enlightenment). Yet, instead, most people are too caught up in fixing their ego-level problems first (which won't matter much at the end of their lives after all). Sadly, modern psychology caters to the needs of the ego, rather than nourishing our soul connection. The purpose of transcendence in human functioning and the illumination of the soul is thus seldom recognized in mainstream psychological science.

Bearing that in mind, although I have a strong interest in transcendence as an area of scientific investigation, this book should not be confused for a research piece. This book is no more than a personal reflection on transcendence states, and how I have interpreted these experiences as a developing practitioner and individual. When writing this book I made the decision that my work would be most helpful to readers if I spoke from direct experience, rather than writing a 100,000 word research dissertation in an attempt to justify the role of transcendental experiences in scientific literature. That is not the purpose I had in mind at all.

Instead, here I have decided to consider the experiential value of transcendental experiences. Instead of evaluating the meaning of transcendence on an intellectual level, it can sometimes be more useful to approach such states from an emotional and experiential frame of mind. This is an approach that will be expanded upon throughout this book as part of a state cultivation model, an approach for fostering consciousness states without having to grasp their meaning on an intellectual level.

I encourage readers to treat the practical explorations found in this book as behavioral experiments, as though you are playing a game with your reality and noticing what comes of it. Taking a playful, experiential approach, is essential for grasping these concepts. If a technique in this book brings you closer to a deeper state of consciousness in life then this is fantastic. If not, that is fine as well. However, I would prefer that readers experiment with these techniques firsthand rather than trusting an author I have cited who has PhD, MD, or some other string of letters after their name for the mere sake of academic standing. The bottom line: This is a book of techniques, not a book of theories and models.

As this is not descriptive book, I'm not going to canvas a vast amount of actual experiences or accounts of transcendental states. The book provides a vehicle for experimenting with unique states of consciousness firsthand and bending the boundaries of self, rather than explaining or defining the meaning of transcendence. Doing so would be futile, and only the strict materialist mind would demand definition above direct experience. If you are rather looking for a book about specific accounts and techniques for inducing specific altered states, I would recommend that you also read a more topic-specific book (from esoteric, transpersonal, or parapsychological literature) alongside this book.

Thus, keep in mind that this book can be utilized as a handbook of techniques and reflections for personal growth. An over-analytical approach is discouraged in the reflection areas of this book, at least, while first experimenting with the techniques. Instead, readers are asked to use their intuition and to keep the following questions in their awareness when considering the practice techniques here:

1) Is the technique consistent with my own personal experience? If not, then what are some of the valuable insights that I can gain from my personal experience with this technique?

2) How might this technique influence how I perceive the world, myself, and how I interact with others?

3) Does this technique have other implications that I could use which are not written about here? How could I come up with some other creative methods to utilize this approach?

Our experience of consciousness is quite personal, and no matter how much scientific investigation surrounds this subject, we cannot gain true inner wisdom until we experience and deepen our consciousness firsthand. When reading about the techniques in this book, you might find it beneficial to reflect on the above questions and to approach each technique with an open heart, rather than over-intellectualizing the tasks involved.

In this book, I will aim to discuss transcendental states of consciousness with the aim of striving toward helping the reader achieve a greater balance and sense of purpose in life. If you are a personal growth enthusiast, a philosopher, or just a casual reader, it is my hope that this book challenges your paradigm of the world and broadens your self-concept. I hope that, with the aid of the techniques here, your journey of self-exploration is enriched by each of the chapter topics I present here. On the other hand, if you are a clinician, it is my hope that this book brings a creative light to transcendence states and their potential place in a therapeutic context. Although this book is written for the general reader, I believe the topics here have wide application in a broad range of life areas.

INTRODUCTION:
CAPTURING MOMENTS
OF TRANSCENDENCE

I woke up one morning and looked outside my window at the sunrise. This
time it seemed somehow different than other mornings. My mind was so
clear and my attention was fully present. For a moment I completely forgot
I even had a body. I felt like my entire being was expanding into the world.
All at once I could focus on the sounds of birds chirping outside, the voices
of children laughing in the background, everything was brighter and clearer.
I felt more alive than ever before.

– Anonymous account

The above anecdote exemplifies an experience in which a person's consciousness
expanded outside of their normal range of perception. It describes a moment
of clarity, richness, and immersion in the moment – a consciousness state that
transcended the person's 'self' as referred to in the anecdote. Throughout this book, I
demonstrate that we can learn to cultivate similar states of expanded consciousness
as we get back in touch with raw experience. Consider, for instance, how often do
we wake up in the early morning just to watch the sunrise, fully present, mindful
and clear, to allow the external environment to saturate each of our senses? For most
people living in the haste of the modern world, not often at all. Most of the time,
our consciousness is in a less-than-active state.

The importance of taking the time to expand our consciousness in this manner
becomes clear when we consider the practical applications discussed later in this
book. For now, imagine how it would feel to focus your awareness when speaking
with your partner, for instance, or when completing an important project, for
example. Just as you can notice each shade of texture in the indigo-glazed clouds
outside and the subtle warmth of sunlight bleeding through your window, you can
too become as immersed, as sensitive toward those who are important in your life.
How much more "clearly," "completely" and "expansively" (to borrow words from
the anecdote) could you perceive and interact with others with this newfound and
expanded consciousness?

I suggest that what makes these experiences transcendental in nature is that they are
truly felt, beyond the intellectual mind, whether the experience is the observation
of the sunset, or an intimate discussion with a close friend. In each of these
experiences, something draws us in. It is as though nature itself places its hand
upon one's chest and touches the soul, filling it with awe. As with all transcendence
experiences, a heightened level of alertness and presence is required in order to
open ourselves to these gifts bestowed by life. A degree of detachment from the
intellect is also helpful in developing openness to transcendental states. Perhaps

the most important point to be made here is that unlike thoughts or opinions, transcendence experiences cannot be replicated – each is unique and each calls upon a person's willingness and acceptance.

The conscious experience of life is ever-flowing, like a stream in motion (yes, I am hinting at William James' famous metaphor of the stream again). Life itself is in perpetual flow, a flow that is ever-unique from moment to moment. However, most of us experience breaks and disruptions in our flow of awareness. It is easy to become detached from conscious experience because we tend to become fused with our thoughts – we play an intellectual game with life too often (rather than living it). Life goes on, but we retreat into the realm of intellectualization. While we intellectualize our experience, we miss the whole show – we miss what it's really about.

Consider a day in your life that really stood out, one of the best days of your life that you might recall. Your wedding day (or any other day of significance), for example, might have made a greater impact than many of the other memories of everyday life that you hold. A wedding day, for instance, might seem clearer and more meaningful in retrospect, when contrast with an entire months' intense work on a particular project. In such stark contrast, we can recognize that sometimes we isolate peak experiences in our lives, and we categorize the remainder as 'just life.' It is the moments that truly inspire us, that evoke a deep emotional response which remain unique in our awareness. This book does not suggest that we must seek out a greater number of peak life experiences, to immerse ourselves in new environments, and wonderful external events as such, however it does suggest that we can learn how to become open, aware, and present in all life experiences, not just the experiences that we decide to label the best parts of life.

Are your experiences in life graded based upon how good or bad each one is in terms of the objective world? Or, do you decide to experience more happiness, more engagement, and more attention during particular events, while remaining disengaged and disconnected during others? If this comes down to a personal decision, then this implies that we can make a decision to become engaged and attentive to each unique experience that we encounter in life, from moment to moment. Here we can draw upon the example of a child who first enters the world, with no differentiation of experiences. He is just willing to explore and experience life for the sake of doing so. The child does not have the worries and burdens of an adult. Perhaps more importantly, the child does not become entrenched in the carousel of events that make up modern life, all the while forgetting how to live.

To demonstrate this a bit further, consider if we take a glass and begin to fill it from a jug of water until the water begins to reach the outer rim of the glass. Then, we place a drop of red colored dye into the glass. The color of the water begins to transform as it is imbued with the red coloring. Each child comes into the world willing to be open to all experiences in life, but throughout life the child's pure and undifferentiated self-consciousness begins to become impacted with the different impressions, different shades. Another drop of dye, this time green, is placed into the glass. Another drop, this time it is blue. Soon, the colors mix to produce a dark, dense texture, and unless future experiences match this texture, we begin to become more closed off, jaded about life.

If we read too much into our life experiences we can find ourselves becoming caught up in pursuing particular outcomes in life, and thus we lose our basic openness and sense of trust. For example, the child in the earlier example does not care about his cholesterol level, whether he will receive a promotion at work, whether his next car will have cruise control steering. These things do not bother him. He just does not care at this point in his life. It is when we place these ideas into our minds in the first place, it is then that these notions gain monumental importance (a self-serving importance I might add, an external observer such as a child still doesn't care!). We assign these notions importance, and hence, we begin to start caring about them, and so we set into motion a continual process of qualifying our level of happiness and engagement with life based on whether we meet the prior criteria we have set for ourselves. If we picture ourselves coming into this world with an open mind and an open heart, we might see life as a process of filling the mind and heart with experiences that shape us into distinct human beings with particular value systems.

Let's further the example of a child, uninhibited and willing to explore the world. The child's mother might point to a bird in the sky and proclaim "look over there, it's a bird," and so the child from then onward has an understanding that this mysterious flying creature is what we call a bird. Although a simplistic example, this analogy of accommodating ideas from the external world has gained increasing recognition in therapeutic modalities based around the social constructionist model. Such approaches presuppose that we build our internal narratives of the world based on external constructs, and we unconsciously repeat these narratives over in our minds in order to make sense of our life experience. It is no wonder counsellors using such approaches have demonstrated impressive results with cases such of depression and trauma. See, when we let go of the expectation to reap a future that was born from ideas we sowed in the past, we live again, we breathe again, anew. We liberate ourselves to experience life with fresh eyes, as we let go of our past constructs, those old mental commentaries no longer serving us.

5

Each construct that we build about the world from childhood into adulthood is instrumental in shaping who we are, and who we believe we are capable of becoming. If a parent tells her daughter, Beth, that she is "smart, gentle and kind," a similar accommodation process occurs. Beth accommodates these newly assigned labels within, and learns to recognize these qualities within herself in future (and within others too).

It is unfortunate that by age 21, most of us have assimilated a broad spectrum of self-limiting concepts, ideas, and beliefs into an amalgamation that we often term our overall self-concept, the constructed self. How we act, what we believe we are capable of, our personality characteristics, and even our values, correspond to the social construction of this self-concept. Yet, in connecting with raw and undifferentiated consciousness states, not too far detached from those we experienced as a child, we discover the chance to re-write our lives, free from the limitations and inhibitions of our past experiences, and free from the limitations within our glass of perception.

This is a rare invitation. Most people do not recognize the ever-present chance to start afresh. Yet, doing so embodies a powerful move toward recognizing our broader unexplored potential as human beings. Upon a plain white canvas we paint our understanding of life with colors of a dense spectrum, seldom broad, and often definitive. As Don Miguel Ruiz suggested, the self-limiting ideas that we hold tend to cast a magical spell upon ourselves and others, and in doing so our thoughts and words hypnotize others to believe in them, so entrenched are these beliefs about the immutable nature of life experience.

Let's consider a phrase like 'clinical depression.' A man, Lucas, might be experiencing sadness and loneliness because he has just moved to a new town and cannot find new friends to connect with. However, upon a visit to his local psychiatrist, it is possible that Lucas' sadness might be diagnosed as depression. In this case, the label 'depression' carries with it a whole new worldview, a new program for experiencing life. Coming from the mouth of a physician, an influential figure of power, just as in the example of Beth's mother above, Lucas might now reinvent his self-image with this new idea of a depressed man. The danger lies in that he could begin to negotiate his potential in these terms, and identify with the stereotypical meaning of depression. As such, Lucas might adjust the parameters of his openness to new life experiences to accommodate this newfound self-concept. For example, Lucas might stop going out altogether and give up on the idea of finding new friends, because he has conceded to his newfound label of being depressed.

Here, we start to see the subtle but critical link between our experience of consciousness and the formation of self-concept. Our self-concept has the power to limit the extent to which we experience the broader flow of life. As we shall explore later in this book, one's self-concept can either work to suppress or cultivate moments of transcendence. Each one of us looks upon the blank canvas of life, and takes a paintbrush and begins painting the canvas to begin making sense of the world. Experiences that are uncomfortable, negative, or painful are sometimes not dealt with at all, and instead we integrate these into our schema of what life is supposed to be like (based on our assumptions), perceiving the world as cruel, negative, and fear-ridden. Our self-concept is then mirrored and reflected in our perception of the external world.

For instance, we might paint the canvas of perception in a bright golden color when we find ourselves having positive experiences, while we might instead paint with black and dark blue oils when we are faced with negative experiences. Then, just like the character Mario in the 'Nintendo 64' video game 'Super Mario 64,' we dive into the portraits we have painted to experience life through a certain shade. Each person lives in their own subjective world in this manner. Oftentimes, however, life aims to teach us to embrace each one of the unique experiences it offers, rather than forming firm inner barriers. Even the melancholy and sadness of a pale blue pastel has variations in shades of blue. But, if we consider our lives in terms of dichotomies and strict definitions, such as 'I am a good driver,' 'I cannot play musical instruments,' 'I am smart,' 'I am depressed,' and so forth, then we define the scope of our experience in black-and-white textures, rather than opening to the limitless possibilities on the spectrum of consciousness.

Transcendence experiences reconnect us with a deeper part of our consciousness – but, what is that part? How can it be defined? This part lies beyond the constructed self. Consider, who are you, really, at the core? Behind the mask? Those readers who have delved into self-development or meditation practice soon might have realized that the question of who we really are at the core, at a deeper level, is not as simple as it might appear. When asked the question "who are you?" a person might first provide a basic response, "I am my personality, my job, my name, my religion" and onward. Looking deeper, we discover that as individual beings, we are more than that. So much more. We consider our drives, our motivations, some of the reasons behind our behaviors.

Ken Wilber referred to the pre-personal self (the amalgamation of unconscious desires and inclinations), the personal self (the conscious experience of self), and the transpersonal self (the self as experienced through the lens of the super-conscious mind or cosmic consciousness) in his work. Most societies have a representation of these three levels of self. However, most modern societies tend to sublimate the pre-personal self and the transpersonal self, bringing to the forefront of experience, and heralding, the personal self – emphasizing it to extremes.

It is not considered wholesome to express our unconscious desires in public. Likewise, there is not much room for deep spiritual exploration in modern societies (and I don't mean religious or New Age affiliation, I mean real inner discovery). Instead, religious and spiritual doctrines are usually built around the intellectualized idea of the transpersonal self. This leads people to believe that experiences of transcendence are reserved for men of God such as priests, shamans, or those indoctrinated into the relevant traditions. This is not true. In modern times, many people believe any state of consciousness outside of our wakeful consciousness is tantamount to mythos, an irrelevant aspect of the self. This is also false. The limitations of self are not as clear-cut as we might believe, and human potential extends beyond the contrived limits we place upon our understanding of mind.

The idea of reconnecting with the super-conscious mind (the meta-mind that connects us with broader consciousness experience) as a means of pursuing personal growth is not a new notion in the personal development field. The work of Maxwell Maltz, for example, introduced the idea that our conscious and unconscious minds are in constant communication with each other, and that we, as conscious individuals, can influence this communication process. In this book, I am not just suggesting that transcendence experiences help us reconnect with deeper realms within the unconscious mind, but that these experiences allow us to connect with something greater than ourselves, something even deeper than the unconscious mind, a cosmic level of awareness. From that standpoint, we open a dialogue between ego-self and spiritual-soul element of ourselves, and discover the deeper secrets of transcendence.

Maxwell Maltz is one of my favorite personal development authors, primarily because his approach to self-transformation works quite well, and his techniques have a powerful effect. The former is only true of a modicum of self-help books, while the latter is rare among all psychological and personal development literature. Maltz worked as a doctor, a plastic surgeon, who molded the appearance of people's faces to their highest expectations. Then, he moved on to mold people's minds instead. His work suggests that at a deeper level, each one of us has an innate intelligence that is ever-guiding us in the correct direction in alignment with our true self. He theorized that it is often the conscious mind that limits the flow of human potential and brings forth doubts, worries, fears, and anxieties that limit us. Once we can let go of these doubts and trust the infinite intelligence at the unconscious level, positive changes begin to occur in rapid bounds, according to Maltz.

Maltz thought that the conscious mind inhibits our full potential of human experience. It would be more accurate to argue here that the limits we place at the surface ego-level perpetuate the perceived limitations of our conscious experience. A plastic surgeon is bound to working within the confines of a person's existing face or body to nip and tuck changes, but the mind is not as predetermined as the physical self. Imagine if your body could be condensed into a blob of potential energy and then re-built from the ground up, this time, you could have the exact facial and body features you imagined. Obviously this cannot be done physically (at least with our modern technology), but the mind is mutable in just this manner.

Robert Monroe considered that when our consciousness becomes altered, we change focus levels from one consciousness state to another. Monroe's argument fits in well with the anecdote presented at the start of this introduction. The individual in that anecdote talked about focusing on her environment to a greater degree. It is not that her experience opened a new environment of the sun rising, birds chirping, and children talking in the background. Rather, the individual became attuned to these features of the environment in a clear and engaged manner. It is remarkable how our entire world transforms and flourishes when we open ourselves to the experiences that life has to offer. Monroe suggested our consciousness can travel to vast realms and infinite worlds, it is just a matter of changing our focus. And, what is focus, if not a concentrated use of our consciousness?

This raises an interesting question: What is the nature of the normal state of consciousness that each one of us experiences? Scientists know little about the true nature of consciousness and whether we can (or should) sum up consciousness into rigid taxonomies of 'normal' consciousness and 'altered' or 'abnormal' states of mind. I believe that there are numerous shades of consciousness that we experience throughout life, and no single explanation that offers a clear-cut classification of consciousness is sufficient. It could well be that we are all experiencing a collective consciousness state that is abnormal (how would we know for certain, after all?).

In addition, accounts of anomalous phenomena and exceptional human experiences (EHEs), in which people appear to break the laws of a normal state of consciousness, challenge the presumptions we might have about whether there is such a concept as a fixed baseline state of consciousness. Individuals who have experienced out-of-body phenomena, telepathic communication with their loved ones, and spontaneous encounters with divine wisdom, among other fascinating accounts, can be considered. No matter how far-fetched experiences such as these seem, this book invites readers to warm to the idea that consciousness states do not just fit into the neat dichotomies of baseline and abnormal, awake and asleep, or normal and altered.

So, transcendence, in its most basic element, can be thought of as an expansion of self. In that expansion we can find a sense of wholeness and integration, as we get back in touch with the original source of our consciousness. A seeming paradox also comes about when we begin to transcend the personal self: We gain more freedom, power and self-wisdom, and yet we become much more attuned to our place within the cosmic continuum of consciousness, our place as conscious beings in the cosmos thus becomes clearer.

In order to illustrate our greater potential as human beings, this book aims to encourage readers to 1) normalize, 2) contextualize, and 3) utilize transcendence experiences.

First of all, this book aims to normalize transcendence as a part of the human consciousness spectrum. Transcendence experiences are not reserved for the special or initiated, thus we ought to strive to cultivate them in our lives for spiritual and emotional growth, and to work toward removing the constructed obstacles to our full consciousness spectrum. I have thus avoided the term 'altered state of consciousness' in this book, because the experiences I refer to here are not altered at all, but rather in-line with a deeper part of ourselves. These are normal parts of the human experience, once we learn to expand ourselves to welcome these new states of being.

The second aim of this book is to contextualize transcendental consciousness states by questioning and critiquing mainstream reluctance toward examining these experiences a little closer. This book can then also be considered a brief examination of how transcendental consciousness states can be contextualized within a philosophical and self-help framework. It aims to ask questions that would pave the road for future exploration, in addition to offering some potential answers to questions about human consciousness that remain unanswered in the works that have come before it.

The final purpose of this book is to encourage, above all, a practical shift in the reader's experience of consciousness. I have developed 200 individual action steps in this book which aim to encourage unique perspectives on how we can cultivate transcendental states and integrate them into our life experience. This book aims to redefine how we engage with our minds and with life overall.

This book consists of eight separate chapters, each with a particular purpose, and a progressive link that builds to subsequent chapters. A similar progression applies to the mission tasks throughout. You are more than welcome to read the book in any order that you so desire, however, do note that some concepts might not make complete sense without first reading the preceding chapters.

In this first chapter, 'The Mind Illusion,' we will consider the nature of the constructed, intellectual mind. The role of the intellectual mind in limiting our experience of raw consciousness states is deliberated. I invite readers to consider the example of communication and how we can learn to re-connect with others at a deeper level when we let go of our impulse to categorize their life experience. The relationship between consciousness and self-image is also considered and the notion of re-connecting with our heart's true purpose is introduced.

Chapter Two ('Sublimated Consciousness') introduces the notion of super-conscious potential. I also discuss numerous practical techniques to highlight the importance of connecting with our deeper experience of self and the unconscious mind. Chapter Three, 'The Reimagined Self,' serves as a bridge between the first two chapters and the chapters that follow, offering an explanation of how the social construction of language can impact on our threshold of consciousness. This chapter also canvasses the value of transcending our outdated self-image to rediscover a new sense of personal power. Again, following a tradition of pragmatism, several behavioral experiments, reflections, and exercises shape the chapter into a practical, applied focus.

The more advanced cultivation of human potential via consciousness exploration begins in Chapter Four ('Reclaiming Disavowed Emotions'). In that chapter, we'll consider the role of emotion in experiencing rich, fulfilling, and vibrant consciousness states. This chapter will perhaps be most beneficial for practitioners reading this book, I wrote it from a perspective of moving toward healing and wholeness, and was sure to keep practitioners in mind when drafting it. Those with an interest in emotional healing will also find this chapter beneficial.

Chapter Five ('Transformational Mind States') invites readers to contemplate meditation experiences that bring about unique states of consciousness. Meditation has often been associated with the development of mental discipline, inner power, and a deep-seated compassion for all living beings. However, the connection between the actual practice of meditation and the humble pursuit of these virtues has become misplaced in much modern literature about the subject. The missing link between meditation and human potential is considered here. Chapter Five approaches meditation from a stance of personal empowerment.

The last three chapters interweave practical examples of how we can learn from transcendence experiences to discover a greater meaning, purpose, and potential in life. In the sixth chapter ('Relational Depth') I invite readers to consider the role of transcendence experiences in enriching our interpersonal relationships, as well as the concept of the conscious relational field. In Chapter Seven ('Ultimate Freedom') I discuss the connection between free will and the creative expression of consciousness. Chapter Eight ('Our Higher Mind Potential') concludes the book with an exploration of some the most interesting experiences I have had the honor of working with during my time consulting as a parapsychologist. This chapter includes cases, metaphors, and reflections that I believe highlight the limitless power of human consciousness and the true potential that each one of us is capable of bringing to the forefront of life experience.

CHAPTER ONE

THE MIND ILLUSION

Idealists live in a fool's paradise, but materialists live in a fool's prison.

Reading a book satisfies the mind, but how often does the act of reading fill the soul with awe? Just as the world's attention has turned to an information age, so our attention too, as citizens of the world, has turned from deepening our experience of life to the pursuit of accumulating momentous volumes of information. In modern times, we much too often substitute wisdom with information, communication with texting, self-expression with preoccupation, and faith with expectation. With robot-like precision we are trained at school, in the workplace, and in family life to micro-manage each and every detail of our existence. Our information obsession has triggered most of us to fall for the mind's illusion and to forge an intellectual wall around ourselves, a wall that fortifies the inner heart and prevents its true expression.

Despite how deep, the cold pulse of the over-intellectualization of modern societies can be felt in our hearts, if we dare to look within. It might feel as though a slight discomfort, something out of place, not quite right, or it might manifest as a deep dissatisfaction with life. It presents itself as the realization that we have become disconnected from ourselves and immersed in the intellectual mind; a schema of thoughts that we ourselves have constructed, a schema that only tangentially informs our reality, and often preoccupies us with meaningless notions.

Consider, how often does the act of reading a book enrich one's soul? How often do we read instead to entertain the intellectual mind and fill it with information instead? How often do we listen to the radio as a distraction, rather than allowing the music to touch our souls? Consider talking with friends, attending a seminar, preparing a meal, and each and every other task that we perform throughout life. How often do we perform these tasks mechanically and with a lack of mindfulness and soulfulness?

To pierce the intellectual wall we must begin "focusing the mind not on the appearance of the envelope, but on the meaning of the letter inside it," as philosopher Neil Kramer suggested in his book, 'The Unfoldment.' Too often we can find ourselves caught up in the impressions, ideas, and notions that we hold about the world, instead of setting aside our intellectual understanding of the world for a moment and beginning to live. As we remain in the mind's illusion, we put ourselves at odds with felt life experience.

The prison-like confinements of this wall do not just extend to those who are intellectually-minded. These self-imposed confines on our conscious experience affect all of us. From childhood, schools do not teach children how to build moral character, techniques to foster emotional intelligence, the importance of using

15

their intuition, or means for living a fulfilling life. Schools instead teach children the sciences, mathematics, languages, and the necessary tools to become effective workers who support society. Most of us thus end up living in society's dream, rather than spending some time figuring out our own desires and dreams. This dilemma keeps us trapped in a constant model of thinking, organizing, and evaluating our world rather than reconnecting with what is important in life.

In our information-driven culture, most of us engage with online media, television, newspapers, and magazines that create a model of reality through the power of words, pictures, and symbols, all of which conveniently tell us all about how the world is, and little about our true nature, little about how we are (or who we really are). The mainstream media bombards us with a constant influx of images intended to incite feelings of fear, inadequacy, worry, and confusion. We substitute our true identity for 'brand identity,' losing our essence to the world of things. Switch on a television for just a few minutes and reflect on the images that are broadcast on the screen to recognize this process in action.

As far back as the commencement of schooling, we are encouraged to continue learning, to accumulate more and more senseless information, to pursue the idea that the more we know, the happier we will be in life, whether in a direct fashion (boosting our prospects of finding a job by having a higher caliber of education) or in an indirect manner (suggesting that knowledge somehow equates to happiness). I believe that knowledge that leads to self-examination does lead to happiness in life. However, reflect on the following question for a moment: Does the knowledge that we accumulate throughout schooling contribute to our overall happiness? To answer this question in depth we must give it more than just a few moments of sincere reflection.

Often, our sense of happiness has no relationship to what societal structures have to offer as such, but rather arises from within. Those who have experienced transcendental consciousness states often come in touch with a deeper sense of happiness and peace within, a sense that is not contingent on societal expectations or exterior goals whatsoever! In fact, moments of transcendence illustrate that society's dream of happiness is false, an empty pursuit.

The earliest moments in life in which I experienced self-transcendence can be best described as my sense of the personal self disappearing for a moment. All of the inhibitions, all of the limitations I had, seemed to vanish and it felt as though anything was possible. Any rationally-minded person might argue that this is just a subjective state of experience, and I would not have been able to experience anything more than I was capable of in the first place. However, my experience has shown me that this is not the case. Moments of transcendence do not just help us connect with a feeling of greater potential, these moments in fact empower us to discover more possibilities in life than we had ever believed existed.

Take an example of creative expression. In moments that we pursue creative endeavors such as writing, or drawing, we have the chance to connect with a deeper part of ourselves, a super-conscious force that we have access to when we allow ourselves to forget our personal sense of self, so to speak. The temporal self-construct disappears, and the wellspring of potential beneath now comes into clear sight.

There is a certain reverence that lies beyond the intellectual wall that many accounts of transcendence capture. When we learn to connect with that transpersonal part of ourselves, it becomes much easier to draw upon this innate power and creative potential. For example, consider Elizabeth Gilbert's 'TED Talk,' in which Gilbert mentioned that she could not understand how some people experience 'writer's block' – creative potential seemed unlimited from her vantage point. This is easier to understand when we consider moments of transcendence. Tuning in that no-self state of being brings about a transcendence into a more expanded, and more approachable consciousness state, a state in which possibilities arise in infinite potential. It is in these states that we tend to experience raw creative potential.

To consider my experience of this process, I can reflect back to when I had a deep dislike for school and the Western educational model in general. During high school education in particular, in my attempt to escape mathematics, physics, and chemistry classes, I strived to switch to as many arts, design, and history classes as possible. It is not that I dislike left-brain, logical thinking, but rather that I was using those faculties too much, and I felt that the creative artistic part of my consciousness was being neglected. Later in this book, I will describe how creative and artistic pursuits open our potential to a much broader range of experience, whilst building logical, structured models of the world tends to limit our interaction with life itself.

During Grade 11, when I transferred into an art subject toward the end of semester, I realized it was not going to be as easy as I thought it would. In fact, I had not been very good at drawing at all, as I had not attempted it before. It didn't help that I did not pay attention to any of the classes until the moment that the final two hour examination arrived. When asked to paint an original piece of work, I panicked immediately, and I honestly believed that I was bound to just stand there for the entire two hours with a blank canvas in front of me the entire time. I think the teacher even told me that there is no chance I would pass the exam (or something along those lines) because I never attended the classes. However, something unusual happened at that moment. Something prompted me to pick up the paintbrush, and I found that I stopped panicking and stopped thinking, and I intuitively began painting.

I was quite surprised by the quality of the work I saw beginning to form in front of me, in particular as I had never been that good at drawing or painting in the past. The aspect of this experience that stood out for me is the lack of intellectual engagement throughout those two hours. It felt as though I was not thinking about what I was doing at all, the two hours felt more like 20 minutes at most, and yet, I ended up with one of the highest grades for Art among all of the subjects I was enrolled in, as the result of the work I had somehow produced during that exam. In retrospect, it was as though I was in a trance state or altered state of consciousness during the experience.

This experience showed me that there is a deep-seated source of intelligence and inspiration that rests just outside of what we can come to understand with the intellect alone. Many artists lose themselves in their work, and at that point discover their full potential to paint. That source of potential is transpersonal, it is not born from the constructed, personal self. It extends to a place of soulfulness and super-conscious potential. Such states of transpersonal connection arise not just during artistic and creative expressions, but can be cultivated in all life pursuits. Although the artistic work that I completed in high school was quite simplistic in contrast to the surges of creative genius we often see in our world, I believe that other works of pure creative expression come about from a similar source of inspiration that transcends the intellectual wall. The works of art by Leonardo da Vinci, Michelangelo, and many other famous creators noted throughout history seem to transcend what is humanly possible. We look at those artworks in awe, as they touch a place beyond our rational understanding. Certain artistic works are so majestic that they seem to reach a place of inspiration far beyond possibilities first fathomed.

Despite claims that moments of creative genius are rare and unique occurrences, I suggest here that the states of consciousness that bring about this creative power are accessible to each of us, on an ongoing basis, if we learn how to cultivate these states. The creative genius of da Vinci, Rembrandt, and Monet arose from this same inner wellspring, this same intuitive-creative source within. During schooling we are not taught to fine-tune these intuitive capabilities, and instead we are taught the methodical approaches of how to think, how to write, how to draw, and so on. On other occasions in school I recall that answers to complex mathematical would seem to just arise in my awareness, I could not provide reasoning or proofs, but I could just receive the answer when I quietened my mind enough. I had many telepathic (mind reading and subtle information transfer) experiences such as these long before I developed a professional interest in studying the extended capabilities of the mind. It was not a methodical thinking and problem-solving process that I was using during those moments. Far from it. It felt more like a meditative trance-like state of knowledge acquisition.

One point for clarification that should be noted in this chapter is that I am not against intellectual thought. However, I believe that as a consequence of the information-driven world that we live in, we have become increasingly dependent on knowledge, facts, data-based information, and micromanaging life, and, particularly in the Western world, we have started to forget how to experience life fully, how to reconnect with our intuition and our emotions. Therefore, this book advocates for a balance between the thinking mind, and the emotional and spiritual facets of the human experience. Too many people in our world spend less than 10% of their time deepening their spiritual and emotional experience of life, and most of their time widening their intellectual knowledge, putting their mental commentaries about the world on repeat rather than engaging with life in the here-and-now.

This detrimental over-intellectualization does not just extend to basic tasks in which we retreat into the mind rather than engaging with life. This process is more subtle than that, it is about the constant reduction of core human values to societal constructs, mental ideas, and concepts we find in the external, rather than cultivating our sacred inner experience. For instance, too many people gossip about others rather than connecting with others at the soul level. Too many follow rules to the letter rather than valuing wisdom above doctrine. Too often we interpret rather than feel; analyze rather than experience. These are all symptoms of being out-of-tune with ourselves as we overemphasize just one shade of conscious experience: The intellectual mind.

Earlier on I stated that the intellectual mind just somewhat informs our experience, and more often than not, separates us from direct felt experience. To expand on this point, consider the myriad conflicts that arise in the modern world. Despite our overall intelligence on the rise on a global scale, we can see more incidences of violence, depression, divorce, and conflict also on the rise. These observations affirm that a balance between the intellect mind and the soul is not just preferable, but essential in our world. No matter how smart, how advanced we become, this constructed intelligence cannot substitute our deeper connection with direct felt experience.

Too often we depend on the intellect alone to deliver us meaning, failing to recognize that meaning can exist on a multitude of levels: Spiritual, emotional, intuitive, and metaphorical, for example. Yet, too often we focus on the rational-intellectual understanding that we hold and herald it as the correct, or complete understanding. What is it that gives intellectual experience that status of being correct, whilst emotional spiritual knowing is often considered of a somehow lesser caliber than rationalized knowledge?

Most people see the world through the lens of the intellectual, rather than creating the much needed space to understand how the world can be perceived through several lenses, intellectual knowing being just one facet of perception. The intellectual mind only tangentially informs our reality by filtering out all incoming information through the five senses that does not match our pre-determined schema of the world. The process of what we choose to filter and experience consciously is determined by our worldview and what we expect to perceive. In many ways, the intellectual wall only alerts us to what we wish to see, discarding all of the other data and experience that our consciousness touches. Consider, for example, someone who acts as a racist. He immediately filters out anything that someone of a different race in the room wishes to verbalize or express. He refuses to validate their experience before even hearing it. It is almost as though his intellectual mind cancels out the real and valid experience altogether, substituting it for an alternative worldview.

Experiments in perception help us observe how our intellectual model of the world can cancel out and eliminate entire fragments of information from our awareness (see 'The Invisible Gorilla' experiments, as well as the theories behind the deletion, generalization, and editing of perceptual information in Neuro-Linguistic Programming; NLP). Accounts of transcendent experiences often discuss coming in touch with a much broader experience of life. This makes much sense when we consider that trillions of bits of information and data make up matter around us. We take a slight percentage of this into our perception, making an even smaller percentage of matter true (valid, in our eyes) by validating it with the intellectual mind and allowing it into our field of perception. How much of physical matter do we really perceive with the five senses? Is it 10% of all that exists in front of us? Is it one percent? Or even less?

It is important to consider here the Taoist idea that all matter is in constant motion. The intellectual mind takes the experience of motion and turns life existence into a static image. Like a metaphorical Medusa, the mind freezes potential realities in time and turns them to stone. The aim of effective self-awareness practice is to recognize the importance of motion when working with transcendental states. It's also critical that we recognize how the intellectual wall can be so static, so immovable. Often we term people who are fixed in their beliefs as acting out in an arrogant or stubborn manner because these individuals are no longer receptive to be constant motion of life, instead deciding to fixate on a particular single point of consciousness even if that point is no longer relevant now.

Thus, our ultimate mission in this book is to create a space in the intellectual wall where we are once again able to reconnect with that eternal motion of consciousness. Most of us have such a space within, a chasm through which we connect to deeper states of being within, but for the most part, we do not recognize this at first. Once a person has broken through the boundaries of their inner wall, we might state that this person has experienced transcendence. In the cases of artistic genius, spiritual attainment, and others in which individuals seem to break through to a different state of being for longer periods of time, we could state that these individuals have stepped over the intellectual wall and discovered what lies on the other side.

The Sanskrit term, 'māyā,' encapsulates how most people experience a multitude of elusive projections and compelling illusions about life, rather than a direct connection with life itself. Māyā is the dream of one who lives in a mental frame his entire life rather than moving past the frame and living in the presence of what is valuable to him now, in the promise of the present moment, rather than in the elusive thought of a moment that might (or might not) follow. Life as we know it on the intellectual level rests upon a cunning tapestry of illusions in which people pursue hollow desires and unfulfillable dreams. It is only when we self-actualize (engage with the here-and-now, with life as-it-is) that we become prepared to move on from the lessons of this world of stone and into the experience of the eternal moment, the endless stream of consciousness.

The idea of enlightenment in spiritual traditions refers to the shattering of the illusion and experiencing the world as it is (see Gabriel Cousens' work on spiritual enlightenment for a good overview of this process). In this book, I refer to this encompassing illusion as the intellectual wall that takes the simple experience of life and makes it something it is not. I believe perceiving life as-is requires one to rebuild trust in one's own intuition and inner heart. The heart sees a clear picture, while the mind theorizes. We could argue that this requires the heart of a child, untainted with societal programming, clear and pure, open to the world. It is possible for each of us to return to this state of innocent perception, if we are willing. In such a state, moments of transcendence come often, as life is magical at its core, it is the intellectual mind that makes it mundane. In the magic of life, we discover that our inner heart, at its depth, cannot lie or hold deceitful illusions of the world, it is the intellectual mind that lies and deceives us into illusions and distortions of perception.

So, I feel that in this chapter it would be worthwhile for us to consider the difference between intellectual knowledge and inner wisdom. Hence, in the subchapters that follow, I invite readers to consider the idea that intellectual knowledge is experienced via the thinking mind as a sort of proxy for life, while true wisdom belongs to the domain of the inner heart, which is felt and experienced with our consciousness in a more direct and intuitive fashion. In these reflections, I ask readers to consider the value of piercing the intellectual wall to reconnect with their intuitive capacities. Toward the end of the chapter, we'll also consider how we tend to pursue our mental goals in life that have been acquired from the external world, rather than connecting with, and listening to, our heart's true intention.

Some practical explorations are also introduced in this chapter, which I refer to as 'mission tasks.' These tasks invite readers to experiment with their own experience of consciousness. Here is how it works: You will find throughout each subchapter in this book subheadings titled 'Exploration,' and under these headings a number of practical tasks will be assigned, along with completion requirements. Some tasks are goal-oriented, and others are non-directional and have no intrinsic purpose apart from deepening self-awareness. In total, 200 personal development action steps can be found throughout this book, these can be found within 120 unique mission tasks that span the book (with 15 core personal mission tasks per chapter). These action-based goals were crafted to give readers proactive steps and unique ideas for engaging with the core themes presented throughout.

You are not required to complete the mission tasks if you would prefer not to. In fact, you could even skip past certain tasks, if you like. However, if you would like to experience some of the concepts spoken about here directly, on a personal level, the mission tasks are a good place to start. I believe that reading a personal development book has little value in and of itself, unless readers use and apply the concepts taught, which is why I have gone to the effort of developing a large number of unique and (hopefully) fun mission tasks to facilitate active engagement with this book. You do not have to complete a particular task prior to moving on to the next, as some tasks can take a while to finish and can be left for later exploration, if this approach is more convenient.

RISE OF A THINKING CULTURE

Just a few moments ago I submitted a Google search query for the word 'love.' The search query returned a total of 8,950,000,000 web page results. The first three results were: 1) a Wikipedia entry, 2) a love calculator and, 3) a website titled 'LOVE.' The Wikipedia entry for 'love' discussed definitions of love, categories of love, and expressions of love in different cultures. The second page, the love calculator, seemed to suggest that it could calculate the success rate of a given relationship based on the spelling of each partner's name (though, if I wrote my name as 'Alexander' instead of 'Alex,' a startling 12% disparity in success was to be seen). The third website loaded a photo of a woman in a wedding dress, smudged with make-up, cupping her breast, with no text on the page except a 'home' button at the bottom.

Then, what can we learn from this short experiment? Even though I just had time to open the first three pages listed on Google's search index, it would be interesting to browse even a small proportion of these almost 10 billion websites to determine which pages can tell us something real about love. A good researcher could find sufficient facts about love online to fill volumes. However, just because someone is able to understand love on this broad intellectual level, does this infer that the individual has understood the true nature of love on a direct, conscious level?

It is clear that there is no lack of information in our world. It is flourishing wherever we look. However, there is a lack of deep understanding. Most of us depend on facts, information, data, details, figures, statistics, answers, and scientific conclusions to inform our lives and make sense of the world in which we live. However, we too often forget to trust ourselves, our intuition, and our direct connection to life itself as an instrument for guidance. I believe that we have come to a crossroad in human civilization, where we now have the potential to move from an information age to a consciousness of connection, wisdom, and felt experience. There is a certain point, a threshold to which we can accumulate information to inform our experience of life. After all, we were not designed as robots, and the way that many of us live in the modern world is completely contrary to how human beings have lived and function throughout the previous two millennia. Our purpose is to experience life rather than spending the major portion of our time staring at screens.

It is ironic how our information obsession has given rise to an over-trust in science. Using the same degree of determination a religious fanatic would use to defend their beliefs, so we too defend our beliefs with qualification, knowledge, accreditation, bureaucracy, procedure, and enshrined process of mind-justification. Just as religious fanatics can be inflexible, rigid, dogmatic, and disconnected from the truth, now we can observe the same trend of inflexible and dogmatic thinking in some of the hard sciences that pride themselves on a supposed accurate understanding of truth.

Experiences are meant to be experienced, not intellectualized. It is not difficult to fall into the appealing frame of mind in which we spend most of our time thinking about our experiences in life and adding mental commentaries to them, rather than immersing ourselves in the experiences. The demands of living in an information age have led us to under-prioritize our felt experiences, while over-prioritizing our thoughts, beliefs, opinions, and ideas about our experience of life. In the modern world, it is common to saturate our minds with constant input via the five senses, but how often do we take the time to stop and to appreciate each experience, to allow it to enrich the soul?

EXPLORATION: INTELLIGENCE VS WISDOM

This book will illustrate that being correct about something or having a sound intellectual understanding of what we believe about life is often less important than the value of felt experience. After all, what proportion of our ideas about the world actually come from within ourselves? How many of these notions originated from parents, teachers, significant others, and those we have encountered in life, persuading us to copy-and-paste their view of reality onto our own? Like puppets echoing memes at an all-important round table, we forget the lack of original substance that we ought to bring to the table, as we elevate the merits of the intellectual mind to new extremes.

Although people living in First World countries such as Australia and the United States should have some of the lowest rates of poverty and crime in the world, most people in the First World experience a poverty of the soul. Their experience of reality is a replica of someone else's, as they have forgotten how to look within and discover their own inner light of wisdom, all the while substituting intuition with intellectualization.

MISSION TASK 1: FELT EXPERIENCE

Sometimes we spend too much time thinking about our experiences rather than embodying them completely. Often, we have mental commentaries and expectations about life rather than just living in the present moment.

Completion Goal:

In this first mission task, recall one experience in life in which you felt completely engaged with the present moment, without expectation or judgment. Take careful notice that during such an experience you might not have even recalled thinking at all, or analyzing at all, you just completely allowed yourself to be in the present moment as-it-is, without expectations or anticipations. Reflect on what that experience of 'just being' felt like. Did your self-awareness differ during that moment, as opposed to, say, right now? And if so, how so?

MISSION TASK 2: WHAT IS WISDOM?

Is intelligence the same as wisdom? In many cultures, elders are considered wise, and are often sought out for their advice and guidance. Thus, age seems to be associated with wisdom in our modern world. But what is it that brings about true wisdom? Reading a lot of books? Having a college degree? Having a breadth of life experiences? What is wisdom, at the core of it? And, how does that differ from intelligence? In this book I often contrast the intellectual mind with the inner heart. I argue that the wisdom of the inner heart is infinite, while the intelligence of the intellectual mind is limited to theories and models about the world. Of course, this is just my own personal opinion. I would like to invite you to reflect on your own personal view of wisdom.

Completion Goal:

Consider, what is wisdom? For this mission, think about particular parts of your life in which you had to exercise the use of wisdom or intuition, rather than depending upon your intellect, and acquired knowledge. Have you ever ignored what your logical mind was suggesting and just trusted in your heart? What was that experience like for you? Reflect.

Alexander De Foe

MISSION TASK 3: INTUITION

Your mission is to consider the following question: 'What does the word 'intuition' mean to me?' Find three articles on the world-wide-web about intuition that seem interesting, each of which has at least some depth of discussion (over 500 words) about what it means to listen to one's intuition. Do you agree with the ideas presented in each of the articles? Do you disagree? What is your own personal experience with intuition in contrast to the ideas presented in each article?

Completion Goal:

Read at least three web articles about intuition and reflect on the idea of intuition.

THE HEART'S PROMISE

It is far more valuable to ask ourselves what we love most in our lives, what we believe to be real, rather than becoming consumed in the constructs about the world that we hold within the confines of the intellectual wall. Often, felt experience is so much more valuable than intellectualization. For example, consider when someone asks, "why is this crisis happening to me?" or more complex questions such as "what is the purpose of this life?" Let's take the latter question and reflect on its true felt meaning. Usually, when someone asks a question such as this, they are seeking a deeper understanding, rather than an intellectual response. Yet, how often do people offer their own opinions, beliefs, or ideas in place of an empathic understanding? This is not just true of complex philosophical questions, but also true in general conversation.

The issue arises when people take preference in consulting their intellectual mind rather than connecting with their felt experience. Consider this. A person asks "what is the purpose of life?" Now, instead of thinking of an answer, I can decide to listen to the meaning behind the words. This individual might lack a sense of purpose in their own life, something might be missing in their life experience. "What prompted this individual to ask this question now?" I might wonder. I can look for the energy, the motivator, behind their words, rather than looking to the phrasing on the face. I do not think to myself: "hmm, this individual is trying to test my intellectual understanding about metaphysics, I wonder how I could outwit her and present a thorough ontological analysis on the purpose of life." The latter attitude is a product of over-intellectualization, rather than connecting to felt experience.

26

How often do we answer questions to demonstrate our own understanding, instead of perceiving questions as invitations to connect? How often is our focus placed upon the intellectual wall as opposed to the inner heart? How often do we seek for a logical understanding rather than an empathic understanding?

One of the presuppositions of NLP practice states that the meaning of communication can be found in the response it elicits. In our society, we are often taught the inverse of this, that there is a common absolute worldview somewhere (out there), rather than a deep and profound truth that can be found within if we look inside ourselves. This NLP presupposition can teach us much about the nature of communication. Communicating is not just about validating each other's logical understanding of the world. It is also about deepening our level of connection with others.

For instance, an individual who is questioning the meaning of life might have been led to this process via several possible routes. For example: 1) A feeling that life itself does not make sense at all, 2) a feeling that some things in life are just not making sense, the seeming lack of worth or value of certain tasks makes them becomes questionable, or 3) a feeling that death is the end of the road and feeling as though there is no reason to move forward. Which approach, then, is more important: To methodically figure out the correct response to a question? Or, to come to a greater empathetic understanding of the individual's experience beyond the mere wording of their question?

The intellectual wall fools us into thinking that the more logical, intellectual, rational, and scientific we are, the more precise our experience of life, the more precisely we can address our human needs. The paradox is that as we surrender the intellectual wall, human experience becomes all the more rewarding – we then connect on a heart-to-heart level and experience true understanding and empathic engagement. Therefore, it is important to place our attention inward, to tease out our inner potential. In doing this, we also encourage others to express themselves and to recognize their true selves as well.

Instead of reacting to surface-level communication with others, it is far more rewarding to connect with the deeper meaning beyond the mere words, to step into another's inner world for a moment. As we step beyond the intellectual wall, we move from merely believing in something intellectually, to knowing it in our hearts. This book goes so far as to state that even complex understandings that depend on faith, such as our knowledge of God, can be integrated into our experience of life. Instead of interacting with our intellectual beliefs about God, for example, we go inward to establish a real and authentic connection with God (but, more on that later in the book).

When most people communicate, their communication occurs not with another individual, but with their ideas about that individual. Often, we interact with our intellectual wall, rather than connecting with others on a felt level. A strong believer in a particular idea is out to prove something. A nonbeliever is out to prove something too. Thus, with heart-to-heart listening, our aim might not be to prove a point at all, but rather to observe just how things are. Careful observation, rather than intellectual critique and judgment, can often bring us closer to climbing over the intellectual wall and into real life experience and connection.

Upon running into someone we know in public, we might as well be visualizing endless labels above her head: 'female,' 'attractive,' 'left-wing beliefs,' 'Catholic,' 'likes bowling,' and so forth, in addition to our recollections about our past experiences with this individual. An issue of concern arises when we engage with our thoughts about this individual, rather than the individual herself in the present moment as she is now. Reflect on this statement for a moment. It is not difficult to overlook just how rare and wonderful authentic human connections are in-the-moment. Unless we are able to look 'past the past,' so to speak, and to embrace others without holding particular judgments or ideas about them, it becomes difficult to foster deeper friendships and relationships. In our world, people seldom search for a connection with others at the soul-level, and instead settle for a superficial understanding.

EXPLORATION: REFLECTIVE LISTENING

In the previous few paragraphs we discussed the importance of focusing the connection we experience with others rather than getting caught up in the musings of the intellectual mind. Re-focusing our communication is one of the easiest approaches for practice shifting our awareness from the intellectual wall toward authentic conscious connection. Conscious connections are unique and magical experiences, whilst intellectual communication is often repetitive and boring, reducing people to things of concern. It is in moments of conscious communication that the ineffable qualities of connection, growth, and experience arise in our relationships. However, one of the major issues with communication in our modern world is that we hear what we choose to hear, shaped by our own preconditions and assumptions. Often, we do not allow ourselves sufficient space to feel what a person is saying, and rather react in a split-second fashion based on what we hear through our limited filters of perception.

MISSION TASK 4: TRUE LISTENING

In future conversations, take notice of what you are thinking about. Does the conversation trigger you to remember something similar in your own experience? Or, are you perhaps thinking about what to say next? If each individual in a conversation focuses on their own thinking process, then to what extent is each connecting with the other? This distracting thought process is perhaps what keeps us from being satisfied in the connections that we develop with others.

This exploration invites you to spend the following few days practicing reflective listening. Your mission task is to become aware of what you are thinking about during each conversation that you have throughout the day. You might like to decide upon three conversations to practice with specifically and note whether your own internal thinking process differs during each of these conversations.

Then, as soon as you become aware of your thinking process, aim to connect more deeply with each individual you speak with instead of getting caught up in those thoughts.

Remember the previous example about the individual who pondered the meaning of life? Just as I demonstrated in that example, aim to connect to the core of what each person is striving to communicate during the conversation, aim to listen beneath the surface of what is being said. Focus on the intention behind the words. What is it that the person's words are pointing to? Can you gain a glimpse into their inner world? Practicing this technique for a week will help improve your communication skills and reflective listening capacity. Practicing for longer periods of time helps develop the process of heart-to-heart communication, a rewarding experience of transcending the boundaries of language and connecting on a wholehearted level.

Completion Goal:

Instead of listening to specific words during a conversation, aim to focus on the intention that a person is projecting. Consider: Do the person's words align with the apparent intention behind the words? Aim to get an emotional sense of the meaning projected behind the words. You could start with focusing on their tone, facial expression, and overall 'feeling' of their words. Reflect on how having an awareness of this new process of listening could be valuable during conversations.

MISSION TASK 5: TAPESTRIES OF MIND

After practicing the previous mission task at least a few times, move on to this task. In each of your longer conversations (over five minutes in length) during the following day, take note of what goes on in your own mind during each conversation. Take note of what sort of things you are thinking about during conversations with others. Can you notice any particular patterns in your thoughts and mental commentaries? You may also find it easier to choose someone who talks a lot and usually dominates the conversation for the purposes of this exercise. Now, what is your mind doing while listening to that person? Are you completely focused, engaged, and in-tune with them during the conversation? Is your self-awareness centered in the moment?

Completion Goal:

After each substantial conversation, recall and mentally list at least five things you were thinking about. Did a common pattern emerge? If so, take note of it for now. If not, consider practicing a few more times and notice whether a pattern of similar thoughts or thought-patterns emerges, if not, move on to the next task. The purpose of this task will make more sense as this book unfolds.

MISSION TASK 6: SACRED CONNECTION

After completing the previous mission, consider this task. In each of your conversations over the next day, treat each conversation as a sacred experience of connecting with the person you are speaking with. Catch yourself getting caught in your own mental commentaries, beliefs, and judgments about your experience of the interaction, and then bring your conscious awareness into the experience of just listening. During each of the conversations you participate in, ensure to listen reflectively by keeping your awareness focused fully on those who you interact and connect with.

Completion Goal:

Reflect on whether it makes a difference (or not) to treat each conversation as a unique chance to foster a sacred connection with another human being. If so, how does this perspective influence your experience of communication?

MISSION TASK 7: COMFORTABLE SILENCE

The following day, participate in a conversation in which you avoid asking any questions at all, just listen. You may make comments, as long as your comments are not in the form of questions. Experiment with expression, empathy, and gathering information using intuitive means (for example, statements such as 'go on,' 'I see,' and nonverbal cues) rather than questioning. The aim here is to see how long you are able to practice until the conversation concludes. Note that short periods of silence are acceptable. Reflect on what this experience of not asking a single question was like for you and for the other individual in the conversation. Could you carry a meaningful connection without the use of questioning? Take note of whether this was a beneficial or detrimental process, and the reasons that this was the case.

Completion Goal:

Complete the practice of having a conversation without asking a single question until you are able to maintain a meaningful conversation for at least five minutes using this approach.

MISSION TASK 8: MOTIVATION

The above technique of avoiding questions during conversations is a useful experiment that illustrates how often we ask questions just for the sake of filling the silence or gathering information for our own purposes. Often, people will tell us what is most important to them, what is on their minds and in their hearts, if we allow them the chance to do so, rather than asking questions that we believe most relevant from our limited understanding of their subjective experience.

Alexander De Foe

Completion Goal I:

In this action step, I encourage you to consider some of the future motivations that you hold for asking certain questions during conversations. Are these motivations linked to a genuine sense of being curious, or just intended to fill the silence? Consider how your conversational approach could be better framed toward connecting with others rather than intellectual information-gathering through questioning.

Side Notes:

Although I advocate for developing a deeper emotional and spiritual connection throughout this book, it is worthwhile finding a balance that allows us to use our discernment, as well as our emotional faculties, rather than over-depending on the former to extremes. Thus, striking a balance between reflective statements and the use of direct questions in conversation is ideal.

Let's examine this further, by reflecting on NLP practice, in which we can draw upon two models, the Milton Model and the Meta Model. The Meta Model deals with tangible, concrete ideas, specific information and details that are useful and can be elicited through specific questioning. These targeted questioning techniques help shape a specific, logical, and structured understanding of a person's inner experience.

The Milton Model (based on the hypnotic language patterns devised by Milton Erickson), on the other hand, utilizes less specific and more reflective language with the aim of eliciting a person's inner dreams, wishes, and hopes – these are more abstract and focused on feelings rather than thoughts. Both models are useful, but in a world that is obsessed with building the intellectual wall, the previous exercise can be an effective approach for moving past the wall that human beings build with their language, and into the heart of one's inner world. From that place of understanding, silence can be more meaningful than questioning. In terms of consciousness, the Meta Model clearly defines worlds, bringing problems and concerns into a clear focus that is approachable, while the Milton Model weaves new worlds of experience and is explorative in nature.

Based on the above considerations, it can be useful to reflect upon moments in which exploring a person's inner world is the main focus of conversation, in contrast to just having a conversation for the sake of covering particular details, specifics, and information about a person. These two aims are quite different, with different results in terms of the connections that we form with others. Sometimes, when we communicate we become unconscious of our deeper motivations for connecting and can fall into the habit of circling an intellectual leash of discussion, rather than delving deeper and exploring beneath the surface.

Completion Goal II:

Consider your true motivation prior to engaging in a new conversation with someone. Is your ultimate motivation to gain information from that person, or to foster a meaningful connection with them? Aim to remind yourself of your ultimate goal prior to your next three encounters.

MISSION TASK 9: MAKING MEANING

Practice at least a few of the above mission tasks again, and this time consider the overall impact of these practices, if any. The purpose of this exploration is to encourage you to notice what it feels like to connect with the real experience of being present with another human being, rather than mechanically reacting at the surface-level of language and thought. When two souls connect for the sake of the experience, the experience is beautiful, it transcends the mere connection of two constructed selves.

Which challenges did this practice bring? If you are reading this book with a partner or someone who has read this book as well, discuss some of these difficulties with them. Which aspects of the experience did you find most rewarding? Finally, consider how you could utilize some of these practices using alternate creative variations.

Completion Goal:

Ask at least one person what their definition of 'real human connection' is, and share your own definition with them.

LESSER MAGIC

Jack Elias, a therapist in the field of Transpersonal NLP, stated that most human beings in the modern world live in a consciousness state of hypnotic trance – the trance of the masses. Elias argued that people live in a hypnotic trance from day-to-day, even though they believe that they are fully awake and conscious. The way in which we engage with the intellectual wall is consistent with Elias' observations of how people live in modern societies. So strong are our beliefs in the definition of ourselves that we forget our true potential as human beings.

For example, a mother of four children can so strongly invest her energy into her self-image as a mother that she forgets her capabilities in other areas of life. For instance, this woman might have been a great artist or a successful businessperson in the past, but her self-image has altered to a new view about herself: She now sees herself as nothing more than a good mother. Is that all she amounts to as a person, however? The other potential states of being, and embodiment in other roles, take a back seat to the current self-image that we have hypnotized ourselves into believing, and so we perpetuate the ideas that persist, telling us who we are, and all we are.

We hypnotize ourselves, with the lesser magic of the mind, into believing in the fairy tales of our recurring mental commentaries. Slaves to the subconscious, we believe our experience to represent a satisfactorily limited frame of reality, when in truth, we experience just a fraction, a miniature portion, of possibilities. We take all potential and condense it into a small portion of what is possible. This is what clinical hypnosis techniques are all about at the core: A strong focus in a particular direction. In the case of our daily lives, we focus so strongly on our own self-image that we cancel out all other possibilities. In light of this, perhaps one of the most curious features of transcendental consciousness states is that a person can sometimes find themselves breaking free from this continuous trance of limited perspectives, and into a more encompassing self-awareness.

The mythical maenad in the television program 'True Blood' convinced herself that she was invincible, and so that reality came to pass, nothing could challenge her immortality. But when the maenad began to believe that her god, Dionysus, was the only one who can kill her, sure enough, Dionysus manifested and the maenad was forever cast into oblivion. Clearly, human beings perform a similar process of defining their limitations, far less drastically, but with a similar focus on convincing themselves as to their talents, limitations, potentials, and impossibilities in life. As children, we take everything that the world has to offer and build constructs of reality by modelling our parents, teachers, and those we look up to – we adopt their behaviors and worldviews as our own – we hypnotize ourselves into existence. However, most of us forget that the worldviews we have adopted are just maps for experience. These maps act as mere guides toward real experience.

Elias suggested that the role of an effective hypnotherapist is not to hypnotize his client at all, but rather to break his client's self-limiting trance. In his book, 'Finding True Magic,' Elias suggested that "everyone is hypnotizing you—telling you what you are, and what your actions mean regarding your worthiness – by delivering suggestions to you with repetition and emotional force." Following, it is the role of a good hypnotherapist to de-hypnotize his clients from unconscious programming. Likewise, when an individual experiences a transcendental state, that person breaks from the normal threshold of consciousness that others are experiencing. Their experience is so foreign that others label the experience an altered consciousness state or an experience of transcendence (of course, transcending the normal consciousness range). Their once narrow focus on self becomes broad and difficult to define. In these moments of breaking free from trance, we have a chance to take a step back from ourselves, so to speak.

Time and again literature has referred to the idea of pure undifferentiated being that occurs prior to the construction of a defined self. For instance, Ken Wilber's exploration of cosmic consciousness states, the no-self state referred to in in Buddhism, as well as the idea of self-as-context presented in models of Acceptance and Commitment Therapy (ACT), all allude to a state of direct experience without constant mental dialogue and judgments. Throughout this book I argue that it is from this no-self state that we begin to build our constructed self – we take limitless potential realities and decide to cultivate a certain frame of existence. However, after some time, we forget our ultimate creative power and become slaves to our created self-image, which, now, appears immutable. Yet, through the greater creative potential of consciousness, we have the power to re-invent the self-image in a new light.

EXPLORATION: PERSONAL NARRATIVES

As the child in the introduction to this book quickly learned that all birds have particular attributes and features, so the child would have also gone on to learn what this reality is like – what men are like, what women are like, what work is like, and a broad summary of the world's characteristics. Each of us perform a similar process, but we forget to recognize that we are just scribing words on a notepad, just creating a tentative map of the world. Instead, we pretend as though we are writing our own personal encyclopedia of the world. Instead of adopting an approach of 'thoughts = impressions of reality' we tend to perceive our thoughts more strictly as direct reflections of reality: 'thoughts = reality.'

Some of our narratives and maps of the world serve a purpose. For example, knowing the principles of mathematics on a theoretical level can be useful when purchasing an item from the shopping center. Yet, narratives such as 'I am a stupid person' are self-detrimental and serve no real purpose. Often, people tend to equate their thoughts with truth in such a manner, however, whether the thoughts pertain to a scientific fact, or an opinion about ourselves, we tend to weigh each on the same scale. Thoughts that reiterate our self-concept often repeat themselves based on our engrained unconscious programming. A woman whose mother consistently told her "you are stupid" as a child whenever she did something wrong would have adopted such a belief at the unconscious level. This belief would have taken root quite strongly, as children have less of a critical faculty to evaluate whether a certain statement is a fact or not, and even less so when such a statement comes from an authority figure such as a parent or a teacher.

Although as adults, we might recognize that statements such as these are not facts, this programming might well have already been encoded at the unconscious level during our childhood as it continues to manifest in subtle thinking patterns despite our best conscious efforts to thwart them. Thoughts even as simple as feeling like an idiot when making very minor and completely acceptable mistakes in life manifest even as we mature into adults. Life narratives such as these continue to generate negative mental commentaries that people treat as facts about themselves, reinforcing their self-concept. In the following mission tasks, let's consider that the thoughts we have about ourselves are more like creative imaginations, rather than firm facts; we will also consider the benefit of adopting this new conscious stance in the chapters that follow.

In the first part of this exploration, your mission will be to determine what sort of narratives and mental commentaries you make about your own life on an ongoing basis. In the second part of the practice, I would like you to consider which commentaries you would prefer to make about your life experience instead. Imagine you are writing a story about your life up until this point. What will the next chapter be about?

MISSION TASK 10: MENTAL COMMENTARIES

Notice the experiences throughout your day that cause the strongest and most powerful emotional reactions. Notice which mental commentaries and self-talk you engaged in during these experiences.

Often, when we experience intense emotional responses to life we tag these responses with a string of mental commentaries, however most of us are not aware of this tagging process until we bring our conscious awareness to it. For example, consider that a driver cuts you off on the road. You might feel furious in response and scream or honk the horn at the other driver. Or, you may experience an entirely different reaction, such as fear for your safety, slamming on the car footbrake immediately. In any case, we tend not to notice the actual mental commentaries that we play in our minds around emotional experiences until we take the time to notice the subtleties. For instance, in this example, the mental commentary might be targeted toward the other driver, "he should not have a license," "he is an idiot," or "he must be drunk and shouldn't be driving."

However, perhaps the more important mental commentaries arise about ourselves, these inform our self-concept and repetitive behaviors in life, and becoming conscious of them is quite important. In the above example, you might have experienced more self-directed commentaries such as "I should have been paying more attention," or "I live in a dangerous world and must be more careful in future."

Consider the idea that all life experiences have a certain level of neutrality to them, and we take these experiences and color them with our own impressions, narratives, and ideas. The purpose of this exercise is to help recognize the chasm between the neutral experience of reality and the experiences as we perceive them through the lens of our own mental commentaries about the world.

Completion Goal:

Note the mental commentaries (self-talk) that you made during and after at least three highly-emotional events that occurred throughout the week. You might like to write these mental commentaries down in a notepad for reference in future explorations.

Side Note: At the start, it can take some time to notice what goes on in our minds during intense emotional events, but as we quiet our minds, some interesting observations about our inner narratives can be noted.

MISSION TASK 11: SELF-IMAGE

This evening, reflect on some of the mental commentaries you made throughout the day. If you were describing your day to a close friend who you trust completely, how would you describe yourself as the main character during the story of your day? Consider in particular your thoughts, feelings, and impressions throughout the day. Also notice how you perceived yourself, your self-image, throughout the day.

Now, imagine that your friend handed you a magical eraser, with which you could wipe any details that you did not like in the story, and rewrite them as you would have preferred the story to turn out. Now, note how you would perceive yourself if you were limited only by your imagination. Would you re-write the events and your behaviors the same way, would you re-write the narrative? How would you write it this time?

The above mission encourages you to recognize some of the ways in which you might define yourself on an everyday basis. Many of the labels that we assign ourselves are contrived from societally-formed notions of who we believe ourselves to be rather than our true nature emanating from within. The second part of the mission asks you to re-write how you would narrate your life story in an ideal world. This exercise asks you to really connect with your inner heart, and instead of applying common social definitions, aim to connect with who you really are as an individual, how you would act as your true self. Developing a deeper connection with ourselves becomes easier when we step back and recognize that we can imagine ourselves in any form possible with the power of consciousness. So, consider where your imagination led you in rewriting your own personal narrative.

Completion Goal:

Spend about 10 minutes daydreaming about how you would rewrite your own personal narrative in one particular event or interaction that you have had in the past. How would you do things differently? How would you feel? How would you see yourself? How would others see you? Treat this as a creative brainstorming exercise.

MISSION TASK 12: AUTHENTIC NARRATIVES

For this mission, a piece of paper and a pen are required. Firstly, write down the following question: "what do I want from my life?" Next, write down your response – write down the very first thing that comes to mind. This can be a single word, a sentence, or a paragraph. Continue the process until you write a response that seems to come from your heart, rather than merely an intellectual answer. You will know the difference, because at a certain point you will feel more emotionally connected to one particular point that you wrote down than all of the others. You may find yourself sincerely smiling, laughing, or even crying when you stumble upon this point.

Completion Goal:

Reflect on how you knew the response you wrote down came from your heart rather than from the thinking mind. Did it feel different, was there a sense of deeper wisdom about the response that seemed to resonate within you? Take notice of what the heart-response felt like.

EAVESDROP ON LIFE'S SECRETS

In this subchapter let's consider the idea that life is ever inviting us to reconnect with the deeper meaning behind the surface. I believe it is just a matter of listening to the meaning all around us. If we do not listen, our experiences of life become substituted with outdated ideas, concepts, and mental commentaries. The intellectual wall is like a fortress that we build around our experience of the world. It takes our direct experience of life and filters it in an attempt to keep us safe from the dangers of the world. However, the real danger lies in becoming trapped within our thoughts, and becoming distanced from the direct experience of life.

In this subchapter I would like to play with the idea that in order to step out of the intellectual fortress we reside in, first we must reconnect with the inner heart, with our original dreams, hopes, and inspirations for life. This is an exercise in rediscovering the core of our consciousness, the seat of the soul. As we explored in the previous exercises, this process often involves taking a break from the constant mental commentaries that consume the mind. It is important to get a feel for the sensation of listening to your heart rather than merely listening to your thought process. This is the key to reconnecting with oneself. Once we learn to reconnect, we can move past the conceptual version of life and toward the real, direct, felt experience of life.

Unfortunately, such a large proportion of people remain driven by the expectations that they believe others hold them to, rather than being congruent with themselves. These might be simple expectations, such as feeling a need to dress up when meeting friends for fear of what others might think. However, often the expectations are much larger and more complex. We pursue dreams of success in life based on how we believe others will judge and evaluate our successes. How often do we spend time caring about what our parents, partners, friends, co-workers, and bosses think in comparison to the time we spend caring about our own goals and desires that we hold within the heart?

It's sad to see that most people do not care enough about authentic congruence to pursue it above all other goals in life, rather most people mindlessly replicate what is being said on the television, online, and in the popular information sources, without thought, question, or feeling. The constant barrage of television, online media, magazines, and other outlets for information are plagued with negative, incorrect, misleading notions about what it means to be happy, to find success, or to find love. The impressions that these media sources hold about these pursuits in life are no more than remnants of society's false dream, echoed over and over, as our minds absorb them with senseless acquiescence.

There are two points I'd like to finish this chapter on. First it's important to become mindful about how we construct our ideas about the world within. You would not drink six coffees for breakfast or eat eight burgers for lunch, because this would cause undesirable consequences for your body. However we often subject our minds to a similar floodgate of sensorial input. Just as you would nurture your body by being careful about what you put into it, it is just as important to nurture the mind also. Become like a frugal consumer, but with your mind. Note what you place into your mind, as the notions that are placed into the mind are like seeds that flourish into thought patterns. As the old Buddhist proverb suggests, thoughts become habits, habits become mannerisms, which form character, and character forms virtue, leading to fortitude of being.

The second point relates to a concept from ACT: Psychological flexibility (1, refer to 'Appendix D: Notes'). We all experience a chasm between life as it is, and life as we believe it to be in our minds. In short, psychological flexibility is the willingness to treat our thoughts as non-absolute guides about life, tentative maps of the world. Someone who is psychologically flexible avoids forming rigid beliefs and is often willing to change their mind, to see things in a new light. Psychological flexibility can be learned, and likewise, most of us learn to become psychologically inflexible via social conditioning in the first place, which is what makes close-mindedness and rigid thought patterns so important to unlearn.

This process turns an intellectual wall made of stone into a wall made of rubber, much more flexible and amenable to new perspectives and new experiences in life. Russ Harris, a pioneer author in the ACT field, suggested that the space between direct experience and intellectualization determines just how fused we are with our thoughts, unwilling to divorce them in place of felt experience. Those who are unwilling to let go of their adoration of the intellectual notions that they have formed about the world are most fused with their minds, unwilling to compromise or create a space for consciousness to open their hearts to new experiences in life.

Once we let go of some of the barriers within the intellectual wall, our entire life experience changes. Remember how earlier on we discussed the idea of accommodating certain experiences into our conceptual understanding of the world? The child in the example saw a bird flying in the sky and did not know what to make of it. However, the mother gave the child a reference point. "This is what we call a bird," the mother might have said. From that point forward the child would have categorized all other birds despite their different colors, sizes, and features as nonetheless birds. By age 18 each adult has a concrete understanding of the world and the features that make it up. However, when we come across a concept that is foreign to the intellectual wall that we have constructed, we will either take a leap of faith to accommodate this new experience (as the child did upon the first time of seeing a bird) or we will hide behind the intellectual wall and reject the experience outright (insisting that a plane is a bird on first sight, for instance). All encountered concepts in the external world are either shaped to our mind illusion or experienced with an open and embracing consciousness.

An individual who acts in opposition to certain cultures or certain races might hold the point of view that 'this is just a foreigner, he doesn't know anything' upon meeting someone who just relocated to the country from the other side of the globe. If this individual took a different approach and became open to the experience of learning about the foreigner's culture, he might find that this process opens up an entirely new world of possibilities and experience for him. Mark Twain wrote that "travel is fatal to prejudice, bigotry, and narrow-mindedness, and many of our people need it sorely on these accounts. Broad, wholesome, charitable views of men and things cannot be acquired by vegetating in one little corner of the earth all one's lifetime." It is imperative to experience the world consciously in our hearts, and to leave our conditioning, rife with expectations and false beliefs, behind. An open heart reveals new worlds before us and demonstrates that our prior experience of life was less than a raindrop in an ocean of possibilities – possibilities that await the simple act of receptiveness.

EXPLORATION: LISTENING TO OUR HEARTS

This exploration involves discovering a core sense of purpose in life. Are your tangible life goals in alignment with what you seek in your heart? Or are these pursuits simply reflections of other's expectations and ideas that you have assimilated along your journey?

During a stage of my life when I was practicing as an NLP practitioner, a client had come to see me about his dilemma of not being able to find a girlfriend. He said that his ideal future partner has to be beautiful; she has to have certain physical characteristics such as being tall and having blond hair, because he deserves a beautiful girlfriend. This goal of deserving a beautiful partner was toward the top of his list of personal goals about what he needs in a partner in order to know for certain that he has attained a good relationship. He would reject previous partners because they did not match this requirement, and he took their lack of model-like appearance as indication that he was not good enough to deserve a beautiful woman (note the mental commentary, 'not good enough').

Most of the time in life we might seek for something external to us, an attractive partner, an expensive car, a respectable job, for example. It is the attraction to the initial appeal of these features that draw us in. However, often the attainment of such things will not lead to what we expect, because we are attempting to fill an inner void with an outer objective – this very idea will begin to seem more and more nonsensical the further this book progresses.

To offer an example, people who search for a good partner might value the principle of companionship or love. However, if their intellectual image of a good partner comes down to particular physical characteristic or a feature that they simply hold intellectually, then this person may be disappointed to find what lies beneath the surface after getting to know that person a bit better. Many people think they know what they want, but they haven't really connected with their hearts in order to determine the deeper-level desire beneath their constructed goals.

Likewise, if we search for a respectable job, then we might be holding our pre-geared principles of success or respect in the intellectual mind. Let's consider those who invest time training to become a lawyer or a doctor because certain people associate success and respect with these roles. Are all lawyers and doctors successful? Are all lawyers and doctors respected in the workplace? In fact, we often find that the external idea of what makes for a respectful and successful career and work environment differs from what respect and success means to each individual person. For example, respect from one's boss might mean having creativity, autonomy, and flexibility at work. Oftentimes, we do not examine the deeper desires we hold in our hearts, and just go with the societal or cultural definition of what makes a good partner, a good job, a good lifestyle, and so forth. It's worth digging a bit deeper prior to making such major life decisions.

The following exercise is intended to help clarify life goals and life direction by encouraging you to reflect on your personal goals and how these relate to the deeper-level core principles that you value most in your life. This exercise involves asking yourself what you truly value. It is a simple practice that involves asking yourself why you are moving in a particular direction in life, and then, awaiting the response from your heart to reflect on this life direction. I have included a worksheet in Appendix C ('Hierarchical Model of Principles') that corresponds to this practice.

MISSION TASK 13: RECEPTIVENESS

In the previous mission task about intuition, I asked you to find a few articles that discussed techniques for connecting with your intuition. These articles might have discussed meditation, visualization, or other approaches for forming such a connection. Do you recall which three articles particularly stood out for you? Which of the three strategies did you find most helpful in terms of developing a connection with your intuition? Finally, based on what you have read in this chapter, what do you think it truly means to connect with one's intuition? Aim to respond to this question from the heart rather than coming up with an intellectual answer.

Completion Goal:

Reflect on what it means to connect with one's intuition. How does an intuitive mode of living differ from a deductive, logical mode of living? Are there advantages and disadvantages to both? Attempt to answer this question using the intellectual mind first, and then ask this question again, this time answering based on what the response 'feels' like within. I will ask you to answer the questions in the following task in a similar fashion, using your intuitive capacities rather than intellectual thought alone.

MISSION TASK 14: CORE PRINCIPLES

For this practice, print and complete the worksheet, 'Hierarchical Model of Principles' (see Appendix C). You may start with any initial idea, this can be an answer to the question: 'what do I want most out of life?' Or it could just be belief, mental commentary, or expectation of yourself or others that you consider important for your happiness, security, or general satisfaction in life.

Intellectual response (the societal manifestations): Under the first column, following the initial idea, write down which mental commentaries, ideas, and beliefs you hold about this particular goal or expectation. If nothing comes to mind, write down what society values most about this particular idea. For example, if you wrote down 'I want to be successful at … (a particular task),' consider what success means by society's standards in that particular task.

Heart response (your felt experience associated with the idea): Next, take a few deep breaths and turn to your intuition. What is your intuitive response to this original idea that you wrote down? Look inside your heart and listen for the guidance and insight that arises within. At a deeper level, you already know why this idea is so important, don't you? If you are unsure, search for the deeper meaning that lies behind any rationalizations you may have made about this idea. At the core of it, why is it really important to you? What is the true meaning, beyond any social or rational statements? Be patient with this column, await the authentic response from your intuition.

Personal core principle: In this column, aim to sum up your response for the 'heart response' column in one single word or phrase that captures the true essence of the idea you originally wrote down. The aim of this column is to condense the previous columns into a singular essential driving idea. What is it really about? Note whether you can intuitively arrive at a single principle or central value that you hold dearly that corresponds to the original goal or idea that you came up with. You might find this differs quite a bit from the original idea, yet this principle will usually always have some relation to the original idea.

Example: If we continue with an example of achieving success and accomplishment at a particular task in life, then the 'personal core principle' could have something to do with a sense of purpose or confidence in oneself. Note, however, that the principle will be completely unique to you depending on what you write down and no-one else will be able to tell you what it is, because it arises from within your own heart. Ultimately, this step is all about getting to the true meaning behind our actions, goals, and behaviors in life. What is the core principle that is driving your main expectations, goals, and pursuits associated with this specific starting idea?

Sometimes you will encounter a situation with a no-principle outcome. This is common when the 'initial idea' corresponds to someone else's demands or expectations of you. You might not actually value the idea at all personally. In these cases, write down what keeps you motivated toward this goal. Is it about showing respect or care for the other person's demand, or something else? Aim to get to the core of the feeling.

Completion Goal I:

Complete the 'Hierarchical Model of Principles' worksheet (see Appendix C), reflecting on and refining each idea and finishing with at least 10 core principles on the sheet.

Completion Goal II:

Upon completing all columns in the worksheet except for the last one (Rank), re-evaluate whether any of the ideas you originally wrote in the first column have shifted in priority, once you have spent some time reflecting on the deeper motivation behind each idea. Now, assign each of the principles a number value from 1-10 (1 being the most important principle in your life right now, and 10 being the least important on the list). Then, consider whether your priorities have shifted now that you have had some time to reflect on the deeper personal motivation behind each of the points in the table.

MISSION TASK 15: MEANINGFUL INTENTIONS

Consider how often your goals and behaviors in life are driven by other people's expectations, society's expectations, or your own presumptions about life (based on the second column responses). How much of the time are your goals and behaviors driven by what you truly value in your heart? Can you see a benefit in identifying personal motivations and filtering out those which are simply based on social beliefs that you have assimilated throughout life?

Based on the 1-10 ranking method, you would have noticed that some of your initial ideas were more aligned with your true inner motivations than others. In certain life pursuits, your direction will likely be more authentic and congruent than in others. Sometimes you will do things in life because other people pressure you, and at other times you will follow your own heart. I hope that by the end of this book, I have convinced you, or at least persuaded you, about the value of the latter approach. It's important to prioritize what we hold dear in our hearts, at a deeper consciousness level, not what others expect of us. I encourage you to utilize this exercise to identify those areas in your life which you may like to work on crystallizing a more meaningful motivation and sense of purpose around.

Completion Goal I:

Over the next three days, consider whether the actions you take in your life are congruent with your top three core principles or not. How could you alter your life direction (even so slightly) to align with your personal principles in life more?

Side Notes:

In future, next time you interact with someone and notice something that has stood out about their behavior, focus your awareness toward the question of 'I wonder why that person acted that way?' This is a useful task in times when you find someone's behaviors or choices are unusual or difficult to make sense of. Instead of judging the person's behavior, ask yourself what sort of mental commentaries might have been going on in the person's mind that led him or her to act this way. Also consider: What sort of motivation was he or she connecting with (column 1)? Which surface-level societal programming might be pertinent (column 2)? Was this person's heart in the right place (column 3)?

As you practice with observing other people's motivations, you may also find it easier to notice their true purpose from the heart, and the potential reasons that they choose to instead act from a rationalized idea rather than connecting with their true purpose.

Completion Goal II:

Notice whether you can determine the deeper-level reasons (or principle-focused reasons) that people might act in certain ways during at least three of your conversations over the next few days.

CHAPTER TWO

SUBLIMATED CONSCIOUSNESS

Each moment contains within it infinite potential, eager to
explode new realities upon the blank canvas of life.

In Gestalt thought, there is a notion which suggests the whole is greater than the sum of its parts. In this book, I consider that a holistic, integrated approach to consciousness helps us to better understand ourselves on all levels. In contrast, from a reductionist perspective, we could consider that all learning and all communication occurs through a process of transmission. A person utters a few words, and our brain receives the vibration signal and converts it into meaningful language. Yet, from a holistic perspective, all minds are connected, and this process is less a case of transmission-reception, and more of a case of direct conscious experience and connection. Some go so far as to state that mind cannot be plural, rather each human being is connected to a greater all-encompassing consciousness, all-mind-consciousness. This concept will set the scene for this chapter.

This chapter aims to challenge how we might perceive the construction of our personal consciousness, and how we tend to filter out alternative thresholds of experience. Boundaries between these experiences of consciousness are not as clear cut as we might like to believe. However, for the purposes of this chapter, we will be considering different levels of consciousness in terms of thresholds of experience: The conscious, unconscious, and super-conscious minds. When we broaden our experience, we learn to access more sensory information – we literally broaden our experience of reality, and in doing so we deepen our understanding.

In Gnosticism, there is a teaching that states most human beings are only about three percent conscious, and 97% unconscious, or asleep. The teaching suggests that we can learn to broaden this small percentage of conscious awareness and learn to expand our consciousness. Many psychologists and philosophers refute such an idea, as they believe that our conscious awareness is more like the spotlight, we can choose to shine awareness in one small area of the mind, or another small area, but not a large area all at once. In other words, some believe that we can move our consciousness in various directions, but cannot expand it to new proportions. Yet, this presupposition is false, as consciousness can in fact be expanded and experienced in greater proportion. Indeed, some people are less conscious than others. If we consider teachings such as those in Gnosticism, then our threshold of consciousness can be expanded using specific techniques and practices.

Theorists such as Rick Hanson (author of 'Buddha's Brain') suggest that spiritual gurus who have achieved a much higher level of consciousness had done this by strengthening certain neural pathways and bridging the connection between the left-right brain hemispheres. Although this is just one neurological example, many other examples have been shown to demonstrate an expansion of one's consciousness by intention alone. This further suggest that consciousness is not just a product of the human brain, but rather of force in and of itself that can expand and flourish in a direct fashion. Indeed, studies into neuroplasticity demonstrate that focused conscious awareness can cause neurological circuits to alter, thus creating a tangible change in our neurochemistry.

Drawing upon the unconscious mind, we can cultivate our hidden potential, realities unrealized, into the foreground of our conscious experience. First, it's important to recognize that most of our thoughts are not our own, these come from acquisition from our combined life experiences. Yet, there is a part of us within that is unique to our core essence, a conscious willpower, or soul. This is the true essence of our consciousness, and we can learn to engage with this element on a profound level.

In this chapter we will consider how nonsensical it is to just trust in the intellectual mind and nothing else, and we'll look at approaches for understanding the broader picture of human experience, delving into the nature of the unconscious and super-conscious minds. Later in the chapter, I expand on the idea that true personal power arises from within the conscious heart, not from the intellectual mind. Ultimately, this chapter lays the foundation for ideas that I will be presenting in Chapter Three about how direct, conscious experience, can transform our self-image and open us to new realities.

DETOX FROM THE MIND ILLUSION

Human experience encompasses multiple dimensions of being (for example, unconscious, conscious, and super-conscious realms). In esoteric traditions, some have suggested that these planes of consciousness exist as actual separate worlds in different dimensions of experience. This is not so far-fetched when considered alongside string theories which consider an 11-dimension universe. Theories are not that important for the purposes of this book though. The more compelling question is: Can we experience these broader levels of consciousness and dimensions of being firsthand?

Buddhist monks can meditate for hours in a row, but to the idle observer it appears as though these monks are just sitting starring at a blank spot for hours and hours. Yet, their inner world is alive, more alive than yours or mine, which is rife with repetitive mental commentaries that are mechanical, not conscious. To sit still in pure meditation helps one to raise and accentuate one's consciousness, this is a prime example of cultivating higher states of being. Practices such as meditation, hypnosis, and visualization also show us that consciousness can expand to new frontiers, it is not just grounded in the constructed self, as some would like to believe.

In that sense, the individual unconscious mind and the collective super-conscious mind is available to each of us once we learn how to engage with these deeper thresholds of human experience. All that we can imagine has some degree of essence, it has some level of power, or energy, if you will. For example, although dinosaurs are now extinct, as they did exist at one period in the history of planet Earth, we still give power to the construct, the idea, the essence of 'dinosaur.' People recreate the mythos of dinosaurs in books, films, and historical exhibits. Although dinosaurs no longer exist, the idea, the essence of dinosaurs, is still real, the notion still has power if we choose to infuse it with power and continue to breathe new life into the concept.

Archetypal concepts from a long time ago have a way of seeping through into our conscious awareness. This is perhaps most evident in dreams, but it is also quite evident in our everyday lives, for example, in the music we listen to, the films we watch, and the books we read. Human beings have a tendency to create mythological narratives based on their own lives as well. The prodigal son, the damsel in distress, the victim, the teacher, the seeker, the martyr, the hero, and so forth, are all fine examples. Often, these mythological archetypes tend to have a much more powerful effect over our lives when we integrate them into our self-concept, much more powerful than our action-driven decisions. Yet, we seldom acknowledge these archetypal qualities that arise within, instead most people perceive their decision-making process as part of their own free will. In fact, stereotypes (unconscious societal structures) and archetypes (super-conscious timeless constructs) have a much more powerful influence over our lives than the constructed self.

Learning to communicate with the language of metaphor, symbolism, and archetypes can have a powerful impact on coming to grips with who we are as human beings, and our sense of autonomy and purpose in life. Consider, for example, a marriage reception or a birthday. It is the power, the essence, the connection, the mental, emotional and spiritual investment on our part that gives these events their real-ness, not their physical nature as such. What is the meaning of the fabric that makes up a bridal gown, the structure of the building in which the reception takes place in, or the words that the celebrant announces? Do these features, in themselves, hold meaning at all? No, it is the symbolism behind the event that holds the true power. The energetic potential.

Consider another example. My birthday is on the 31st of October. Does the month of October, or the date '31st' have any meaning in itself? Would a cake, or perhaps a gathering of people, give this event meaning? What actually makes the day a birthday, what gives it the spirit, the essence of 'birthday?' Some might argue that the years gone by give the date significance. But, what are years? Are years not just a social construct to measure time? If we had decided that there ought to be 480 days in each year, then the same birthdays we celebrate would lose their meaning, unless of course there is something more to it than just the date itself. It is the essence of a birthday that I am speaking about here, not the date itself. Here we can note that experiences such as birthdays, weddings, meetings we have with friends, and a broad spectrum of other human experiences have almost nothing to do with the physical composition that makes up these events. It is the conscious experience itself that is most relevant, not the material construct.

It is important to recognize that the essence we give to others, to ourselves, to our reality, is a type of mental and spiritual energy, rather than a physical act as such. To remain in line with the examples above, consider the number of arguments some people have about the formalities of their wedding. Lovers squabble over the choice of flowers, dress, where the reception will be held, and so forth, rather than focusing the true essence of the experience, what it is all about (note: recall the core principles exercise in the prior chapter, which was intended to focus on essential qualities, rather than societal constructs). In this example, if we reconnect with the symbolism of love instead, then how can physical objects cause debate? This idea highlights the imperative to move past our intellectual notions of meaning and toward the essence of the experience.

We infuse power into life experiences from the past as we continue to revive them with a fresh breath of life in the present. Most people do not recognize that from moment to moment they make a willful decision to give essence, or power, to certain aspects of their lives, while negating others. A counsellor who works with archetypes, for example, might ask a client about the reasons for cultivating a repeating narrative in her life. We bring certain stories about ourselves to the forefront of our consciousness, manifesting them and making them true in the present moment. This process is perhaps most evident in the broader social arena. Just about now, there must be at least a dozen zombie and vampire shows broadcasting during the television season. What is it that causes us to draw upon these mythological creatures in particular, and not others?

As soon as someone has an idea, or even a single thought, that notion gains power and momentum on some level. The idea contains energy, power, and potential, from first instance. Imagination is the mediating force between the realm of the un-manifest unconscious mind and the active conscious mind. Thus, our reality fluctuates between these two forms of motion: 1) Essence, what is possible, and 2) existence, that which exists right now. Just as dinosaurs existed and were considered to be real in prehistoric times, so too modern technologies, such as computers, emerge in domain of 'realness' in modern times. However, just like dinosaurs were, computers are bound to fade out of existence and into essence, moving from form to spirit, from shape to potential.

Carl Jung suggested that intuition, openness, and receptiveness, are central requirements for reconnecting with the super-conscious mind where all potential essence rests, awaiting for us to cultivate it. Here lies the true miracle of imagination and the sovereign power of the mind. Here can be found the source of what inspired da Vinci to envision modern machines centuries ahead of his time. It is what leads innovators to design, create, and inspire new worlds and to break through the paradigm of the world we deem so real and tangible. Thus, the entire aim of cultivating transcendental consciousness states is to inspire a broader vision of the world and ourselves. It involves softening the soil of the mind so that new realities can flourish.

Philosophers have pondered the ideas of essence and existence throughout the centuries, however this book is not just a philosophical discussion, and it asks more practical questions, such as: What is the true power and potential of a flexible mind to create new worlds? The flexible mind is not just capable of infusing new creations and realities into our world, but to also reimagine itself in a new light. This power of creative imagination allows someone who has low self-confidence, for example, to move past the social construction of what it means to be confident and to connect and align with the original archetype of a confident individual (as just one basic example).

We renegotiate the terms of our world on a consistent basis, based on what we choose to accept, value, and create in our lives. Just as the ground-figure illusions in Gestalt psychology illustrate how our perception changes based on whether we look to the figure or the ground, so too we can begin to appreciate how our life realities negotiate between consciousness and unconsciousness, cross-fading being and non-being, existence and essence, on a continual basis. Our conscious awareness is the foreground of the scene, but the entire show rests asleep behind the stage. The mind illusion ignores this process, it states that all that exists, exists, and nothing more. But, experiences of transcendence have shown that there exists a far broader energetic potential awaiting to be fostered and nurtured into existence.

EXPLORATION: THE SOURCE

In this exploration we will endeavor to capture the core essence in a number of life experiences: 1) Experiences of 'just being' as opposed to engaging with our thoughts, 2) experiences of learning and acquiring essential knowledge, and 3) experiences with particular significant life events. Aim to focus on the essential experience during these tasks, rather than the judgment or analysis that might arise intellectually about the experience. Consider, what is the core energy that gives rise to each of these experiences? What is its essential nature?

MISSION TASKS 16: PRESENCE

Over the next week, take notice of experiences in your life in which your consciousness is fully present in-the-moment, times when you are interacting with your reality wholeheartedly, rather than simply engaging with your reality on an intellectual level. We can notice the difference in shades of human consciousness quite easily when we become aware of how engaged or non-engaged we are with the intellectual mind. Notice experiences in which you are particularly involved in thinking, analyzing, and evaluating your reality, when all of your energy seems to be placed inside the mind of thoughts. Then, notice experiences that bring you completely into reality and out of the intellectual processes of the mind. These experiences are often marked by a very clear state of presence, sensing what it feels like to 'just be' without the constant barrage of mental commentaries.

Note that although this mission might seem like a rehash of the first few missions in Chapter One, the aim here is to distinguish between the two distinct modes of functioning in the world, via thought-engagement, and via conscious engagement. These are two distinct states, or thresholds, of consciousness that are worth exploring.

Completion Goal:

Notice the differences between these two consciousness states during this practice: 1) Intellectual thought and 2) present-moment awareness. Note how it feels to be engaged in each distinct mode of consciousness during at least three separate periods throughout the day.

MISSION TASK 17: EXPERIENCE-BASED LEARNING

Most people have differing definitions and understandings of what lucid dreams are and how we come to grasp them. Just so, most people have a conflicting understanding about a whole range of different ideas, differing cultures, and even concepts that seem universal, such as our understanding of God. As I suggested earlier, much of this conflict in perception can be explained when we consider the over-intellectualization of our culture, and the disconnection from felt experience. I have read over 1,000 articles and several books about lucid dreams, out-of-body experiences (OBEs), and astral projection, and I have found that perhaps a handful of the authors who wrote those works had these experiences themselves firsthand. Even fewer wrote about their own experiences, and most avoided self-disclosure. Most wrote from a theoretical understanding.

To further this example, when I was younger, I didn't know about the concept of lucid dreaming. Hence, I automatically assimilated the term into my existing intellectual model of the world. I assumed that lucid dreaming was a neurological term related to the REM sleep cycle. That's all. About half a decade later, when I actually experienced a lucid dream myself firsthand, this experience shattered my previous model of how lucid dreaming can be defined. My previous model instantly became invalid, and my whole experience of the word changed. This is an example in which my conscious experience was more valid and real than my intellectual understanding of the concept.

This lucid experience illustrated just how foolishly I relied upon my mental constructs about a particular idea, when I was completely and utterly wrong. As mentioned in this chapter, too often we simply fit new knowledge into our pre-existing worldview. We close our eyes to the world so much, we do not see most of what is possible and available to us in the here-and-now.

Consider the difference between experiential knowledge and intellectual knowledge. What does it mean to truly know something? Reflect on the benefits of reading about the particular topic, taking a course, or participating in specialized training about a specific subject. Now, consider the benefits of learning via direct action. What are the differences between these two forms of gathering knowledge, and what are the advantages and disadvantages of each?

Completion Goal:

Reflect on few of the best (or one of the best) skills, or talents that you have. Consider to what degree this skill came about from intellectual learning, and to what extent you acquired this skill through direct practice.

MISSION TASK 18: RITUALS AS METAPHORS

In the modern world, we tend to favor a scientific, rational explanation for most things. In fact, ever since the Age of Reason, human beings have valued the merits of the intellectual over emotional and spiritual wisdom. Further, many scientists today do not even give credence to the dualism debate at all, and consider our entire reality material, physical – with nothing existing outside of the material. However, even though we have sublimated much of our connection to the mystical, transpersonal, aspects of life, this connection to the collective unconscious still comes through in pockets of modern living. Most people tend to see rituals as something tantamount to tribal thinking, or perhaps religion, an outdated set of behaviors with no rational basis. Yet, we participate in rituals on a continuous basis. As mentioned earlier, birthdays and weddings are two such rituals. These events have no meaning in and of themselves, it is rather the symbolism and the conscious experience itself that holds meaning. Through these rituals, we cast an anchor to the unconscious and super-conscious realms.

Christmas, New Year's celebrations, and Easter celebrations, all mark events that have no meaning in and of themselves, but point to something greater. This process of creating rituals is an indication that on some level we still maintain a connection to a deeper part of ourselves. It is unfortunate to see that most rituals have been associated with societal value systems, such as accumulating and maximizing personal wealth. Just look at the consumerism culture of events such as Christmas or Easter. Have we lost the true value of these rituals, and what they point to? It would appear so. It seems that we have kept the rituals, but dissociated from their essential meaning and replaced that meaning with something else altogether.

In this mission task, I'll ask you to reflect again on some of the main ideas presented in the 'Hierarchical Model of Principles' (see Appendix C) worksheet and how these can be applied to significant life rituals. In this mission, consider some of the rituals that you celebrate in your own life. What are the metaphors, the greater principles that these rituals refer to? Do you notice the stark contrast between what societal values related to these particular rituals and their true meaning? Finally, consider how you could keep true to these rituals, expressing their true meaning, rather than reinforcing society's dream about these particular rituals.

Completion Goal:

For this exercise, choose any particular celebration that will be held in the coming weeks, or select a particular date of significance to you personally (such as an anniversary or a birthday) and reflect on the core principle this particular ritual represents.

Side Note: At first, it might seem easier to identify with the societal association with such rituals (such as giving gifts, drinking wine, having fun, and so forth). Aim to dig deeper and discover the essential energy, the primary motivation, behind this ritual.

BETWEEN REALITIES

No part of the unclassed residuum has usually been treated with a more contemptuous scientific disregard than the mass of phenomena generally called mystical. Physiology will have nothing to do with them. Orthodox psychology turns its back upon them. Medicine sweeps them out; or, at most, when in an anecdotal vein, records a few of them as 'effects of the imagination,' a phrase of mere dismissal whose meaning, in this connection, it is impossible to make precise. All the while, however, the phenomena are there, lying broadcast over the surface of history. No matter where you open its pages, you find things recorded under the name of divinations, inspirations, demoniacal possessions, apparitions, trances, ecstasies, miraculous healings and productions of disease, and occult powers possessed by peculiar individuals over persons and things in their neighborhood.

– William James

The potential to phase in and out of consciousness states demonstrates that we can interact with elements of being at the unconscious and super-conscious levels. We are not limited to just the restrictive framework of our self-construct. To offer an example of this phasing process we can consider a number of theories, such as Eric Pepin's 'in-between' state of consciousness, David Hawkins' consciousness levels, or Robert Monroe's focus levels. Let's first explore Robert Monroe's model for now, as this model offers a workable metaphor for how consciousness states are more fluid then we might first suspect. We'll come back to the other models a little later on.

Research at 'The Monroe Institute' found that consciousness can be represented in terms of one's level of focus. Based on that model, we can consider 'focus 1' as our normal everyday waking state of consciousness (predominated by beta brainwave activity), whereas 'focus 10 state,' according to Robert Monroe, can be considered the 'mind awake / body asleep' state, and 'focus 21 state' relates to broader realities, such as those people encounter during OBEs and experiences with mystical dimensions. Lower focus levels appear to be dominated by consciousness experiences grounded in our local self-construct, while higher focus levels appear to correlate with a broader conscious experience and higher degree of connectedness with one's broader environment. These states tend to arise in a non-local frame of experience and encompass the broader transpersonal self.

A workable metaphor for different focus levels is that of a radio. In tuning the radio, broader experiences with consciousness become possible. You can think of the example of dream consciousness, for instance. Have you ever noticed that when you wake up in the morning, it is easier to remember dreams than it is in the middle of the day? Sometimes when we are about to fall asleep, it is easier to remember dreams that we had long ago, and it is even possible to continue the narrative of previous dream states. About a month ago I went through a time during which dream elements became superimposed in my waking state for a few seconds before fading out of existence, this demonstrated an overflow between dream and waking consciousness. Some people experience a similar phenomenon in greater prominence.

It's interesting to consider that most people associate dream states with a drowsy, low-level awareness functioning. Yet, conscious or lucid dreaming techniques illustrate that sometimes we can be even more conscious, or lucid in dreams, than we are in the waking state. This challenges people's understanding about the nature of being awake or asleep. Carl Jung's quote "who looks outside, dreams; who looks inside, awakes" captures this idea well. It is, in fact, the inner world that is often more alive and consciously-engaging than the outer world, when we learn to re-connect with that deeper plane of experience.

As Lynne Levitan and Stephen LaBerge (researchers at the 'The Lucidity Institute') noted, some lucid dreams can be even more real than waking life, causing one to become confused about which is the true reality, the dream world or the 'real' world (2). When I became conscious during a dream a while back, I felt a rush of engagement and excitement in the dream world and I decided to fly off the ground and around the city, I found that I could do so with little effort. This differed from other dreams, in which I would just go through the motions and passively observe the dream realm. In lucid dreams, on the other hand, it is possible to explore vast worlds with our conscious intention. The drowsy dream realm of potential existence suddenly becomes awake and alive as our consciousness permeates it.

In that sense, certain dreams capture higher levels of consciousness, in which we experience worlds that are more vivid than physical reality. These worlds enrich our consciousness with colors, sounds, and even emotional experiences that transcend the spectrum of what is possible in our material world. Indeed, dream realms have often represented passages into hell, heaven, and other worlds. The recent report of Father Steven Scheier's near-death experience (NDE) exemplifies this, as Scheier reported a negative NDE riddled with hellish imagery. Christians sometimes take such vivid experiences as actual encounters with God or the devil. In the larger proportion of NDEs, a person tends to report a positive experience with a white light, encountering their deceased relatives. However, in Scheier's case, like a number of others, he reported an encounter with the demonic realms. Our once faded mythos of hell, heaven, and all in between, becomes enlivened and transformed from unconscious essence into conscious existence, as we experience these realities in the awakened dream realms. The greater magic of consciousness dreams new realities, and draws in both unconscious and super-conscious aspects of being. Yet in our world, the notion of dreams and dreaming is often disregarded.

Some years back, I hosted an online radio program called 'Self Growth Talks,' and I invited some of my favorite authors to discuss the connection between human consciousness and personal development. One of the most frequent speakers on the program was author and healer Hillary Raimo (3). Hillary speaks and writes about human consciousness, meditation, and awakening experiences, and she made an outstanding contribution to the program. I recall in one of our discussions, Hillary pointed out that in her home, her family spends a significant portion of time discussing their dreams and their significance. Hillary also pointed out that most people do not give their dreams much thought at all, and that this is detrimental, as negating our dreams, in effect, suppresses an essential aspect of ourselves.

If a child experiences a nightmare, or a significant dream that stood out for them, their parents will often exclaim "oh, it was just a dream, go back to bed, Billy," rather than respecting the sanctity of the dream realm and the connection that it represents to the inner realms. In 2013 Kelly Roncace published an article in the 'South Jersey Times' titled 'Paranormal Corner: Kids who talk to 'invisible friends' may be sensitive to spirits, experts say.' The article received a barrage of negative responses from the general public. But, there is some truth to the statement in the title. Children are more sensitive to the subtle, broader, realms of existence, and not all of their experiences are hallucinations and products of the imagination. In fact, dreams are sacred realms of consciousness that show us greater potentials of experience and should never be trivialized.

The power of imagination and dreaming is the most suppressed power of the human being, this is the magic of the mind that has been lost to the ages. To imagine is to create, but in our world we tend to regard imagination as tantamount to daydreaming and hallucination. Few people have the mental discipline to focus their attention on the cultivation of pure creative power, instead, their minds are scattered and full of chaotic mental commentaries. Using the lesser magic of the mind, people confuse themselves into a room with smoke and mirrors, their imagination equates to mental masturbation, rather than sacred connection with their core creative power.

According to Hillary Raimo, for the trained clairvoyant, imagination and creation become one and the same. As Hillary stated in our discussion program, when a regular person closes their eyes, they see darkness, blotches of color, random imagery; yet, when a clairvoyant closes their eyes, they see true precognitive images, intuitive glimpses into another's world, and mirrored reflections of reality itself. The clear dreaming lens perceives broader truths, whereas the muddied lens of perception (overwhelmed with programming and indoctrination) perceives images reflecting the mind's delusion. In the one case, consciousness works through the restricted pallet of the intellectual wall, and in the other, consciousness experiences a clear signal to the super-conscious.

Our lack of balance between exploring the conscious, personal experience of being human, and our unconscious, un-manifest potential, causes us to disconnect from the deeper meaning beneath the surface of life. To offer one personal example, I was bewildered during primary school when teachers talked about how primitive and uneducated the ancient aborigines of Australia were. The teachers took us on school excursions to museums to discuss the 'archaic' beliefs and mythos of the Australian Aborigines. Yet, like aboriginal beliefs, a number ancient belief systems serve as cultural representations and metaphors for a greater, all-encompassing, consciousness. There is a deep and moving essence behind those beliefs. It is the intellectual mind that diminishes their power to that of nonsensical rituals and arcane mythos. Even as a child I recognized that there was something profound about the art and traditions of these ancient cultures, whilst most fail to recognize the hidden meaning, the hidden essence, amongst these sublimated forms of expression that can be found in most civilizations from our historic past.

For example, the aborigines in Australia held beliefs about dreamtime and the rainbow serpent, however most people living in Australia now have a close-to-zero understanding of the deeper significance of these concepts, their true meaning. If we examine the metaphor behind these particular beliefs, the serpent can be related to the creative force of the 'kundalini,' which is no myth at all, in fact each one of us hold within the kundalini dreaming power of creation. Each of the colors on the rainbow spectrum (represented by the rainbow serpent in Aboriginal artwork and culture) relate to the seven energy centers in the etheric body represented through several religious and cultures discourses.

Hence, considering the realm of the super-conscious mind leads us into somewhat complicated terrain. For instance, most debates on the topic of transcendental states center on whether these experiences are real or just hallucinations. Thus, the aim of this chapter is to encourage readers to consider what is real and what is not real, and whether we can make such clear distinctions at all. I personally believe that it is much more pragmatic to reflect on realities in terms of their essence and existence, in terms of what occurs in the foreground of consciousness, and what remains uncovered.

Real and unreal, on the other hand, are such subjective terms, and even in reference to seeming objective proof are often grounded in human observation (and fall apart when a human aspect is lacking). Yet, there is another question to consider here, the question of truth and falsehood. In this book, I place quite a great emphasis on personal truth, encouraging readers to trust their own intuition and experiment firsthand with all of the points I make here, rather than depending on theories. Thus, it's important to keep this focus on personal truth in the practices that flow throughout this chapter.

In a 2014 debate broadcast on the online program 'Intelligence Squared,' two believers in the afterlife (Eben Alexander and Raymond Moody) and two skeptics (Sean Carroll and Steven Novella) debated the topic 'Death is Not Final.' Steven Novella, who is current President of the 'New England Skeptical Society,' argued that physically-grounded truths are self-evident, while spiritual concepts are too difficult to conceptualize, and are therefore less valid. Yet, although something as simple as an equation, $1 + 1 = 2$, might appear more true and definitive than a transformative state of consciousness, the latter is often more meaningful and has a deeper level of personal, emotional truth. Therefore, as part of this chapter it is important to consider the notion of truth not in relation to logic, but in terms of broader conscious experience, inclusive of emotional and spiritual experience.

It is more important to search for a greater clarity to discern and distinguish what is true and valid for us, rather than just depending on one tool of the mind in order to distinguish objective truth. The latter would be tantamount to using a flash light during daytime in an attempt to help enhance one's perception, as logic only functions well in closed systems, while the capacities that connect us with the core of our soul essence (such as intuition) encompass the broader self.

Carl Jung often spoke of the external experience of life as a mirror for the internal world, Jung stated that "projections change the world into the replica of one's own unknown face." Hence, while we disown parts of ourselves, terming them unconscious, irrelevant, or unreal, we find that those parts contribute to our ultimate illusion about the world, and the delusion that prevents us a glimpse into our true nature. Once we come to know ourselves at a more subtle level, our experience of, and impact upon, the world broadens to new dimensions. 'Seeing is (not) believing,' as our perceptions are often just illusions of the constructed self that confirm their own existence on the false canvas of the external world.

Let me give an example to illustrate the importance of spiritual and emotional truth, in contrast to an objective truth. Lucid dreaming instructor Charlie Morley facilitates workshops around the world in which he teaches techniques to help people achieve a dream state in which they are more conscious and have a more vivid experiences of dreaming. Once a lucid state is achieved, Morley encourages dreamers to explore their own unconscious projections that often appear in the form of particular entities or certain people. Morley has discussed some of his own experiences in which he faced a frightening demon during his dream (4). Yet, after dialoguing and engaging with the demon, he found that this demonic creature was just a visual manifestation of his own fears. He woke to find that a part of his unconscious had been brought to the surface and integrated, which led to more energy and peace in his overall conscious life experience. Lucid dreaming techniques demonstrate that it is possible to dialogue with our dreams in this manner, rather than perceiving them as a constant barrage of meaningless images.

Then, we can consider, which is the true representation in a dream such as the one Morley described in his presentation – the demon, or the essence behind the demon? If we look just to the surface, in our lives, and in our dreams, then we perceive the surface-level illusion that appears real, tangible, and solid, but the truth, the essence, hides behind our initial impressions so often.

When we suppress a part of ourselves, that part tends to reside in the unconscious as a metaphor or a visual; it hides itself in symbolism because we are not prepared to face it. Yet, in working with metaphorical dream states, it is possible to bring these lost parts of our conscious experience to the surface. Once we work with the unconscious mind, our super-conscious connection becomes clarified, and we can then connect with visions, metaphors, wisdom, and unique states of experience in the cosmic mind.

I awoke, only to find that the rest of the world is still asleep.

– Leonardo da Vinci

Leonardo da Vinci's drawings of helicopters and tanks remained conceptual pieces of artwork, drawings that were taken as no more than fiction. However, in modern times, aerospace engineers can envision complex aircraft and technologies that can in fact be brought into conscious existence. Our dreams weave into realities in a similar fashion, as our external technologies facilitate the expression of our internal dreams. As essence spills into existence, and back and forth in a subtle dance, so the tides of our conscious and unconscious experience in life follow.

EXPLORATION: HIDDEN REALITIES

In this exploration, let's consider the interaction between the unconscious and conscious mind, the flow from potential essence into tangible existence. Readers are asked to experiment with the nature of dreams and symbolism in these tasks.

MISSION TASK 19: DREAM METAPHORS

Thousands of books have been published about dream interpretation, most of these offer predefined interpretations for particular symbolism during dreams. However, psychologists have found that most of these interpretations are unreliable. This is not to suggest that dreams have no meaning whatsoever. Quite to the contrary, dreams have immense meaning and can teach us about the aspects of our reality that we have suppressed or ignored. However, dream meaning is deeply personal and must be investigated firsthand, rather than via a dream interpretation book.

Gestalt psychologists often utilize a technique of dialoguing with a dream realm when assisting their clients to recall specific aspects of a dream. One of the common techniques used is based on dream content embodiment – what would it be like to embody particular elements, characters, entities, or people within a dream? For example, if you encountered a dog in your dream, you may like to embody the consciousness of that dog, and consider, what life would be perceived like from the dog's perspective in your dream. Often, embodying ourselves in a particular dream element helps us to better understand the symbolism and purpose of that dream element, as we recognize that it is an essential part of ourselves, rather than external to our consciousness.

Completion Goal:

Next time you re-collect one of your dreams, take a moment to identify three of the most significant parts of the dream. These could be particular characters, feelings, events, environments, or other dream aspects. Next, instead of considering these elements as external objective realities, aim to embody them. What would it be like to be that particular character, elements, or dream symbol for a moment? Complete this process for a few moments for each of the significant dream elements. Imagine that your consciousness has assumed the awareness of each dream element, and spend a few moments getting to know what it feels like exist from within the vantage point, or the consciousness, of this new frame of perception.

MISSION TASK 20: SYMBOLISM

In this mission task, I would like you to consider the use of symbolism in our world. I will ask you to choose three particular symbols. As I live in Australia, I might pick the Australian emblem, which shows a kangaroo and an emu (native Australian animals) holding a shield. Secondly, I might choose the caduceus, the main symbol used by the medical establishment, and also the symbol of kundalini. And finally, I might choose a white flag. Each of the symbolic elements I have selected are predominantly visual, they do not tell us much in a direct fashion. Yet, a picture speaks a thousand words, and these symbols hold much more power than words alone. Likewise, unconscious symbolism can hold immense hidden power, until we begin to decipher it and understand its basis, then we understand its source of power. In this task, I'll ask you to consider, what does each symbol relate to? Where is its origin? Where does it derive its power from?

Like unconscious dream symbolism, symbolic visuals run through all cultures and are often used as a means of sublimating core states of consciousness, shaping reality in particular ways, and reinforcing certain societal structures. Symbolism is much more powerful than written and spoken language, as it is often based on immortal concepts and ideas that cannot be destroyed, even if the societal structures that they were born from become diminished. On this basis, the role of symbolism in our world should never be understated nor ignored.

Completion Goal I:

Take note of three symbols that you have seen before that you are not completely sure about in terms of their origin. These should be three symbols that are quite predominant in a particular culture, or cross-culturally relevant. Symbols are used in almost all facets of society, and it is possible to find hundreds of symbols all around us if we look carefully. Thus, make sure not to overthink this task, as it can be completed quite quickly.

Completion Goal II:

Rather than spending too much time on choosing the symbols above, I would like you to focus more so on what you have learned from deciphering and understanding the origin of each symbol. Spend five minutes or so researching each of the three symbols that you chose and their true meaning, origin, and source of power (what makes people respond to these symbols in a certain manner?).

Completion Goal III:

Over the next few days, notice whether the above reflections and observations have had an impact your conscious experience of life (in any way whatsoever).

MISSION TASK 21: MENTORS

Throughout life, we often sublimate particular experiences into personal symbols that have a significant meaning in our lives. In this mission task, I would like to explore the idea of symbolism relating to mentors, teachers, or inspiring people who we look up to in life as a means of cultivating personal courage and confidence.

An obvious example of this is the symbol of the mother, which also relates to the archetypal construct: Mother. Consider for a moment, what are some of the qualities and characteristics of the mother archetype that you personally draw upon in your own life? Does this archetype serve a particular purpose in your life?

Another mentor symbol is that of the teacher. As with the mother example, we can associate with such a symbol in either a positive or a negative light. This depends on whether some of your early life experiences at school, or in the presence of teachers were positive or negative, for example. In that sense, you may associate the symbolic notion of a teacher as someone authoritarian and rule-enforcing, rather than someone who inspires and shows you a new way of looking at things. The mentor can be polarized in this manner, in that we may draw upon certain mentors for strength in life, while disowning others.

In our society, many people look to the wrong mentors for inspiration. For instance, people wear branded clothing as a means to boost their confidence by associating with a particular clothing brand ("oh, it's a pair of Nike shoes, I have to get them"). Much too many people choose a Hollywood star as their mentor (whether conscious or unconscious), and endeavor to be like that person, to dress like that person, and to act like that person, to use that person's stereotypical appearance as a source of supposed confidence. Is this helpful, however?

Completion Goal I:

Reflect on three examples of how people misplace their sense of confidence in false mentors.

Completion Goal II:

On the converse, ask yourself, what are some examples of good mentors to associate with? Which archetypal mentors do you resonate with most? Mother? Teacher? Others?

Completion Goal III:

Dwell on the above question and consider which people in your life and in our society in general serve as living embodiments of the above mentors. Do they serve as an authentic source of personal power in your life, or are they false mentors?

ESCAPE FROM PLATO'S CAVE

The intellectual mind is useful for some of our pursuits. But, use of the intellect is not beneficial when exploring the nature of God, the nature of love, or even the nature of consciousness itself. These are spiritual and emotional experiences, not intellectual.

Therefore, when I advocate for a greater awareness of transcendence experiences in our world, I am not advocating for more scientific research to consider transcendental states as valid phenomena. I do not think that it matters whether transcendental consciousness states are considered valid or not. These experiences have nothing to do with intellectual terms such as 'valid' or 'proven' from the outset. The value of exploring transcendence is experiential in its own right, not intellectual, and certainly not contingent on a rigorous process of intellectual prodding and probing. If we pursue moments of transcendence from an intellectual scope, then we are just chasing shadows in Plato's Cave. To experience some of the states of being I discuss in this book, it is important to step out of the Cave (the intellectual wall) and to have firsthand, direct experience.

In that sense, it is important to create space between 'me' and 'my thoughts.' Thought and emotion can comprise of unique, conscious, original experiences, however if we take notice of the patterns of the intellectual wall, we soon notice that 99% of our thoughts and emotions repeat themselves over and over, like a dog chasing its tail. It is that one percent or so that makes up unique and original mental and emotional states within. Oftentimes, in relationships we experience disagreements about the exact same issues, over and over, repeating the same emotional reactions, again and again. The things that get us down and make us feel depressed tend to be quite similar, these ridiculous thoughts come up again and again as single-patterned tapestries. Thus the delusion of mind continues, and we remain asleep, not conscious, but in a perpetual-cognitive trap.

In order to create a space within, to recognize which factors fuse us to our beliefs and thoughts about the world, we must recognize the origin of some of our programming, and some of our beliefs about life. Perhaps a worthwhile example here is that of self-esteem and intelligence. In 2011 I was contracted to teach at Monash University in the 'Diploma of Tertiary Studies' (DoTS) bridging program. In Australia, most students must achieve a high school rank within the top 30% of students nationwide in order to gain acceptance into most undergraduate studies. DoTS is a program organized by Monash University which offers students a second chance, so to speak, by allowing them to complete a first-year of university studies, upon which their enrolment into 2nd year university is evaluated by their performance during their first year (instead of being judged by their high school marks). This allows students with low high school grades to enter the program.

The concept of struggling in high school was quite familiar to me, which drew me to becoming involved with the program. Interestingly, a number of the students enrolled in DoTS that I spoke with reported quite a low self-image, perceiving themselves as unintelligent, incapable, or just confused about the concept of completing academic work. Perhaps they did not have a good mentor, or just did not fit into the schooling system. Yet, toward the end of the program, many students discovered that success in academic work has nothing to do with intelligence and often corresponds to one's ability to think critically, to believe in oneself, and to become open to new experiences. In fact, I believe that these three factors are essential in cultivating intelligence, and that anyone can learn how to be intelligent, just as anyone can learn to do or be anything in life, if they are truly willing to challenge themselves and challenge their prescribed reality. This comes down to self-image and conscious willpower.

Once again, we can draw upon the example of a child who is told that he is not intelligent from a young age. His mother, his teachers, might all endorse this opinion of the child. There is a high chance the child will go on to form a self-image of not being intelligent and will begin to act as though he is not smart at all. The child holds onto the shadows of what it means to be intelligent, rather than connecting with the true experiential (non-intellectual) understanding of intelligence. By beginning to act stupid, others then continue to reinforce this child's reality, recognizing that he is not intelligent and reinforcing the unconscious self-image that he has constructed.

Later on in life, this individual might struggle to gain entrance into a university program, to follow the career that he wishes to pursue, and to create the life that he wants, just because he has subscribed to the image of not being smart and has not even questioned its truth. Here we can see the true power that self-image holds over each aspect of our lives, and hence the importance of changing the self-image to become congruent with our true selves, rather than subservient to the notions that others have told us about ourselves.

As conscious individuals, we imagine ourselves into existence with our creative power all the time, whether we are aware of this process or not. Just as an artist might practice replicating an object such as an apple in as high realism as possible on a canvas, so we too paint our own lives based on the self-image that we hold within. In this manner, we are all artists of our own creations: Ourselves. However, human beings are not static portraits. We are constantly changing and becoming something new. Each moment affords each one of us the chance to become a new and unique person based on how we decide to experience ourselves. So, what is the purpose of perceiving ourselves as static, unchanging beings?

In Buddhism, there is a principle called impermanence – the idea that nothing lasts forever. This notion highlights how important it is to release ourselves from our preconceived expectations and to let go of the images that we hold of ourselves and of other people around us. This also allows us to acquire new images of ourselves, of others, and the world. Some people have taken this concept too far, however, suggesting that as creative beings we have total control over our realities, and in the spirit of books such as 'The Secret,' that we can manifest new worlds with the power of the mind. Don't get me wrong. Human beings have an exceptionally powerful creative potential, but books about manifestation and the law of attraction have misrepresented the true nature of this creative power. As author Thomas Murasso has discussed on the radio program I facilitated, the concept of manifestation is not just about visualizing what we want in life and expecting it to happen overnight at all, like a number of quick-fix self-help books proclaim.

Rather, Murasso suggested that the most powerful process of weaving new realities and human potentials comes from letting go of our expectations, stepping out of our own way, so to speak (3). Our self-image encompasses the rules of what we believe we can and can't do, it dictates the terms of our potential. And that part of ourselves, we can change, however we must do so by connecting with our broader conscious experience, rather than working from within the confines of the intellectual wall itself. People hold so much to their self-image that it projects forth into their external experience of the world, making the world more of a reflection of themselves and their beliefs. While we hold on to a fixed picture of how we expect things to turn out in life, we become more receptive to realities that confirm our portrait of life and neglect potential new opportunities for self-growth.

Researchers suggest that one's personality is most significantly influenced by experiences during the first seven years of one's childhood. Peak, or primary, emotional experiences occur during these ages. Author Laurel Mellin suggested that some of our neural circuits form during our earliest relationships, the relationships we first form with our parents during childhood. Those circuits can remain dormant (according to Mellin) for decades until our first relationship, when we begin to re-experience the same emotional reactions as we did with our first child-parent relationships. There might be no problem here, if someone had a good, nurturing connection with their parents. However, if that connection was negative or emotionally damaging, then this can create strife in future relationships, as the volatile nature of relationships is integrated into our self-concept as an expectation of sorts. In those instances, this entrained-drama-mindset becomes one's sole experience of relationships, negating all other conscious potential for love and happiness.

Robert Anton Wilson also argued that it is the most potent, peak emotional experiences that tend to shape our neurological circuits, and in particular, our self-image. Wilson offered the example of a person who was embarrassed during their first sexual experience. Since then, the individual had many sexual dysfunctions and required extensive psychotherapy to overcome the initial embarrassment which integrated itself into his self-image. Rites of passage such as this, Wilson suggests, are peak points during which our self-image begins to form and become solidified. First experiences, or primary experiences, seem to make us quite vulnerable, and thus the self-image is most amenable to change during these stages. The constructed self becomes quite volatile and amenable to change during these states. This also seems applicable in transcendental experiences, in which a person lets go of their self-image for a moment, and encounters a broader consciousness, a broader potential. In these states, powerful changes can be made in one's self-experience.

In terms of peak emotional experiences, critical points in life can either connect us with ourselves, with others, and with life itself, or they can cause us to become reclusive, isolated, and disconnected (from our core self and the world). It is important to consider how these critical points in self-image construction serve to connect us with reality, to engage us with the present moment, or work to our detriment, keeping us trapped in a mind illusion. Laurel Mellin described the latter as a low-level state of functioning, a highly stressed and isolated state, whereas higher levels of mind-brain functioning give rise a co-creative mindset predominated by states of peace and authentic inner happiness, according to her research.

EXPLORATION: PEAK POINTS

I have observed that most people have hidden talents that have not been explored. I also believe that most people have some awareness of what those talents are even if they are not 100% conscious of them. Once we bring this awareness to the forefront, it becomes easier to align one's self-image with one's true motivations, rather than attempting to shape our self-image to the demands of others.

Further, living life based on the terms that others expect of us, rather than reconnecting with what lies in our hearts, can indicate that we are operating from within the confines of the intellectual wall, rather than reconnecting with our core selves. In these cases it can be helpful to continue the practices in the first chapter of distinguishing between intellectual and heartfelt consciousness states. The soil of the intellectual mind should be softened to a degree that our cognitive process works with the heart, rather than confining it. In such moments, we are able to broaden our conscious experience rather than fixating on entrained aspects of the constructed self.

MISSION TASK 22: YOUR PERSONAL TRUTH

Completion Goal:

Reflect on three particular features or characteristics about yourself that you believe to be positive, and three characteristics that you believe to be negative. How did these qualities come to be? What is their origin, or essence? Did you decide upon them yourself? Do these qualities mirror your soul essence, what really lies within your heart? Or, did these notions come from somewhere, or someone, else?

Side Note: It's interesting to note that a number of ideas we hold about ourselves come from other people, rather than ourselves (even though we call it our own self-image). Concepts such as 'I am not attractive,' 'I am not intelligent,' or 'I am a great athlete,' or 'I am capable of... (...insert a skill or characteristic that you are proud of here)' can be acquired in peak emotional experiences earlier on in life.

MISSION TASK 23: PRIMARY EXPERIENCES

Completion Goal:

10 minutes of reflection time. Reflect on your first day ever at school, your first day in a job, your first kiss, your first attempt at driving a car. Reflect on other primary (or peak) experiences that you have had in life (the very first time you had a significant unique life experience, such as a rite of passage). What were these experiences like for you? Generally positive? Generally negative? Intuitively, which experiences do you believe had a lasting impact on your self-image?

Alexander De Foe

MISSION TASK 24: EMBODIED POTENTIAL PART I

It is important to define ourselves how we wish to see ourselves, rather than how others have defined us in the past. In that sense, it can be useful to consider which mental commentaries we hold on to as part of our core sense of self. For example, a child might have been born with the talent to create beautiful music, but her strict mother did not like how her child was practicing and then told her that "this is all wrong. You are terrible at that instrument and should find some other hobbies." The daughter might have from that point onward abandoned the whole idea of pursuing music or exploring her musical talents. She took her heart and hid it behind the intellectual wall, deciding on an unconscious level that she will never amount to a good musician. However, upon challenging the intellectual wall and reconnecting with her creative power, she can rediscover this gift again in future.

It is sometimes easier to see parts of ourselves as impediments, but more often than not, these parts are just protecting us from perceived potential pain. In the above example, the daughter might not be willing to explore her hidden potential for music due to a fear of disapproval and rejection by her mother. The latter is more important than the former (in her mind). Yet, as we will discover in Chapter Four, a number of these impediments can be overcome with emotional healing, which assists in the process of cultivating our suppressed and hidden talents in life.

Completion Goal I:

Consider a time in life during which you felt you could completely express your full potential in a particular task. You might have felt comfortable sharing your complete self during that moment.

Completion Goal II:

There might have come a time where you were rejected or criticized by someone, and since then you have felt inhibited from sharing that particular skill or part of yourself with others. Alternatively, you may have been encouraged to cultivate that skill or talent. Can you recall a moment in your life when you had to hide a part of your true self in order to avoid certain embarrassment or critique by an authority figure? On the converse, can you recall a moment in your life when you felt encouraged and supported in cultivating your personal talents and true self?

MISSION TASK 25: EMBODIED POTENTIAL PART II

Consider the idea that each person is born with intrinsic qualities, qualities of the soul that can either be cultivated or ignored throughout life. Our self-construct may not always reflect these qualities. The self-construct is born of interactions with the physical world, but our soul nature is eternal.

Some of the most valuable strengths and talents are sometimes visible to other people, but invisible to us. To the objective observer, our true nature is sometimes clearly perceived, whilst we hide behind our own intellectual wall. There are certain parts of yourself that can be considered blind spots, areas of yourself that you have not yet understood or reflected on in much depth. The metaphor of the mountain in Acceptance and Commitment Therapy (ACT) illustrates this notion well. Imagine that you are standing on a mountain top, and a few hundred meters away you see someone else standing on another mountain about the same height as you, this may be a friend or a colleague, for instance. Your friend can see your mountain from a much broader perspective, and you can see his mountain from a more encompassing vantage point.

In this metaphor, you each see each other's mountains, how far you have each climbed, and how much further the path extends. Yet, from your own first-person vantage point, it is difficult to perceive such a broad view. You see things up close, but might miss things up ahead further along the path to the top of the mountain. Yet, your friend can see these potential roadblocks and shortcuts to the top of your mountain from a distance. Likewise, your friend cannot see the entire path that he must follow, yet you can see the trajectory of his journey from your vantage point. This is a workable metaphor for self-serving bias that arises in the constructed self. Each person's self-image can either further their progress, or inhibit it. We see life through the lens of our first-person perspective; yet our friends, mentors, acquaintances, and fellow travelers, can sometimes see our path with a greater degree of objectivity and from a much broader vantage point.

The most well-known psychological representation of this notion is the Johari Window. The Johari Window is used by psychologists as a tool that can represent 1) the personal qualities we are aware of in ourselves and share with others (openly shared qualities), 2) the personal qualities we are aware of in ourselves but do not share with others (hidden qualities), 3) the personal qualities we are unaware of in ourselves, that others are aware of (blind spots), and 4) the personal qualities we are unaware of in ourselves that others are also unaware of (undiscovered potential).

Completion Goal:

Find a pen and piece of paper, or a drawing application, and draw your own Johari Window. You might like to either draw four squares, four quadrants, or just four columns, each representing the four factors above: 1) Openly shared qualities, 2) hidden qualities, 3) blind spots, and 4) undiscovered potential. First, reflect on five of your best or favorite personal qualities or talents. Then, decide which of the first two quadrants (openly shared qualities, or, hidden qualities) each of these attributes would fit into. Do you openly share these qualities with others, or, are they parts of yourself that you keep reserved and hidden from most people? Then, ask a close friend about what they believe your top five qualities or skills are. Note these down in the third quadrant: Blind spots. Did you find that you learned anything about yourself after examining any of the five qualities your friend mentioned? Were you aware of these before to the same extent?

Side Note: This technique provides a chance to peek into the unconscious mind and to consider parts of ourselves that we might have perhaps filtered out or not even considered in the past. Practicing with a few different people (close friends in contrast with acquaintances, for instance) can produce some interesting results and help broaden our self-awareness.

MISSION TASK 26: EMBODIED POTENTIAL PART III

Author Robert Greene stated that the activities we enjoy doing most in our earlier years of life should be cultivated in adulthood. In his 'TED Talk,' Greene offered his personal example of a love for writing. He noted that when he became an adult, he faced tremendous adversity from publishers telling him to pursue a different career path, because they believed he was a poor writer. In spite of their negative remarks and criticism, Greene persisted with his passion and eventually became a bestselling author.

Often, that which we are drawn to earlier in life can seem like just a phase, or an unrealistic life choice, as we become adults and pursue a more responsible or secure career path. Yet, on an intuitive level we naturally gravitate toward certain hobbies and inclinations in life. It is only when we attempt to plan life within the confines of the intellectual wall that factors such as level of income and social prestige seem of utmost importance. Yet, in order to find core happiness in life (joy at a consciousness level, rather than the mentally-enforced idea of happiness) it is important to look within our hearts. What were you truly drawn toward earlier in life? Reflect on the inclinations you had at an intuitive level.

Completion Goal:

Choose one particular inclination, talent, or task that you enjoyed pursuing as a child. This should be something that genuinely sparked a sense of joy in your soul. Reflect on what it is about that particular expression of yourself that you loved (or still love) so much.

MISSION TASK 27: EXPLORING THE UNCONSCIOUS

As adults, we become comfortable with our current level of self-consciousness, and rather than expanding our potential, we find a comfort zone in which to reside for most of our lives, never venturing too far out or exploring the boundaries of our conscious being. The parts of ourselves that are outside of this comfort zone tend to become suppressed and sublimated, transmuted into unconscious potential. Yet, it is possible to re-engage with aspects of ourselves that have been long hidden.

In this mission, let's experiment with exaggerating the polarized parts of the self-image to extremes, in order to experience a direct understanding of the limitations that we place on ourselves. Notably, it is important to use your intuition and discernment with this task, keeping in mind your personal safety and comfort level. The aim of the task is to push the boundaries of your comfort zone to some extent, but not so much that you feel the exercise is detrimental.

This technique is commonly used in Gestalt therapy as a means for balancing aspects of the personality. For our purposes, it is intended to demonstrate that direct conscious experience is far more fluid and far more powerful than the boundaries of the self-image that we choose to hold on to. Like a child in a swimming pool holding on to an inflatable doughnut, this exercise intends to experiment with letting go of the doughnut, to recognize that it is possible to swim freely.

You might like to start by taking a basic personality quiz such as the Big Five personality test in order to brainstorm which features of your self-image you believe are most well-defined (5). If, for example, you are mostly introverted and tend to avoid groups of more than a couple of people, you may like to play out what it is like to be a full-blown extravert by making the effort to talk to a group of four or five friends. If you consider yourself a perfectionist and always keep a very clean and ordered house, you may like to experiment for a day with acting as a very carefree person would, not worrying at all about where you leave things, or whether your desk is in a slight state of disorder (with papers or documents spread out across it).

The first part of this mission goal was intended as a reflection on the boundaries of the self-image, and how we tend to exclude our broader self-potential. The second goal encourages readers to also consider that other people's experience of self and consciousness is not as fixed and immutable as we might believe, this realization can be quite liberating.

Completion Goal I:

As a behavioral experiment, choose any defined aspect of your personality, and in the safety of your own home, role-play the exact opposite of that attribute.

Completion Goal II:

Do you have a particular responsibility to any person or people in your life? If so, ask up to three people which expectations they hold you accountable to. Inquire about what these individuals expect you to do, or how they expect you to act.

Side Notes:

Often, we act in particular ways around certain people because on an unconscious level we believe these people have particular expectations or demands. Yet, often those expectations are self-defined – we assume our people's demands of us without first asking, we assume how other people expect us to act, often without clarifying this or challenging these notions upfront. Once you have completed this advanced task, reflect on whether your own presumed expectations matched the answers you received from each person, or whether there was a discrepancy between your assumptions and their stated expectations of you.

You may find that by asking these people to state their expectations of you, that you were probably too harsh on yourself (and if not, you may find it easier to negotiate or challenge those expectations when you hear them stated explicitly). People generally find that it is harder to love themselves and to be kind to themselves than to be kind to others. Hence, often we might make the judgment call that other people are critical or harsh, because we might hold ourselves to a high standard. Yet, the reality is often a much different one, that is, when we learn to connect with others at a deeper level and understand their true intentions toward us.

RAISE ANIMA'S CREATIVE FIRE

Carl Jung believed that the human being is polarized by two ultimate forces at the unconscious level, the anima (divine feminine) and animus (divine masculine) energies. The union of theses core energies represents undifferentiated creative force. This undifferentiated power can be cultivated and channeled into particular outcomes, hence when we experience peak moments of creative potential, desire, or willpower, the end result or outcome might seem unclear, but these creative forces draw upon the potential to bring new experiences and new realities into focus over time. The power can be felt on some level, but the tangible manifestation might be unclear, undifferentiated force, at that point. This greater creative conscious magic within allows us to transform ourselves from the inside out and to transcend the societal boundaries coded to our self-image. This is a process of awakening to one's true self and reigning over our conscious creations in life – recognizing the power of consciousness to transform our realities.

You might like to think of this as a spiritual process of awakening, or a psychological process of healing and re-engaging one's core self. It doesn't matter what we label it, this process of rediscovering our true selves is paramount to understanding instances of transcendence. In moments of transcendence, we recognize that our consciousness is capable of expanding past the boundaries of the self-image that we have formed. In that peak place of transcendence, it appears as though all possibilities are present in undifferentiated creative force. From the ashes, the phoenix emerges, born anew.

Maxwell Maltz found that a person's aptitude to visualize images in their mind is much more powerful in determining their life outcomes than any other factor such as intelligence or goal-setting. If a person wholeheartedly imagines themselves as a great innovator and businessperson for example, then this process can be far more powerful than anything that individual will gain from attending even the best business schools around the world. This is a process of harnessing our inner creative force. Once we combine the process of visualization, with a process of reconnecting with what is truth and genuine in our hearts, then I believe the move into alignment with our true selves becomes natural and progressive.

> Creative imagination is not something reserved for the poets, the philosophers, the inventors. It enters into our every act. Imagination sets the goal picture that our automatic mechanism works on. We act, or fail to act, not because of will, as is so commonly believed, but because of imagination.

– Maxwell Maltz, 'Psycho-Cybernetics'

Maxwell Maltz discovered that each individual has an in-built Automatic Success Mechanism (ASM) that the over-thinking mind often prevents from being activated. Hence, according to Maltz's theories, all we have to do is let go of the intellectual mind and allow our unconscious to take care of processing tasks. This is quite straightforward in practice. For instance, we do not have to think about breathing in order for our lungs to sustain our bodies. In the same way, by letting go of many of the intellectual control mechanisms that we hold, we find that the unconscious mind will support us and (as Maltz suggested) will also drive us toward the best possible decisions. As the unconscious mind can process the world and our decisions much much faster than the conscious mind, this notion is not only tenable, but provable (see Malcolm Gladwell's work for examples).

Maltz found that when a sportsperson could visualize a favorable outcome of a game, their rate of success was far increased. The simple practice such as visualizing a basketball shooting through the hoop, and then letting go of conscious intention and allowing one's hands to move in a natural direction to throw the ball, is sufficient enough to increase one's success in sports performance. The unconscious mind takes over, and determines how much force and pressure must be applied to throw the ball in order for it to reach its target – this has little to do with conscious, intellectual deliberation. The concept of the ASM is not as applicable in this particular book, because we are not dealing with success as such, however this concept is essential in understanding how the unconscious and super-conscious holds much more power, wisdom, and insight than can be found within the confines of the constructed intellectual wall.

So, how do we go about cultivating this creative potential? I hope this chapter has drawn your attention and led you to consider some of the approaches that we could take along this path. Chapter Three will refine and build on some of the concepts introduced here from a more practical focus. To sum up for now, let's consider the differences between 1) creative sublimation, and 2) creative engagement with consciousness.

Through the lens of the mind's illusion: Creative output must be methodical, it must follow a specific sequence of thought, it must have a self-serving purpose, it must follow specific universal and absolute rules or laws, it must fit within existing methodologies (cultural, societal, traditional, and so forth).

Through the lens of conscious awareness: Creative output is intuition-based, thoughts or assumptions do not matter as much, strict self-definitions and self-serving biases are released in favor of authentic self-growth, the nature of creative exploration is light, fun-oriented, open, and not too concerned with strict rules or dogmas, it is a process in which we are able to distance ourselves from fixed notions of a predetermined structure.

Pure creation, our greatest power, allows us to re-draw our self-image in a new light. Yet, as soon as we begin to define an experience or attempt to hold it close as though to prevent its escape, the experience itself begins to degrade. All creations in the physical world degrade over time, because creative power comes from the eternal soul and infuses the material world, which is finite and temporal. This can be noted often in our world. An artist, musician, or filmmaker produces a work of art that transcends this world. It touches our souls. However, later on, that artist attempts to live from the coattails of prior success, attempting to replicate the supposed formula that led to their success on an intellectual level. Thus, the artist produces inferior, redundant, and repetitive works that are born from the intellectual mind's fear of failure, rather than from the true creative potential from which their original masterpiece rose.

Unless we emerge into and maintain a state of perpetual creative flow and movement, we lose connection with the endless creative reservoir within our souls. If we allow our creations to stagnate, then they begin to degrade. Perhaps an apt metaphor here is that of the Hindu gods, 'Shiva' and 'Shakti.' Shiva represents the un-manifest, the potential essence of all being, and Shakti represents the active force of conscious creation, bringing potential into being and existence. This process seems to continue on a multitude of levels as the un-manifest becomes manifested and vice versa; essence and existence enter a subtle dance. Yet, the intellectual wall ignores this subtle process, and attempts to retain certain creations while ignoring new potential for growth, expansion, purging, and cleansing, at its own peril.

Our self-awareness becomes constricted when we replace these universal energies with strict societal concepts. Here the importance of separating our intellectual understanding from what we feel in our hearts on an intuitive, creative level, becomes apparent. In this manner, the unfoldment of the inner heart is often not just the creative process, but rather also a process of remembering our original being – that which existed before we acquired societal constructs or intellectual ideas about our world. From potential to actual, we reinvent and manifest ourselves on an ongoing basis. We perpetually renegotiate the terms of our existence. No being is static and immutable. When we reconnect with this inherent flow in life, we liberate the self-image that we have created, we recognized that it is fluid, not fixed, and amenable to this ebb and flow of creative flux. In doing so, we break free from the solid, fixed constraints that we have acquired, and re-imagine ourselves in a new light.

EXPLORATION: MIND POWER

MISSION TASK 28: UNCONSCIOUS PROCESSING

The metaphor of the ocean is apt when considering the unconscious mind, because it highlights the intuitive, ever-flowing, and sometimes unpredictable motion of the unconscious. It is impossible to control the ebb and flow of waves in an ocean. Likewise, in order to gain congruence between the conscious and unconscious minds it is important to recognize the importance of letting go. In fact, it is often when we attempt to force or control our unconscious motivations that we come across a negative result, often leading to imbalance and neurosis.

For instance, a person who keeps telling themselves "I will remember to finish this task tomorrow" over and over might find that her forcefulness causes the unconscious mind to become disagreeable and cause her to forget about the exact task she was reminding herself of. This is quite common – the unconscious refuses to co-operate with the conscious. The two minds are out-of-synchrony. It is important to recognize whether one's unconscious mind is working in union with one's conscious intention, or whether the two minds are in opposition and out of congruence.

Completion Goal I:

Think of three other metaphors for the unconscious mind.

Side Note: Here are some examples: 1) An iceberg (with the tip of the iceberg representing the conscious mind, the driver's seat), 2) a horse, with the rider attempting to direct the horse's movements, and 3) the computer software and applications running using the hardware responsible, such as the processor and hard drive.

Completion Goal II:

Reflect on three instances in which your conscious mind had been out of congruence with your unconscious mind.

Side Note: It's useful to further the horse example in the above task. Some horse riders have a very good rapport with their horse, almost as though they merge with the horse's consciousness and each can predict and follow the non-verbal intentions of the other. Yet, other riders are out-of-sync with their horse, and despite their strict commands, the horse might throw them off, rejecting the commands outright. Has your unconscious mind ever done this? For example, you might have had a heated argument with your partner, and then apologized and promised never to argue with them again about that same topic, but find yourself doing so again within a few days despite your best efforts. You might have a homework task or a big project to finish for tomorrow, and even though it will only take you a few hours of work, you just cannot force yourself to just sit down and complete it, no matter how much you consciously intend to, you unconsciously seek out distractions to procrastinate.

Completion Goal III:

Based on your understanding of this chapter, reflect on this question: Is it possible to achieve total congruence of being, at the unconscious, conscious, and super-conscious level? We will return to the notion of congruence in later chapters, however this is worth reflecting on for now.

MISSION TASK 29: CLEAR SIGHT

In this subchapter I introduced the idea that the mind illusion often distorts our clear perception of life. Just as dream realities are often jumbled and riddled with symbolism, our hidden biases, assumptions, and beliefs are often superimposed upon how we see the external world. Often, the images we produce in our minds are false representations of our true nature, and false representations of the objective world. However, just as lucid dreaming practice can help us become more conscious of our dream meanings, so too, becoming conscious and engaging our consciousness in life rather than hiding in the mind's illusion, can allow us to perceive life through a clearer lens of experience.

The conscious and unconscious mind out-of-sync do not work well in conjunction with one another – the unconscious perceives mandates from the conscious as limitations on its creative potential, and hence rebels, while the conscious denies the presence and impact of the unconscious and crowns itself as the supreme ruler of the self. Hence, our inner sight becomes clouded and unclear. Re-establishing a connection with our unconscious mind can be done with the use of active visualization, in order to stimulate creative, abstract, and metaphorical processing.

In this chapter, I introduced Maxwell Maltz's theories about shaping our creative potential with the use of visualization; these approaches are applicable in our current discussion. When certain people practice visualization, they only experience a very hazy, distorted, and vague representation of their reality. Yet, as we improve our visualization skills, it becomes much easier to harness our creative potential, as our reality is more closely represented in the mind's eye, and we can also open a line of communication with the unconscious realms via improving our visualization power.

Completion Goal I:

Close your eyes. Now, attempt to visualize (with your eyes still closed) which objects were closest to your proximity. How many objects were there? How close or far away were they? Can you recall particular details? If you are sitting at home, this might seem trivial enough. But, experiment with this technique out in public and notice just how much the mind guesses about its external environment rather than redrawing an accurate picture of the environment that existed just a few seconds before we close our eyes.

Completion Goal II:

Attempt this practice again, but this time spend 30 seconds observing your immediate environment prior to closing your eyes. Could you recollect the visual details in more depth this time around?

Completion Goal III:

Attempt this practice again, but this time focus on just one object in the room for about 30 seconds prior to closing your eyes. Close your eyes. This time, recollect as much visual detail about that object as possible within your mind's eye. Complete this practice five or more times in a row, until you believe you have replicated the visual qualities of the object as closely as possible in your mind's eye. Reflect on how often our inner vision is an estimate rather than a true representation of our experiences, memories, and life events.

Completion Goal IV:

Next morning, reflect on whether any of your dreams were clearer or more vivid after having practiced the above task. Could active visualization practice better help understand the processes that occur at the unconscious level? If so, how so?

MISSION TASK 30: BOUNDARIES OF BEING

Completion Goal I:

Consider that your constructed sense of self makes up just a small percentage of your entire potential conscious experience. Are there certain parts of your true self that you have not yet brought to the forefront of consciousness, that you would still like to work on? These parts might enter your pre-conscious awareness from time to time, but are not yet fully visible in the foreground of your conscious experience. Consider, are there certain aspects of yourself that you have suppressed and prefer not to face? Consider which personality attributes are conscious, and which traits are unconscious, dormant, but still part of your broader self-experience.

Completion Goal II:

Take note of whether particular parts of yourself that you have suppressed or prefer not to face appear in your dream states from time to time. You might like to return to the earlier dream awareness practices in this chapter to delve deeper into the hidden essence behind these sublimated aspects.

CHAPTER THREE

THE REIMAGINED SELF

Effective communication arises in a mediation of both minds.

This chapter can be considered 'part two' of the previous chapter on the nature of consciousness and self. In the previous chapter, we explored the notion that our sense of self does not just exist at our threshold of awareness, but in fact, we can explore beneath the surface in order to establish a connection with our unconscious and super-conscious aspects. The true self extends much deeper than the constructed self that we have contrived throughout our lifetime. In this chapter, we will consider some practical techniques for broadening self-consciousness and exploring the boundaries of self even further.

The topics in this chapter will center on how language and imagination can either restrict or liberate our essential conscious experience. Our use of conscious language and unconscious language limits our expression, as language itself can turn fluid potentialities into fixed absolutes. Like a fine magnifying glass, language allows us to focus and bend our perception of the world in a certain light. Yet, if we use words carelessly, we forget about the remainder of potentialities outside of our enforced realities. When we become open to it, life can lead us in new and unexpected directions. On the other hand, holding on to our fixed beliefs about the world forces our awareness into a prison of mind. Thus, in this chapter we shall also consider creative approaches for re-imagining ourselves in a new light and opening ourselves to the broader range of human experience.

This chapter offers the broadest range of hands-on techniques, worksheets, and ideas in this book for exploring the link between awareness and self-construct. There are a number of techniques that I will introduce here, including cognitive approaches to challenge some of our self-limiting beliefs, strategies for harnessing our creative potential, as well as a number of reflections and tasks that will highlight the essential link between expanding the boundaries of our consciousness and broadening our self-awareness. Before we get right into it, let's consider the connection between language, power, and consciousness in relation to our experience of 'self.'

LANGUAGE AND POWER

The intellectual wall's most potent expression arises in the use of our language, in particular, the English language, although other languages have similar issues. Language is the mind's most cunning illusion that separates us from the real direct experience of life in-the-moment. The English language is riddled with words that serve our societal purpose, to be good workers – it contains few words that encapsulate a means to express our creative power and potential.

In fact, if we take all of the terms from each of the professional discourses in our world (law, engineering, medical, and so forth) and combine them, we would find that we have more words that tell us about work, work, work, work, work, a bit more work, and work than all of the words in a Standard English Dictionary combined (and that number multiplied tenfold). In contrast, how many of the words in the English language can you recall the express feelings such as love, creativity, spontaneity, pleasure, joy, connectedness, or fun? The ratio is almost insignificant when contrast with negative, limiting, and useless (useless for authentic self-awareness that is, quite useful for societal progression, I am sure) words found in the English language.

Language forces us to perceive the world as man presents it to us.

– Julia Penelope

This is one of the reasons that when connecting with people, we might sometimes notice that the words to communicate our true feelings to others are lacking. When I spoke with Chris and Sheree Geo of 'Truth Frequency Radio' in 2012, Sheree noted just how difficult it is to be empathic and understanding with the use of the English language (6). As she demonstrated in that program, sometimes we might just sit in silence and be lost for words when it comes to expressing deeper empathic emotions to others; these expressions are not common and often discouraged in the Western world. During my chat with Sheree, we explored the idea that it is essential to go behind the words, the language, to engage with the core essence, to delve deeper into the essential nature of one's experience. Then, authentic human interaction can occur.

Have you ever felt as though you wanted to express a particular feeling, but there were no words? Drawing upon the common dialects does not do our inner world justice. That expression is often predefined, a canvas of limited expressions that often fail to capture the unlimited nature of the heart. Language causes us to see others and ourselves through limited predefined doors of perception.

In my early twenties, I travelled to a small village in Thailand where most of the residents had never left the country in the past, let alone the island. When I was introduced to some of the local residents, one of the first people I met was a middle-aged woman who came up to me and proclaimed, with great enthusiasm in her voice, "you look like Harry Potter," and she went on about it for at least 10 minutes – furthermore, she kept calling me Harry Potter in all future interactions. She could hardly speak English, yet she knew who Harry Potter was, and instead of making an effort to connect with me on a deeper level, preferred to think of me in terms of this fictitious character.

From a psychological perspective, this woman's behavior was based on a perceptual process of comparing facial features to one's pre-set knowledge. Each face is unique, but we have perceptual processes that evaluate certain features, causing us to assimilate one face into the likeness of another, rather than perceiving it as original and fundamentally unique. Often, we do this with other facets of human experiences too, not just faces, but this process occurs at the unconscious level without our awareness. We anchor the societal ideals that have been impregnated at the unconscious level, rather than waking up to our direct conscious experience in the moment.

Throughout my early travels to Southeast Asia, I had expected that I would be greatly saddened by many of the problems faced by the people living there, however it turned out that what saddened me the most was the fact that Western culture had infiltrated so many of the countries in the region. Western television, fast food, colloquialisms, and mannerisms are mimicked by so many of the locals. This is a clear example in which culture predominates one's own conscious expression to such a degree that it appears to overtake it and consume it whole. People often substitute their connection with their true self for cultural, traditional, societal values, as I alluded to in Chapter One.

Most people are not sovereign in their consciousness, they do not weave their personal reality tunnel, to borrow Timothy Leary's famous words, and instead copy-and-paste other people's realities in place of their own. Like in the facial recognition example, we assimilate rather than accommodate, shape ourselves to match others rather than shaping the world for the better; we act as passive recipients of external realities, rather than creating new, bolder worlds. Language embedded throughout symbolism, memes, and traditions keeps us trapped in a particular frame of perception, at a specific level of collective consciousness.

Language can contract our experience of consciousness, rather than expanding it, in that manner. Instead of using our creative potential to connect with higher states of being on a practical level, we have instead invented hundreds upon hundreds of religious and cultural systems, each with opposing views and conflicting doctrines – doctrines that rest on the assumptions within the intellectual wall. Although various religious doctrines assert that they have attained the correct perception of the nature of God, we can still note millions of people in argument, in conflict over their religious beliefs. What causes this to happen? It seems, over the course of civilization, language has created numerous problems and restricted our deeper level understanding, segregating each person into their own private mind illusion.

Let's consider religion further as an example. How often have you heard a preacher talk about morality and proper behavior, and then to find that same preacher himself often practices a complete inverse of what he teaches in church or temple? Of all the people that have attended church, what number of these have had authentic transcendence experiences of a direct, personal connection with God? Do priests teach us how to cultivate such a connection? Or do priests just give us doctrines, beliefs, and rituals to practice? Often we get caught up in the actual beliefs and language surrounding our life experiences, rather than engaging the direct experience with an open heart and an open mind.

We can also consider an example from medical science here. The 'DSM V' (Diagnostic and Statistical Manual of Mental Disorders) has recently been published by American Psychiatric Association. This manual provides definitions for hundreds of officially recognized mental health disorders such as schizophrenia and depression. The main problem with manuals such as these arises when doctors utilize complex terminologies when diagnosing patients. Often, patients do not even know what the words mean. Though a diagnosis of clinical depression might be straightforward enough, we can still find that this definition references a vague classification, rather than the personal experience of the individual experiencing this so-called depression. The clinical diagnosis references the intellectual concept rather than the personal experience on a case-to-case basis.

There is an immense difference between someone pointing upward and proclaiming that the sky is a bright blue today, with few white clouds, and a scientist explaining the particular mechanics leading to the formation of specific types of clouds and the particular shade of blue in the sky. Sometimes it is more useful to call the sky blue and to see it for what it is. If we know what it is, then we understand it on a personal level. However, as we become lost in the use of language, we disconnect from the experience and do not even understand the nature of our human condition, while still insisting on striving to decode it with the scientific precision of the intellectual mind. It is more purposeful for a person to understand their depression, anxiety, or mental health firsthand, rather than listening to the endless complex neuropsychological mechanics and medical approaches for treating their so-called 'disorder.' The latter is a disempowering process, a process that essentially takes a person's own power over their mind and places that power in the hands of certain authorities that know nothing about that individual's personal conscious experience.

In these instances, language acts as a mere map, just a shell for the essence of experience. Yet, how many people overemphasize the shell and negate the essence? Shouldn't this be inversed? The preoccupation with getting caught up in the constrictive use of language is an aspect that seems to affect all of us living in the modern world, it is not localized to particular groups or ideologies. It is a central component of getting caught up in the intellectual wall and forgetting to step past it into the heart of experience.

EXPLORATION: MIND BENDING

In the previous chapter, we considered the importance of stepping past our intellectual constructs to reconnect with the real and direct experience of life, free from our judgments, criticisms, and mental commentaries about it. How often do our beliefs about the world serve a real, useful purpose? Life would go on with or without the beliefs that we choose to hold about it. The issue arises when we invest all of our trust in theoretical understandings that we hold about the world. Thus, the purpose of this exploration is to bend the mind a little bit, to shake things up, and to make the intellectual wall cast of stone into a more fluid barrier for consciousness, more amenable to new ideas, life possibilities, and fruitful experiences.

Most of the maps of the world that we draw within our minds are developed during schooling. We have an understanding that the world is round, our planet is a certain distance from the sun, and all matter is made up of atoms. Maps about objective facts are not so much an issue. However, most of us also hold subjective maps about ourselves, such as the idea that material wealth is desirable or that physical attractiveness entails certain characteristics, incorporating societal constructs, rather than facts, into our awareness, and weighing both on the same scale of truth. These mental maps of the world can guide our experience through life. Yet, a danger arises when we trust the maps more than our own personal, direct experience.

How much of our knowledge has been validated via personal experience? Oftentimes, the vast reservoir of knowledge that we have accumulated by adulthood goes unquestioned and unexamined.

Consider these two basic premises: 1) Thoughts ≠ truth (thoughts do not equate to truth), and 2) a direct experience is a closer approximate to truth than our thoughts about an experience.

For the purpose of this exploration, we will be dividing the idea of knowledge and truth into four separate categories to demonstrate that our thoughts have differing levels of depth and meaning. Not all thoughts equate to the same degree of truth. Consider these classifications of thoughts related to: 1) Beliefs, 2) knowledge, 3) truth, and 4) raw direct experience. These categories help us recognize that we have a tremendous amount of power over what goes into our minds and whether we choose to invest in all of our thoughts. Refer to the worksheet, 'Belief vs Experience' (Appendix C) for the following exploration.

In the 'Beliefs' quadrant, consider things that you believe about yourself, the world in general, or about other people. Beliefs constitute knowledge that you have about the world, but haven't rigorously validated. Most of us have thousands upon thousands of beliefs about life that we do not validate. The point of this practice is to illustrate that the beliefs we hold about the world should not be taken as validated knowledge, until we are certain.

In the 'Knowledge' quadrant, consider things that you know for certain, or with a high degree of sureness. These things are distinguished from beliefs about the world because there is some level of truth beyond our subjective value judgments. This quadrant refers to knowledge that has been proven and known as a fact to most people in the world; it could refer to common knowledge, for instance, or it might refer to things that you know with a greater degree of certainty than mere beliefs.

In the 'Truths' quadrant, consider things that you know are absolutely true, without question. These are the statements about reality that all people agree with, without contention, these are things that seem to have an intrinsic level of truth – for example: $1 + 1 = 2$, or the statement that all matter is made up of atoms. The purpose of this part of the practice involves separating knowledge from absolute truth, that which is true in all cases, all the time, for all people, and remains true regardless of social factors.

In the 'Direct Experiences' quadrant, consider that which you have experienced on a personal level and have known to be true via personal experience. These things are true because you know them to be true, beyond contention, within your heart. This type of truth comes from pure experience-based conviction, rather than intellectualization. This level of truth is distinguished from hard truths about the world, and instead is concerned with personal truth (the truth of the heart rather than the truth of the intellectual mind).

One common example that we can consider here in regard to quadrant four is the idea of true love. Many people believe that true love does not exist. It is difficult to test this out, we can't just consult scientific research about the matter. There are also no means of knowing the truth of whether true love is real or not, because this is a matter that concerns the human condition and is not related to hard facts about the world. The bottom line is, we can know whether true love exist or not via personal experience, but no other forms of knowledge or truth-seeking can lead us to such a conclusion. Likewise, how can we know whether God is real, or whether life after death exists? The answers to these questions lie within the human heart, not within cognitive beliefs, knowledge disciplines, or hard facts. So, when reflecting on the 'Direct Experiences' quadrant, consider what you have experienced on a personal, direct level.

MISSION TASK 31: BELIEF CHECK

The three most common tests that psychologists use to establish the truth (or lack of truth) behind personal beliefs include: 1) Logic (is the belief logical? Is it factual? Is it true? Is it rational and reasonable?), 2) empiricism (can I observe the belief to be true in the real world? Does empirical data support it?), and 3) pragmatism (does the belief hold real-life value for me? When did I first adopt the belief? Who was I as a person before I adopted the belief? What would happen if I didn't have that belief now? How would my life change without this belief?).

Epictetus stated that "Men are disturbed not by things, but by the views which they take of them." In fact, if something causes us fear or concern, it is important to test whether there is something out there in the real world to be concerned about, or whether the concern originates within our minds, grounded in our subjective mental commentaries about the world.

You can consider personal beliefs tied to self-image here. For example, a belief such as 'I am not attractive' can be assimilated when someone makes a hurtful comment. Often people hold onto trivial beliefs such as this, blowing them out of proportion. Instead of just putting stock in one person's evaluation of you as an individual, it's important to test these assumptions on an ongoing basis in order to align your self-image with your true self rather than with other people's imposed perceptions.

Consider the example belief, 'I am not attractive.' This belief cannot be absolutely true, as attractiveness is a social measure. Yet, it may be true within temporary systems of logic in certain cultures in which particular facial or bodily features are considered attractive.

Can the belief, 'I am not attractive' be tested empirically? Yes, it can. It is possible to ask people either directly or indirectly (for instance, using the Johari Window technique in an earlier mission task) to identify your best (and worst) personal characteristics (note that people often over-estimate the bad things others have to say about them, and under-estimate the good things others have to say about them, thus, you may be pleasantly surprised).

Even if the empiricism approach provides some support for that belief about one's level of attractiveness, that person might then test this belief using the tool of pragmatism. Is the belief, 'I am not attractive,' useful in any way whatsoever? Does it enrich or detriment one's life? Is there any benefit or use at all in holding it? Is it possible to let go of the belief right now (does anything stop you from just dropping it and adopting a more life-enhancing belief)?

Completion Goal I:

Find a stopwatch or a timer and set it to two minutes. You have 120 seconds to write down as many things you can think of that you believe about yourself.

Side Notes:

If you are unsure how to start, imagine that an alien being has just come down from the clouds and knocked on your door. When you open the door, the alien says: "Hi there, I am from a different world and have come here to study what human beings are like, I only have two minutes to make observations and then report back to my homeland, what can you tell me about what it's like being (insert your name here)"?

After you have completed this quick preparation task, consider the types of descriptions about yourself that you made. Did these self-descriptions have any particular context or slanting? Were they mostly positive? Negative? Grounded in your local culture, or more universal? Next, after making these considerations, I would like you to test out some of these beliefs and whether they serve a particular benefit or not for you personally. Are some of these beliefs useful to hold on to, or can some of them be let go of? Would letting go of some of those beliefs (or deleting them from your mind) have any benefit toward seeing things in a more objective light? How so?

Completion Goal II:

Once you have completed the two minute preparation exercise to see how many beliefs you can write down before the timer stops, evaluate three of the beliefs that you have written down based on either one of the evaluation tools that we spoke about, either: Logic, empiricism, or pragmatism.

Completion Goal III:

Choose one of these beliefs and evaluate it with the remaining two tools. Which tool was most useful? Did the belief change at all? How has this exercise impacted your direct life experience (if at all)?

Side Note: Sometimes we continue to hold onto beliefs that are irrational, disprovable via observation, and not useful at all, due to secondary gain. Secondary gain refers to a trade-off at the unconscious level. For instance, if I hold the belief 'money is the root of all evil,' I might not want to let go of that belief because it serves as a comfortable justification for instances in life that money or income becomes problematic to obtain. Secondary gains make our beliefs seem more compelling, even when we know them to be false, as certain beliefs to validate our subjective suffering in life.

Completion Goal IV:

Choose a belief about the world, or other people, or even yourself, that you know intuitively to probably be false, but one that you continue to express on an ongoing basis regardless. Perform the three cognitive tests above to evaluate that belief. Is the belief as strong afterward? Next, consider, are there any secondary emotional gains that you receive, any trade-offs, for keeping this belief? Reflect on these points. Then, repeat this process with two other beliefs that you know intuitively to probably be false, but continue to hold and express on an ongoing basis.

Alexander De Foe

MISSION TASK 32: BELIEF VS EXPERIENCE

Completion Goal:

Refer to the 'Belief vs Experience' worksheet (see Appendix C) and write down up to five examples or more for each of the four quadrants: Beliefs, knowledge, truths, and direct experiences in life.

MISSION TASK 33: TESTING TRUTH

Have you ever considered that your thoughts about the world could have different shades of truth? Is it worthwhile to separate the thinking process into the four quadrants suggested above? If so, how has this practice been beneficial? On that point, have you considered that you do not need to take your beliefs as seriously as you take factual knowledge or truths about the world? Evaluating our beliefs is quite important when we consider some of the mental commentaries we have been holding onto (at the unconscious level) since childhood.

Completion Goal:

Reflect on the benefits of becoming more discerning in what you label as 'truth' in your own mind and what you might choose to instead label as personal subjective belief instead. Does de-classifying certain thoughts from the all-high status of Truth make those thoughts less powerful? Reflect.

Side Notes:

Note the clear difference between the 'Beliefs' quadrant and the 'Direct Experiences' quadrant throughout these mission tasks. Beliefs refer to ideas others have told us about and mental commentaries about the world that we have not validated for ourselves. However, when we begin to value our direct experiences, we begin to value what we have felt and understood in our hearts, rather than just with the intellect. The real importance of these missions is to highlight the value of actual, real experiences, that we can know firsthand.

I'd also like to make another note on the fluid nature of beliefs. Beliefs are meant to be fluid and non-permanent. Paul McKenna provided a fantastic example of this in his creative use of Neuro-Linguistic Programming (NLP) sub-modalities (7). A basic example involves changing our mental representation of certain life events, to weaken the power of negative beliefs. For instance, consider if you have ever had a boss or an authoritative figure who has put you down by saying something along the lines of "you are terrible at doing this, can you do anything right? You are worthless," and other negative remarks. McKenna suggested that you might imagine that your boss is actually 100 times smaller than he really is and that he has a squeaky childish voice. Shifting our perception of how other people express their opinions and statements in this manner often reduces their negative impact on us. We recognize that words are just beliefs, and beliefs are just opinions – neither true nor permanent. This helps break the false programming of 'beliefs = truth' that we so often seem to harbor at the unconscious level.

As a final note, similar concepts can exist in different quadrants of understanding. For example, one individual might believe that God is real. However if this conviction exists in the 'Beliefs' quadrant, then that person is just following from what her religion has convinced her to think or believe. Has this individual established a real tangible connection with God? If someone is speaking about God in terms of the 'Direct Experiences' quadrant, then she moves past mere intellectual theorizing and into real, practical, direct, core experience. She has connected with God in a direct fashion (whether through prayer or meditation, for instance) rather than just talking about connecting with God on an intellectual level. It can be useful to reflect on how people communicate certain terms, whether their communication is referring to an instilled belief or a direct personal experience with a particular subject of understanding.

MISSION TASK 34: THE MIRACLE QUESTION

Consider this. From childhood, our parents create particular expectations of who we will become. In school, teachers hold particular expectations and demands over us, even from first grade. Then, our bosses, peers, and partners hold specific requirements for how we ought to act to fit a particular template. Has anyone ever asked you, "what do you want out of life, what is in your heart?" without holding an expectation for a template answer? A technique from solution-focused counselling called 'the miracle question' sets forth to do just that.

Though it is preferable to utilize the miracle question within a counselling session, I would like to introduce a shorter, more streamlined version here, as I believe it is one of the most powerful therapeutic tools available, and hence should be shared with others. Utilizing the miracle question with the support of a trained practitioner can be helpful, as we are prone to undermining the power of our own imagination, and a practitioner can help prompt us along. Therefore, during the miracle question task, it is important to remain in a creative space, leaving all possibilities on the table. The miracle question is perhaps the most fun one can have in a counselling session, and it works best when we have fun with the process rather than striving to be too serious about it. Thus, have fun with the technique when using it. Keep in mind: This is a creative, brainstorming process, with no limitations except one's imagination.

Imagine you could be anything or anyone that you wanted to be for a day. Ask yourself the miracle question, in specific terms: 'What would happen if I woke up tomorrow morning and found that a miracle had occurred, and suddenly all of my problems disappeared – what would my life look would like during this ideal change of events? What are some of the things I would be doing as a result of the miracle?' Go into as much depth as possible. Most importantly, focus on what you see as you imagine your miracle in detail, and, what do you feel? Embrace the feelings that are noticeable. The miracle question is intended as a technique to develop creative unique solutions to life problems. However, in this book I encourage readers to utilize it as a general creative imagination exercise.

Indulge in the imaginative process and have fun with the exercise. In transforming how we visualize certain perceptions about life, we begin to create the seeds for new solutions and personal growth at the unconscious level. Sometimes, a strong imagination does not even require follow-up action. Having a clear self-image and a new vision of ourselves is often enough for our life-script to re-adjust in order to meet our newfound vision for the future. The idea behind this is explained in the personal development action steps that follow.

Completion Goal:

Find 20 minutes during the day when you can create some quiet time for yourself and you will not be disturbed. Close your eyes and take a deep breath. Allow your imagination to wander and ask yourself: 'What would tomorrow be like if I woke up to find that a miracle had happened and all of my problems had disappeared?' Go into as much detail as possible and imagine how the miracle would unfold. What do you see? What are you doing during the miracle? How do you know that the miracle has truly happened? How do you feel during the miracle?

MISSION TASK 35: LIFE SCRIBING

I'd like to introduce a technique I developed called 'Life Scribing' here, which helps re-write the self-image in new, more flexible terms, and also assists readers to engage with their self-consciousness at a deeper level. First, it is important to determine how we sometimes limit the expression of our self-consciousness. Some questions that I recommend asking: 'How do I define myself as a person on an everyday basis? Am I circling off parts of myself that I know still exist at a deeper level? Could I express myself in new ways that I haven't allowed myself to do in the past? What held me back then? What do I gain from holding onto the particular self-image that I hold at the present moment?' Some of these points may, or may not, relate to the earlier belief evaluation practices we considered, in this practice we will be focusing more so on how we perceive our self-image.

The idea here is to recognize that consciousness is not static, we are ever expanding into new dimensions of experience. Refer to the 'Life Scribing' worksheet in Appendix C and complete the exercise based on a particular goal or self-image that you are aim to cultivating in life.

1) Decide on a goal or outcome state: Decide on something that you would like to change in your life that would enrich it and make it better. This can be something external, such as a particular goal that you would like to achieve. Or, it could be something within, a change in your self-image, or a change in how you feel about life.

2) Examine your true principles and values: Refer back to the principles exercise from Chapter One, how does the statement that you wrote down relate to your deeper-level personal principles? The key here is to make sure that your goal or outcome is not grounded in social demands or other people's expectations, but that it arises from within – it is something you truly value and hold important in your heart.

3) Utilize guided imagery to embrace the new state: Refer back to the idea of the miracle question. Imagine that tomorrow morning the goal or outcome that you decided upon had become fully realized. How would you know that this has happened? Notice how you would feel as a result and what you would be doing differently in your life.

4) Transform your goal into a flexible possibility for personal transformation: Finally, refer back to Step 1 of this process and the original statement that

you had written down. Consider how the statement aligns with your personal principles identified in Step 2 and the miracle image that you experienced in Step 3. In this step, rewrite the statement so that it aligns with your deeper intention. Also ensure that you make the goal present-focused (for instance, instead of stating that 'I will start to diet next week to lose weight,' link the goal to the present moment, 'I am feeling healthier from moment to moment'). Make sure that the goal you have written down aligns with a positive outcome. Have you written down what you truly want, or simply stated that which you do not want, what you wish to avoid?

Ensure that the statement above captures what you want to achieve, by eliminating any self-defeating, limiting or negative words, such as, 'will not,' 'should not,' 'must,' or 'cannot,' in the statement. These words cause inflexibility and rigidity of thought. Our aim here is to create a flexible and open goal statement that you will be able to utilize as a mantra (or symbol) for personal transformation.

Completion Goal:

Complete the 'Life Scribing' worksheet (in Appendix C) for at least one goal or desired state of being.

MISSION TASK 36: CREATIVE MINDS

Before author Napoleon Hill published his bestselling book about wealth accumulation, he struggled coming up with a good title. One evening he set the intention to come up with a creative title and fell asleep. Upon waking up in the morning, he found that he woke up with the perfect title for his book, which became a bestseller: 'Think and Grow Rich.' His unconscious mind came up with the ideal creative title based on what his book was about, while he slept.

Napoleon Hill brainstormed some creative ideas to start with, but had no certain title in mind. The creative brainstorms did not have to make sense on a rational level because his unconscious mind took care of the rest and crafted a title for him while he slept. Our unconscious minds are capable of working in this process, the unconscious acquires our conscious intention and uses its mass resources to come up with creative, emotional, or even practical solutions to our life problems and obstacles. Practicing the miracle question achieves a similar outcome, but during a wakeful, conscious state. Remember, the language of the unconscious mind consists of images, and metaphors, and feelings. Therefore, practicing imagination-based techniques, no matter how far-fetched, can be a powerful approach to expand the boundaries of our self-image and our potential as human beings.

Completion Goal I:

Test the following proposed belief using the three tools of logic, empiricism, and pragmatism: 'One's experience of self-consciousness depends on one's potential to mediate between the unconscious and the super-conscious.'

Side Note: This is an interesting belief, one that I ask readers to consider throughout this book. However, now that we are mid-way through Chapter Three, and you have had a chance to practice some of the mission tasks here, consider this. Do you believe that our level of consciousness relates to how fixed or amenable our constructed self-concept is, and how willing we are to mediate other potential realities?

Completion Goal II:

Test the effectiveness of Napoleon Hill's method. Aim to see whether you can replicate this creative technique by attempting it yourself. Refer to the notes below for some ideas.

Side Notes:

You might have heard of the 80-20 rule often used in business, suggesting that 20% of the work toward a particular business idea results in 80% of the profits or end results. I believe this principle is grounded in harnessing the power of the unconscious mind. I have my own version of this rule that I use: The one percent rule.

Remember how earlier on in the book we described the conscious mind as the tip of the iceberg, just a few percent making up the visible body of ice below the surface, the unconscious? In this manner, we can often use the conscious mind as an intention-setting mechanism, one that trickles down and allows the unconscious to do most of the work toward a given task or intention.

The best example I can offer related to this is that of education. Most college and university students have a knack for procrastination. Most students I have taught at undergraduate level do not start their assignments until one day or two days before the due date (some start after the due date), even though they have up to a month or more of advanced preparation time. This seems to just be a given assumption of undergraduate studies, at least in Australia. Many students (not all) are major procrastinators. Instead of convincing students to start working on their assignments earlier in the semester, I sometimes introduce them to the one percent rule of unconscious power. "If you put in just one percent of work toward your assignment today (on the day the assignment is first available), I guarantee you that the remaining 99% will be far easier to complete."

Just one percent might seem infinitesimally small, but as in Napoleon Hill's example, the effectiveness of this approach can be empirically shown. The problem is that most students put zero effort into their assignments for the first few weeks, putting the assignments out of their minds until the last minute, when panic-mode arrives. Yet, placing just a droplet of effort into a new project, writing one sentence, or just a few words, or even just coming up with a base idea, can create a powerful momentum at the unconscious, a momentum that grows in power like a rolling snowball.

I use this approach often. For example, I find that if I have a presentation to prepare, usually on the first day I will decide upon the topic, then I allow my mind to rest. I then usually notice that throughout the weeks leading up to the presentation I will begin to pick up on things relevant to the topic without having to consciously think about them. For instance, take a trivial topic such as having to prepare a speech about the different types of trees in your neighborhood. If you set this topic in your conscious awareness, and then just forget about it, you will notice that over the next week or so you will begin to pick up on the different varieties and qualities of trees each time you go for a walk, take a drive, or even just go outside. This happens automatically, even if you attempt to struggle against it. The unconscious mind will automatically prioritizes 'trees' as a center of focus for generating creative ideas. Often, by the day of the presentation, you may well find that you hardly need to prepare, because you already have so many ideas stored in your awareness that have been collected throughout the week.

Just as placing one dollar into a bank account and leaving it for several years can accumulate interest that would cause this value to multiply several times, placing a humble idea into the mind and allowing it to grow over the next few days or weeks can allow it to cultivate. Practicing this technique allows you to take the stress and attention from your conscious thinking process, which allows your mind to rest. Nowadays, this method has become a sort of Zen technique for me, a new approach to thinking, in which I treat ideas as droplets of potential, rather than feeling a need to think about them for hours, plan, develop, articulate, and design – I find a lot of these processes happen all on their own when I set the intention and allow all my unconscious mind to do the rest.

BUILDING SELVES

Each moment, we decide the person we want to become, through our actions, and more importantly, through how we imagine ourselves. Although our understanding of time makes us believe that the process of forming self-image can take a decade or longer, the truth is that each singular moment contains within it infinite potential for transformation. It is just that we have chosen to augment each previous moment before the present into a cascade that shapes who we are and how we choose to interact with the world.

Imagine a child whose father continually tells him that in order to be successful in life he must pursue a prestigious profession like medicine or law. The father imagines his son in a certain light. He has built up an expectation of who his son is, or ought to become. Often, we build our expectations of others (and ourselves) in the same manner – holding a clear image in our minds of how the person should act and be – we build a template that we expect others to fit. Like a magician with a wand, we attempt to conjure a certain person in front of us.

Throughout human civilization language has been used to restrict, suppress, repress, and imprison our greater conscious potential; however, language has also been used to foster the powers of creative imagination, love, and to liberate the conscious soul. It is when our words do not mirror the truth within that we begin to express ourselves from a state of incongruence. Remember earlier on we discussed the idea of congruence in relation to the conscious and unconscious mind? Here, we can consider that language can encapsulate the true meaning that we hold within the soul, but this is limited to a large extent. The words we use are the shadows that fall around us, projected from our inner light. The aim of transcending language is found in connecting with the deeper soul-essence, to form heart-to-heart connections – to read behind the words and gaze into the inner world of those we connect with.

> We may treat of the Soul as in-the-body - whether it be set above it or actually within it - since the association of the two constitutes the one thing called the living organism, the Animate. Now from this relation, from the Soul using the body as an instrument, it does not follow that the Soul must

share the body's experiences: a man does not himself feel all the experiences of the tools with which he is working.

– Plotinus, 'The Enneads'

When I completed a minor in philosophy units during my undergraduate education, I found it difficult to enjoy the subjects taught because the lecturers and tutors would critique each philosopher's theories, pointing out limitations based on the language and logic used. When I read philosophical works, I attempt to go behind the words to connect with what the philosopher was attempting to express, what his experience of the world was like, to strive to understand the essence of the meaning. In that place of pure essence there is no right or wrong, or agreement or disagreement, just clear understanding. In that sense, I found that I had acquired real and valuable lessons from most of the philosophical works that I have read. I did not see the sense in comparing these works or deciding which is better than the other.

In the same manner, it is important to recognize that all books, all people, and all expressions of language have some hidden meaning behind them if we dare to look past the words on the page and into the hearts of those expressing the words. This is perhaps one of the biggest secrets of human connection that has been lost in our modern understanding of what makes for effective communication.

As we explored in the previous mission tasks, how we construct certain ideas and patterns can shape who we are as human beings. However, the main contention in this book is that we are so much more than these parameters that we set – the beliefs, and creations, and understandings that we have about ourselves and the world are just temporal forms.

Have you ever held on to a point of view even when it didn't serve you? Have you ever held on to an emotion even though there was nothing you could do to satisfy it, make it right, or change the situation that appeared to cause it? Have you ever held on to tension or anxiety even after the initial event that triggered it was long over?

– Hale Dwoskin, 'The Sedona Method'

As Hale Dwoskin pointed out above, we often hold on to the past. To past experiences, to past emotions and to past events we cling, no matter how long ago these experiences occurred. However, we also hold on to our mental images of others, and when we hold a particular image of someone, that person has a much higher likelihood of mirroring our expectations. If we offer others less than our pure present-moment awareness, then in doing so we limit the self-expression of those we interact with. I have no right to say to you "I limit you to being this name, this profession, or this aptitude level," nor does a single person have sovereign rule over limiting another. Once we let go of our past concepts of others, we allow others to then experience the freedom to discover their true selves.

Yet, when we respond at the definitive language-level, from the cognitive stance of the intellectual wall, we miss the true nature of others and their inner world. From millions of bits of potential unconscious information, we take a small percentage and make it real based on how we expect others will act. Even more problematic, in doing so, we fail to recognize that the true nature of a person's consciousness cannot be confined to static constructs. No person can be captured with the mental commentaries we have about them. The nature of an individual soul cannot be confined like that. It's nonsensical to believe it ever could be.

For example, if a woman is diagnosed with depression and all of her family members begin unconsciously reinforcing this particular image of a depressed woman, it becomes much more difficult for this woman to change her self-image from being depressed to becoming contented and fulfilled in life. Even if she changes her self-image, her friends and family keep the old reference of her: The depressed woman. As a result, how difficult does it become for this woman to break free and to redefine herself as a sovereign individual? It seems that familiar realities persist.

Most people hold onto even the most insignificant details about their worldview (such as historical dates or concepts, anything just to hold their reality together as a concrete form). In much the same manner, we tend to embrace the familiar in those around us, persisting to see them through the image of past impressions. Though, is it not far more important to let go of others, to allow them to express their full nature? This is difficult to achieve, as it is far more comfortable to bask in the familiar, to cling to small details of what we know about those closest to us, rather than embracing the beautiful chaos of limitless potentials of being.

EXPLORATION: HIDDEN DEPTHS

It is through the process of connecting to the deeper intention behind words that we develop a deeper understanding of the meaning past language constructs. Again, we can draw upon examples here of the two different worlds of meaning: Intellectual meaning and experiential meaning. A doctor can collect a comprehensive chart of information about a patient, with data about the patient's gender, age, occupation, education, sleeping habits and much more. However, does the doctor know who this person is, despite having collected a vast range of information and details before seeing this patient? Perhaps even a 10 minute conversation can hold more meaning; even if the purpose of that meeting is not about collecting information as such. It is when we connect on a heart-to-heart level that we begin to know someone, not just their ego, but we come to know their true self.

MISSION TASK 37: MULTIDIMENSIONAL BEINGS

Most people tend to have a very strong association with their constructed self. This is problematic, as people often define and refine their self-definitions within a limited scope. If you are to imagine yourself as an unlimited spirit, or soul, or whatever terminology you prefer to use (I use the term 'conscious being'), then it becomes abundantly clear that the limitations we place on our self-experience are temporal.

Completion Goal:

Next time that you connect with someone or have a conversation, notice whether you can perceive that individual as a multidimensional conscious being, rather than just a personality. Reflect on whether this makes a difference in your experience, and in your connection with that person.

MISSION TASK 38: BENEATH THE MASK

Have you noticed that most people in this world are on a constant mission to define you, to classify you into some sort of consistent version of yourself? We have a habit of doing this, whenever we ask people we have just met about their occupation, their age, their interests, and so forth in an effort to capture their essence. Yet, at the core, our essence as human beings is not meant to be captured, it is meant to be liberated. In fact, the greatest gift we can give another person is the gift of our presence, to liberate all false past images we might have held against them.

It is sad to see that in our world we tend to do the opposite, holding people to incarnations of their prior selves. If you examine our society closely, this is evident in many domains. Yet, even mainstream physicians have shown that the cells in the body perpetually regenerate and are in continuous movement, therefore not only do we not inhabit the same physical body from moment to moment, but the expression of our essence in this world is in perpetual flow. So few people seem interested in discovering their true essence as multidimensional beings, and inviting others to do the same. Instead, it's almost as though it is a comfortable reality for many people to remain contented with the dull song of their constructed self. Yet, there are so much more, so much more to be explored beneath the surface, if we dare look beyond our so tightly-strung definitions on the face of life.

Completion Goal:

Consider five of your closest friends. Are these individuals mainly close friends because you share personality-level interests, or are they primarily close friends because you have a deeper connection with them that is difficult to describe in tangible terms? What is the nature of such a connection? Reflect.

MISSION TASK 39: META MIND

Completion Goal:

Have you ever felt a connection with someone that could not be described with the use of language or particular expressions? Reflect on at least one instance. This might have been more of a feeling rather than a tangible reason that you connected with that individual. Instances of connecting with someone on this level demonstrate that broader levels of connection (beyond spoken or written language) are possible.

MISSION TASK 40: EXTERNAL ENFORCERS

In this mission task, consider some of the external factors that have contributed to shaping your self-image. In particular, consider which personal strengths and limitations you have acquired via social entrainment, whether that be from parents, significant others, mentors, friends, or social factors in general, and that you believe have influenced how you perceive yourself at present.

Completion Goal I:

Reflect on your ultimate self-actualized potential, who would you be if you could become the most ideal of perfect version of yourself tomorrow? How would your self-image change?

Completion Goal II:

Which limitations did you have to mentally remove in order to creatively brainstorm your ideal self-image? Consider which factors are stopping you from removing those self-limitations right now.

Side Note: In the previous few mission tasks, we considered how it's important to see other people as multidimensional beings, rather than enforcing our definitions of them to self-limiting constraints. Our potential to expand our self-concept, and thus our conscious experience, is limitless, yet we seldom connect with this potential, rather settling for a clear-cut and familiar mode of experience. In addition to projecting perceived limits and ideas onto others, we also do this quite often within our own lives. In this practice, the aim is consider further the power of imagination to re-create how we perceive ourselves and the boundaries of our true potential.

MISSION TASK 41: INTERNAL ENFORCERS

Remember how earlier in this chapter we considered the difference between beliefs, knowledge, and truth? For this task, your mission is to recall 10 self-defeating, self-limiting, beliefs about yourself that you believe stop or hinder your process of self-actualization and becoming your best self.

Completion Goal I:

Recollect 10 self-limiting beliefs that have prevented you from cultivating your full potential in life in the past. Consider when you first made the decision to invest into each one of these negative beliefs. Then, consider which current forces in your life perpetuate or challenge the continued existence of these beliefs.

Completion Goal II:

Complete the cognitive tests (we discussed earlier) on each of these beliefs, testing each one on the merits of logic (is it absolutely true?), empiricism (is it observable?), and pragmatism (is it useful?). After completing this process for each belief, ask yourself the question: What would it take for me to release this belief from my self-image and no longer perpetuate its existence from this moment onward? Reflect on the answer from an intuitive, heartfelt level, rather than attempting to come up with an intellectual response. Reflect on how this belief might contribute to, and shape, your current self-experience, and whether this serves your ultimate best interests or not.

Completion Goal III:

List the negative beliefs that are still prevalent in your awareness after completing the above exercise, despite having completed the above task. You may find that some beliefs are easy to let go, as you embrace new potential opportunities for self-growth, while others are more stagnant and rooted in your self-image. For this task, make a list of some of the more stagnant beliefs and complete the above exercise again, but this time perform each of the cognitive tests on the version of each belief based on when it first came into your life.

Side Note: In this exercise, you will be required to use your memory to bring each key point that you wrote down into your imagination, and recollect when you first acquired each of these stagnant negative beliefs. Some of these might have been recently integrated into your self-image, while others could have been acquired earlier on in life. You may not remember when you acquired particular beliefs, in this case think back to a time when the particular belief in question shaped your behavior and experiences in life in a negative way, a time when this part of you did not serve you well. It is best to choose the most potent memory of this experience for the purpose of this task.

MISSION TASK 42: THE UNLIMITED SELF

Researcher Rupert Sheldrake stated that it makes little sense to consider that the human mind is imprisoned in the physical brain. Sheldrake instead postulated that the energy field of consciousness extends far beyond the physical brain and body – although the physical brain is a material substance, the mind transcends the physical realm. If we play with this idea further, questions such as what makes a person intelligent, creative, productive, happy, calm, motivated, and so forth can be considered as factors that do not just arise from one's cognitive make-up, but rather qualities that are central to one's self-consciousness, to one's unique soul.

There are many ways in which we limit our self-image, we have discussed several throughout this chapter. Yet, at a core level, what really limits us, if anything at all? Are there any definitive limits on self-potential? Are there any intrinsic limits on the power of the human mind?

Completion Goal:

Reflect on the above two paragraphs.

THIS MEANINGLESS WORLD

In the work, 'A Course in Miracles,' it is proposed that we live in a meaningless world, all the meaning we assign to the external world has been painted in a contrived light, and thus only remains true while we lend our belief to it. Once we erase all the social conditioning from the face of the world, what meaning remains? We then recognized the neutral nature of all things. The world becomes a meaningless place, replete with un-actualized potential. In its stark emptiness, the world can become full again. In moving toward re-imagining our world, we recognize that all that is true, all that is real, arise from the eternal realm within, not from temporal societal structures.

A good example of this can be found in maps. When astronauts look at the earth from space, they perceive continents and oceans. Yet, when we look at maps, we perceive countries with clear borders. However, the borders are not there in reality, are they? These borders are socially constructed, not absolute. A similar process occurs with our minds – we fill our minds with temporal notions that only make sense within specific and finite societal contexts.

However, the intellectual wall coaxes us into believing that its ideas are ultimate. The truth is, human beings create themselves from infinite possibilities. Once we focus too much on the attachment we have to a particular facet of the self-image, we seem to develop a somewhat tunnel vision, a vision through which all other possibilities becomes somehow distant and inaccessible to us. Yet, the road into the inner heart shows us that we are capable of achieving our dreams and life, if we step outside of the limiting image that we have created for ourselves at the intellectual level.

It would be fitting to end this chapter on a note about creative potential, as we have discussed the benefit of cleansing the mind, but have not considered techniques for cultivating the conscious soul from the emptiness that is left behind – something the following chapter centers on. For now, consider the origin of our core principles in life. Is the origin limited to the material world, such as having a good upbringing or acquiring ethical values, or is there a deeper part of us where these core principles arise? For instance, are our authentic life values informed from a place even deeper, beneath the personality, a soul-connection, so to speak? Is this possible?

Russ Harris argued that the best treatment approach for someone who is experiencing low self-confidence does not involve building new mental commentaries of a confident person. Rather, it involves letting go of the mental commentaries about low confidence, letting go of the meaning altogether, and seeing what comes of it. What comes is the origin of the true self, not a false bolstered confidence, but an authentic neutral self-expression that was there in the first place, awaiting beneath the surface, hidden under the mask of the false persona. As we let go of our intellectual understanding of what it means to be non-confident, we allow what remains to flourish; our true nature. Consider most children, for example. Until someone tells a child that he is not good enough or not smart enough, for instance, the child does not even know what it means to have low self-confidence, hence most children just express themselves in terms of their true self. There is no need to undercompensate or overcompensate for certain character features. It is later on in adult life that these mental commentaries become acquired and restrict certain aspects of our potential conscious experience.

All mental commentaries, all self-images, not just those that are negative and self-defeating, are restrictive in nature. Holding onto the image of being a confident person, or a great mother, or a great musician, can limit our creative expression just as much as holding on to a negative self-image of not being good enough or not being smart enough, for example. As I briefly mentioned earlier, a great deal of artists, authors, and musicians tend to produce inferior works after gaining a certain degree of fame. The expectation of millions of people around the world that define someone as an excellent musician or an excellent author hold a collective image that places so much expectation on the person. The construct of being good at a particular task or skill can restrict the creative process and the unlimited nature of the conscious soul just as much as a self-defeating construct. Good and bad qualities are dualities, dichotomies of the intellectual wall rather than non-definable infinite expressions of the unlimited self.

To sum up this chapter: No definition, word, or term could encapsulate the unlimited nature of consciousness. Our language and definitions do little justice to the ineffable potential of the soul. This chapter suggested that changing the self-image is an important process on the road to recognizing that we are not just who we define ourselves to be. Yet, the strongest self-image is perhaps one that is most amenable to change, open to possibilities and free-flowing, just as the true nature of consciousness is.

EXPLORATION: NON-CONCEPTUAL BEING

The following mission tasks begin to ask the big questions that set the stage for the remainder of the book. What is the true origin of the constructed self? How is our self-image linked to our direct conscious experience of life? And, what is the origin of the soul? As always, reflect on these tasks based on your own personal, direct, experience with them.

MISSION TASK 43: TABULA RASA

Strict materialist tend to believe that the sum of a person's essence is based on their personality that they have developed throughout this lifetime, and that without the personality there is just a blank slate of potential awaiting to be realized. Although this is true to some extent, when we dig a little deeper beyond the constructed self, we can come into contact with a unique soul essence. This is something that makes each person's experience of consciousness unique.

Completion Goal I:

Consider the following question and reflect on this for a few moments: 'Who would I be without my personality?'

Completion Goal II:

Consider the following question and reflect on this for a few moments: 'If I did not have any of my five senses, sight, smell, hearing, touch, or taste, would anything remain that is conscious within me? Would I know that I am still here?'

Side Note: These mission goals are intended to sum up the first three chapters of the book and to encourage readers to consider the deeper aspects of themselves that might not be immediately obvious at the surface level. The extension to this task is based on a technique my partner often uses in order to challenge people to consider whether reality is limited to a five-sensory representation, and whether consciousness can be deemed to arise from an interplay of these five senses, or whether it transcends sensorial experience altogether. Note, as always, there is no agenda or presupposition with these mission tasks, and the main aim is to encourage readers to experiment with these questions themselves in order to come to their own conclusions based on direct experience.

MISSION TASK 44: PROJECTIONS

In his book, 'The Four Agreements,' Don Miguel Ruiz stated that one of the keys to happiness is not to take things personally. This may seem a simplistic statement on first glance, however this important lesson is grounded in the understanding that most aspects of objective reality do not reflect on us directly. Yet we believe they do, to our peril. People intrinsically have a self-serving bias that causes them to assume events happening around them are somehow related to them in a direct, personal fashion. Often, we see parts of ourselves in other people, and indeed we project elements of our inner world onto the outer world before us, in doing so we create a biased representation of life experience. When we take things personally too often, we assume that everything that happens around us is, in fact, about us (it seldom is).

Taking the converse attitude allows us to more objectively engage with the world and to more authentically connect with those around us. In doing so, at first we might recognize that most people are too concerned with their own internal dialogue to even bother with those assumptions we might believe them to hold toward us. On the other hand, in stepping outside of ourselves for a moment and focusing on others, and the world, we temporarily break from our projected biases.

Completion Goal:

Recollect up to five instances when you reacted to other people in a particular manner because you believed they were judging you in a certain way. Retrospect on how you could perceive those situations differently, recognizing that these individuals were perhaps merely expressing their own personal view of reality, rather than judging your experience.

Side Note: On that point, consider whether it is in fact possible to judge another person's experience, at the core of it. Many judgments that people make about others are made through the filters of their own worldview, therefore their judgments are often misinformed, as it is impossible to know another person's experience unless we step into the depths of their inner world. Thus, most judgments are misinformed surface-level beliefs, and are flawed in their nature.

MISSION TASK 45: THE CENTER

Completion Goal:

10 minutes of reflection time. Consider what it means to operate from the center of your being. Take note of where you consider the center of your power and creativity to reside. This could be a physiological location in your body, or more of a metaphorical center. Where does the core of your consciousness arise?

CHAPTER FOUR

RECLAIMING DISAVOWED EMOTIONS

If I live to dream, then I may not wake.
Am I as I seem?
Or, do I pretend for your sake?

Our unique soul expression cannot be constrained, it is rather the intellectual mind that attempts to define and confine the nature of self to a tangible concept. We strive for particular markers of success, happiness, love, and satisfaction in life based on our self-concept, rather than striving to align with the true nature of our soul – the consciousness within. In that sense, the idea of self-development is a strange notion. It implies building up the self, improving on, and strengthening particular parts of ourselves. Yet, the approach that we have taken to self-growth in this book so far is more of a self-releasing process – as we release some of the fixed images of ourselves, we allow a new perspectives, and new experiences to flourish. Our consciousness expands in this manner.

Our potential to expand our conscious experience can be boiled down to clearing the filters of perception, so that we might once again see things through the lens of our own souls, rather than from the lens of the constructed mind-self matrix. On a conceptual level, a person might believe that having more money, more respect from others, a better partner, a better job, a better body, and so forth, would lead to happiness. Yet, depending on external sources to achieve inner happiness is a fruitless pursuit. Hence, we can dream-weave new realities and re-invent ourselves with the power of imagination all we like, but unless we learn to experience a deeper connection with ourselves at the soul-level, our creative power becomes misused, as it is misguided. It's important to thus align our creative potential with our hearts.

The first three chapters of this book have dealt with the idea of clearing our vision beyond the mind illusion, in order to reconnect with felt experience. This chapter explores felt experience further, what it means to connect with ourselves on a deeper level, and the nature of our soul essence beneath the surface.

In order to venture into this area, I'd like to explore the dimension of emotional consciousness. Author Robert Augustus Masters' work highlighted a number of fascinating discoveries about the nature of emotion. First of all, Masters noted that emotional processing complements the quality of logical, rational processing, as our decisions become better-rounded and more informed. Second, in his book 'Emotional Intimacy,' Masters noted a direct correlation between emotional intelligence and practical, or relational intelligence, suggesting that a person with a high intelligence quotient (IQ) who has a low-level emotional intelligence would struggle with processing the world and their life experience in a manner other than one that is linear, logical, and rational – negating abstract and emotional means of understanding.

Perhaps the most interesting point that Masters made in his work is that logical thinking is in fact a less intensive means of engaging with the world than emotional engagement, the latter requires more refined self-awareness. Further, emotional awareness often requires more complex processing and helps develop our overall logical-emotional connection, which leads to more holistic functioning overall. As we know, challenging ourselves intellectually strengthens our mental capabilities – yet, few people realize that the same is true of our emotional and spiritual faculties. Few people spend sufficient time developing these. An approach to life that incorporates both intellectual and emotional awareness fosters a more satisfying experience of human connection, Masters found.

It would be naive to consider that logic and rational thinking is the single method of acquiring knowledge and intelligence. Bryan Roche of 'The National University of Ireland' went as far as to argue that brain training games that are advertised as preventative means for Alzheimer's and dementia are not even near as effective as relational training, in which a person expands their awareness of the world and its relational structures, rather than just building up the intellectual capacities and conceptual understandings. Notably, the effectiveness of brain training techniques for increasing one's IQ has been in contention for some time. On some level, I believe that we intuitively know that strengthening our capacity for emotional and spiritual understanding would serve to complement our use of logic and rational thought, yet strangely, in our world most people have abandoned the former in place of the latter, almost raising it to a superior status. In our society, especially in the West, we have a tendency to avoid excessive emotion, and emotion is often associated with the lack of clear thinking. This causes people to feel disempowered when they respond emotionally rather than logically; logic is thus often misperceived as a more definitive, correct mode of processing the world.

It is rare to see the practice of cultivating emotion for the sake of feeling, rather than for an end result in our world. Instead, there are all sorts of rules and unspoken presumptions about how a person should feel in certain circumstances – most of these are tied into logical, intellectual understandings, and do not represent the value of emotional and spiritual experience for the sake of it. Therefore, in this chapter will we will be experimenting with the potential value of embodying certain emotions fully for the sake of coming to a better understanding of ourselves and our human potential.

So, how is emotional awareness related to consciousness? First, coming to a broader understanding of our emotions, their origin, and their connectedness with our core self helps us to understand ourselves better, this process broadens our self-consciousness. Second, we also broaden our consciousness of other people's experience on a felt level in doing so. This is a process at the heart of true felt conscious experience, piercing the wall to reconnect with other people's true nature in a direct, unfiltered manner – authentic human connection. Therefore, this process allows us to develop greater capacities for empathic connection and understanding.

In the previous chapter, we explored the idea that a number of our thoughts and desires are not our own, they are acquired through a social transfer process. These thoughts come from friends, our parents, and societal influences. Yet, how can someone experience true happiness when pursuing someone else's dream of happiness? Is it possible? The same case arises when we pursue someone else's vision of love, freedom, or other endeavors in life. Unless the vision is personal and unique to us, there is little chance of realizing it.

Mental preconditions often reference the external world, as though others, or 'the world' owes us some semblance of happiness, or success. 'I will experience true happiness when x occurs, I will feel loved when x occurs, I will be successful when I have achieved x.'

For example, consider a woman who holds the belief that 'I will talk with my father when he speaks to me in 'x' way.' The daughter conditions her connection with another human being based on specific rules and requirements that she made on an intellectual level. In creating these requirements, this woman is also preventing herself a connection with her father and causing self-pain in the process of doing so. Some people avoid connecting with their family members for over 20 years over a single conflict that occurred all that time back. In the previous chapter, I aimed to illustrate the importance of connecting beyond the language restrictions that we have set up for ourselves. Recall that it is important to stop viewing other human beings through the social conditions that we have acquired and to instead recognize that no social construct or language construct could contain the true nature of an individual's soul. That which lies within the heart of each human being transcends that which we can come to know through mere societal or intellectual constructs.

Let's explore this idea a bit further. Do we experience our true consciousness, our soul essence, in a direct manner? Thus far, I have suggested that we are limited in our conscious experience, through the filters of the constructed self. Remember in the previous chapter how I suggested that dual states of mind are limited in that they fail to capture the true nature of the eternal soul? Pursuing the self-concept of 'I am a confident person' can have as much detriment as holding a self-image of low confidence. Both are dualities, polarized sides of the same coin. People who have an inferiority complex often overcompensate and can even begin to develop a superiority complex after a while – attempting to balance out the scales of the personality is a futile endeavor. Instead, it's a much more rewarding pursuit to strive toward self-acceptance and self-understanding – to understand our soul nature, rather than attempting to somehow capture or define it in permanent terms.

Bill O'Hanlon, a pioneer of 'Inclusive Therapy,' proposed a process of allowing both desirable and undesirable aspects of our being to be present (both at once). This process helps illustrate some of the ideas in our discussion so far. Recognizing the dual nature of the constructed self allows us to release self-limiting mental commentaries, while embracing new feelings and perspectives on life. Such a technique might seem somewhat awkward at first, but this process makes quite a lot of sense when we reflect on an emotional level.

Consider this example. When was the last time you had a conversation with someone in which a major life decision was involved? Have you ever noticed that the person's decision was influenced by your attitude toward them at the time? For example, imagine that you are planning on investing $10,000 in the stock market, and you inform your partner about this decision. Your partner is quite angry about this, and feels a sense of outrage that you did not consult with her first. On the other hand, let's take one step back and consider that you ask your partner again, but this time you frame the question like this: "What do you think we should do with the extra $10,000 we have saved, how can we make good use of those savings?," and this time you may find that your partner is more amenable to investing the savings. What has changed between these two scenarios?

In the second scenario, there is an element of choice, having the freedom to decide a direction. In the first scenario the choice is lacking, causing the partner to feel trapped. Her response is also geared toward an emotion of heaviness and control, rather than the content of the actual issue at hand. You would be surprised to find how often we respond in a similar way to everyday life situations, if you become mindful of your inner dynamics (8). O'Hanlon suggested that it is important to practice using inclusive language to allow our broad spectrum of emotions into our field of consciousness rather than striving for a clear logical answer a solution when faced with problematic life events or inner obstacles. The point here is not to look for the correct or right way to feel toward something, but rather to acknowledge the freedom to feel (no matter what the emotion is).

You can choose to "feel angry and you don't have to feel angry," to "forgive and not forgive at the same time," O'Hanlon illustrated. O'Hanlon highlighted that this process of allowing multiple emotions to arise at the same time, and being okay with this, can have a significant role to play in healing and arriving at a state of inner peace, a state in which we feel a greater sense of freedom and connectedness with our broader range of emotions beneath the surface.

It is important to let go of intellectual judgments and instead to value the experience of creating a space within ourselves in which we feel free and uninhibited in our conscious expression (no matter how ridiculous or trivial or value judgments on the surface might seem). For example, even though a son might want to find compassion in his heart for his father, as his father caused him so much trauma in the past, it is almost as though a distinct part of the son wants to forgive and move on, but another part seeks to hold on and perpetuate the anger toward the father. Both parts seem in conflict. In such a case, it is important to acknowledge both aspects and to experience them in full, rather than attempting to figure out which emotional expression is the correct one. It is when the son embraces both feelings toward his father (the deep anger and resentment, as well as the compassion and love) that the feelings can begin to resolve, leading to emotional strength, a more encompassing and liberated attitude can then be embraced toward his father.

Here the aim is to move past pursuing a desirable outcome and instead to reconnect with ourselves at a deeper level – to embrace both light and dark aspects of ourselves. In doing so, we come to a better core understanding of ourselves, rather than building up just one polarized characteristic that we hold within our self-image.

In a well-known passage, Richard Buckminster (1895-1983) stated that "in order to change an existing paradigm you do not struggle to try and change the problematic model. You create a new model and make the old one obsolete." This is not just true of societal structures, but also of intrapersonal structures. Instead of holding our mental commentaries about having a particular feeling or experience, we have the freedom to connect with the conscious, here-and-now emotional experience.

The aim here is to avoid identification with the surface-level mental commentaries, and instead to look within. Unless we do so, we fail to recognize the true face of genuine confidence or genuine love, for instance. Instead, we just see the shadows of the constructed self. Sure, it is easier to have a clear-cut idea of which societal values relate to feelings of confidence, or love, or happiness. If we watch the television, it seems to suggest that holding a can of Pepsi is all that is needed to experience happiness, for example. Yet, when we hold someone else's vision in place of our true self, we disconnect from our souls, our authentic conscious experience. The example of Pepsi might seem trivial on the surface, but from what we have learned about the power of metaphor in shaping one's conscious experience, the question of whose image of love, or happiness, or success we are cultivating in life becomes clearer and clearer.

Consider, what does the true nature of love feel like? What does the true nature of happiness feel like? What does the true nature of success feel like? We have developed a complex language describing these concepts in depth, however none of these definitions take us to the heart of the experience. Societal definitions of success, for instance, are flawed in many ways, yet people still seek outrageous amounts of prosperity, fame, and popularity in order to meet their mental pre-requisite thresholds for success. Once a person turns inward, he instead discovers the true personal meaning of success for him. Seldom in this world are we encouraged to practice introspection techniques such as this, and this chapter encourages readers to do just that, to deepen their understanding of their true nature. Yet, coming to a broader understanding of our emotional-spiritual aspects allows us to touch the felt experience of love, of happiness, of success, rather than just mentalizing these potential experiences.

LOST PARTS OF OURSELVES

Spiritual practices such as 'soul retrieval' and 'soul realignment' tend to be underlined by the assumption that we have lost our true selves, or lost touch with our souls. Considering this, the importance of finding ourselves again, reconnecting with our essence, becomes paramount. Most people are not living the most actualized, individuated, version of themselves. It is an inferior version, an inferior image born from societal structures, rather than having been derived from true soul connection. Thus, what are these lost parts of ourselves that we can reclaim in order to reconnect with our soul aspect?

The world tends to capture our attention and we spend so much of our time looking 'out there,' that we lose touch with ourselves. Indeed, some Gnostic teachings suggest that our immersion in the ego-self, the mask, quite literally captures parts of our consciousness and keeps these aspects prisoner, causing fragmentation and disconnection from our true self. If we take this literal interpretation, then the importance of coming to a greater sense of personal congruence becomes clear. The tale of the Buddhist monk who arrives in Times Square and, upon witnessing all of the billboards, proclaims "they are trying to steal our minds," is another stance for considering this. If we get too caught up in external notions, we forget about the importance and value of listening to our own hearts. We lose ourselves in the flood of content all around us and lose our inner balance.

Throughout our time between birth and death, we encounter millions of experiences, each of which either reinforce our constructed self, or facilitate our soul's expression in this lifetime. Some esoteric scholars believe that there is a higher dimension above the fourth dimension of time, and that beyond the linear process of life and death, a more constant connection to soul-consciousness can be experienced. Some suggest that the realm of emotion transcends the realm of time. From that stance, we can consider that most people might experience a life of 80 plus years in length, but the experiences during that time might differ in quality and in the degree of personal growth experienced. One's quality of emotional exploration and consciousness progression is therefore more important than the actual age or length of time that has passed in one's life. Isn't it?

Just as we are given a certain amount of time on this planet to live our lives, we also have a certain amount of opportunities available in this lifetime for emotional and spiritual development. Learning to love, learning to experience happiness, learning to understand ourselves at a deeper level, are pursuits far more valuable on the emotional plane than the sheer quantity of time, or length of time, dedicated to certain life goals. At times in our life, we experience challenging tribulations and obstacles that require self-growth to overcome, at other times we might experience periods of little self-growth whatsoever, spending several months working overtime in a monotonous job, for example. Yet, a single moment of personal realization can be worth much more than thousands of hours of mental repetition without progression, for instance.

What then, do we make of linear time? How does it relate to emotional growth and consciousness progression? Consider a conflict between a mother and a son that caused each to stop talking to the other for 10 years, before the son finally decided to reconnect with his mother. The process could have gone on for 40 years or for 40 minutes. The actual physical quantity of time does not matter. It is rather the emotional experience of learning to overcome a grudge and forgive that is most valuable. Regardless of whether this process took one of the individuals 40 minutes or four decades to initiate, the emotional nature of this experience is as valuable.

In a similar light, an individual might remain in countless demeaning and depressing jobs because he is experiencing low self-confidence. Once he learns to value himself more and begins to gain a greater level of confidence, he refuses to be treated in an unfair manner at work and starts establishing a better career at an organization in which he will respected and valued for his true self. This process might take him two or three years, or it might take 20 years. Again, the actual physical length of time does not matter. It is the consciousness expansion that we are looking at here, the individual's progress on their emotional timeline.

I can also offer another example here. Some people believe in the notion of past lives, stating that if we do not learn what we are intended to learn in this lifetime, we will reincarnate in a similar situation in our next life. I do not speculate to what degree reincarnation occurs, or if it occurs at all, however the idea of emotional timelines does fit in well with the concept of past lives discussed in Buddhist texts.

In primary school, one of the kids that I used to play with during lunchtime once decided to pour water over some ants that were crawling along the concrete outside. I objected to the fact that he was drowning and killing the ants with the water. His response was something along the lines of "but it's okay, I'm only killing a few." Since then, he might have grown up to value the sanctity of life (whether human or animal) more (or he might not have). Again, I propose here that it is not the amount of physical time that has passed which would determine such things, but rather one's progression on the road to emotional growth.

Perhaps such learnings have something to do with the progression of the soul across several lifetimes, mediating whether one reincarnates in less or more favorable circumstances. But again, this is difficult to speculate on. What we can observe, using our present-moment awareness, is that emotional progression has a real and tangible impact on our consciousness level in this lifetime.

Another interesting reflection to note is that most countries have a specific age requirement for drinking, driving a car, having sex, and so forth. For example, in some areas a person has to be at least 18 years old in order to have sex. However, if we consider the idea of emotional timelines, does the age 18 really have as much meaning physically as it does on an emotional timeline? Are all Canadians somehow much more mature than all Americans? Despite the fact that we could take a leap of faith and believe this to be true, how could we possibly discern this for each single individual, each soul? It seems a bit ridiculous when we create a mental construct to suggest that a certain age can be applied across all individuals, across all souls, incarnated in this world.

You might know some people in your circle who act more maturely than their physical age, and others who act quite immaturely for their age. I suggest here that age is not all that important after all. In examples such as those cited above, we can recognize that it might take an individual a short or a much longer period of time to experience the same emotional insights and to expand their self-awareness. The process is more so about reaching a broader threshold of consciousness overall, rather than how long or how little time this process takes based on our conventional tools for measuring time – the intellectual cognitive model of time.

Connirae Andreas and Tamara Andreas proposed an elegant approach for harnessing the process of emotional and spiritual growth through the reclamation of the parts of ourselves that have been lost in previous instances of trauma, pain, or just peak points in life in which we were unable to deal with the experiences that life presented. At certain points during our emotional timeline, we get stuck, or find it too painful to move forward, so we leave behind a part of ourselves in the past, it becomes frozen in time.

For instance, an adult might act maturely about most things in life, but when it comes to certain emotions, she might begin to act like a five-year-old. That could mean that a part of herself experienced great emotional pain at age five, that part and hasn't move on, it hasn't "grown up," as Connirae Andreas suggested in some of the examples in her work. Andreas and Andreas introduced the 'Core Transformation' process as a method for reintegrating the lost parts of ourselves, this process helps open a dialogue with the parts of ourselves that are trapped, missing, or lost; calling for reintegration into our whole self.

Andreas and Andreas proposed that each lost part seeks for a particular emotional acknowledgment in order to be found again (love, approval, or encouragement, for instance), to return home, to integrate with our complete soul experience. Often, when we explore the true intention behind the lost parts of ourselves, we reach into what Andreas and Andreas refer to as 'core states' of consciousness. In this book, I consider these as points of emotional transcendence, during which we reach a state of feeling that seems to encapsulate our entire being, integrating previous emotional pain, detachment, suffering, and confusion into a new state of wholeness and deeper self-recognition. The experience of a core state is difficult to transcribe into words, however Andreas and Andreas noted that each core state encapsulates a level of consciousness that transcends just the persona (the constructed ego). In the below passage, Andreas and Andreas introduce their experience of the core state of love.

> What a great experience it is, to love and be loved! For thousands of years, storytellers, poets and song writers have spoken and written about the

value of love. Most of them talk about loving others, or others loving them. The kind of love we experience as a Core State is much more complete and encompassing than the feeling we normally mean by the word "love." It is deeper than romantic love, deeper than loving and being loved. It is also deeper than self-love. With self-love, I am loving myself–one part of me is loving another part of me. The core State of love includes everyone and everything. It is the love spoken of by many prophets and mystics; one that transcends the boundaries within myself, and boundaries between people.

– Connirae Andreas and Tamara Andreas, 'Core Transformation'

Certain negative emotions can be considered lost parts of ourselves that have been neglected for so long – as we recognize and reintegrate these parts, we experience higher emotional states of peace, love, and acceptance. For example, imagine that a mother leaves her child in the lounge room, while she goes to the office for a moment. After she has not returned for a few moments, the child begins crying. If the mother now returns straight away and holds the child, he will stop crying as he begins to feel comforted. Yet, if the mother stays in the office for an entire two hours, the crying will increase and the child will begin to feel abandoned, isolated, and alone.

This same process occurs with a number of our emotions. At the start, our emotions call for us to recognize them, to acknowledge their presence. Yet, if we ignore them, we cut off parts of ourselves, and cause self-pain. The disavowed emotions begin to get louder, more uncomfortable, more painful, and more negative, that is, until we are willing to face them and recognize them as parts of our lost self. Behind most (if not all) emotions is a call to love, a call to acceptance of ourselves. Beneath the surface, many of these emotions are not negative at all, but simply appear as such because we have faced away from them and have refused to acknowledge their existence, severing a part of ourselves. Our hidden monsters are not what we think they are.

The charge of destructive emotions such as anger, envy, and greed can seem to last longer than peak emotional states that are blissful, all-encompassing, and transcendental, seeming to last just for a few seconds. Yet, once we learn how to recognize them, peak emotions no longer seem temporal, as we acknowledge these states arising within rather than being conditional on external stimuli (as most negative culturally-entrained emotions are). In active recognition, we notice that most destructive emotions are just recycled continuously, which gives them an illusionary long emotional life-span. In actuality, upon experiencing a core state of consciousness, we recognize that these states represent our true nature as human beings.

Other emotional states can be distinguished from core states because they come and go in a sporadic fashion – branches and leaves falling from the trees as the seasons change. Our peak, or core, emotional connections, can be considered the stable roots of the tree, while the reactive, conditioned emotions of negativity, pain, and suffering arise within physical reality and just as plainly leave physical reality, never lasting forever.

If you yearn for a particular emotion that you believe you lack, then this could indicate that there is a part of you that you have neglected in the past, a part that wishes to reunite with your broader self-experience. It is easy to fall for the intellectual mind's trick of 'no-one loves me,' and to isolate ourselves, for example, and to then believe that we are disconnected from love. The truth of the matter is quite the opposite. If we hold a desire for something that we feel we cannot attain, then on some level this implies that we hold a small essence of this state within, a remnant of something we recognized from the past. We project our emotional needs outward onto others, but if we didn't do so, we would not even recognize that we are lacking this inner aspect in the first place. This projection of a desire or need for love, happiness, approval, success, and so forth from other people, is, in fact, a call to reconnect with these very states within ourselves.

One must know what it is to have something prior to having the feeling of longing for that same thing. If we feel we lack happiness, or love, for example, then this is an indication that there is a part within that comprises of happiness or love that is trapped, awaiting recognition and expression. Socrates' fool does not pine for happiness, for he is happy with his menial and plain life, Yet the person who feels frustration, wishes for more, and feels a sense of lacking within, is then called to recognize these signals as invitations toward rediscovering their once lost aspects.

EXPLORATION: REUNION OF SELF

Consider which parts of yourself you have neglected in the past, and how it would be possible to reconnect with and reintegrate these inner aspects into your center of being once again.

MISSION TASK 46: OWNING OUR HIDDEN ASPECTS

In this mission, consider whether it is useful to imagine the human being as a fragmented set of parts that are out-of-congruence. If we take this approach, would a search for inner wholeness, and self-congruence, be a good measure of spiritual growth? Spend some time researching some techniques that work with the hidden parts of ourselves in order to move toward inner wholeness.

Some ideas: 1) Core Transformation, 2) the empty chair technique from Gestalt psychotherapy, 3) voice dialoguing, 4) parts integration techniques from Neuro-Linguistic Programming (NLP), 5) the 'Wholeness Process' (another method devised by Connirae Andreas). I recommend choosing one of these techniques, spending half an hour or so reading about it (in books or articles), and then spending a few moments reflecting on how the ideas introduced relate to some of the reflections you have had so far in this chapter.

Completion Goal I:

Research one of the techniques considered above and reflect on how the idea of individual parts relate to principles such as wholeness and self-congruence.

Completion Goal II:

For courageous readers: Research all of the techniques considered above. Consider the implications of such techniques in how we view ourselves as either whole individuals, or as fragmented into multiple sub-parts of consciousness.

MISSION TASK 47: RECONNECTING WITH SUB-PARTS

Find a comfortable space and spend a few minutes relaxing and turning your attention inward. Choose a particular part of yourself that you feel has been neglected or misheard in the past. Consider how this part has acted out in the past. Reflect on what the true intention behind this part is. What does it seek for?

The purpose of this mission is to connect and listen to some of the parts of ourselves that we have disconnected from in the past. Refer to the listening techniques in Chapter One again. How can we learn to listen to the neglected parts within ourselves from a heartfelt level?

Completion Goal I:

Identify a part of yourself that you have disowned, such as a part of you that you feel ashamed of or uncomfortable about. This time, instead of judging and rejecting the part, allow it to be as it is, become aware of its deeper purpose for being present. There is no need to react to its presence, just allow it to come into awareness. What can you learn from this part's existence?

Completion Goal II:

Reflect on when you first left this part of yourself behind, when you first disowned it as part of your true self. Reflect on your emotional timeline using your intuition, rather than attempting to form an actual linear timeline.

MISSION TASK 48: RELINQUISHING CONTROL

Reflect on the idea of control: 1) How often do you aim to control how you feel instead of just allowing certain emotions to be present? 2) How often do you think about how things could have turned out instead of accepting how things did turn out? 3) How often do you have the illusion of control, when in truth you have no control over certain circumstances? 4) Do you ever feel pushed around or controlled by certain thoughts or emotions? 5) Does recognizing your lack of control diminish your personal power in any way whatsoever? 6) Can you see how giving up control could instead be empowering (and if so, how? If not, how?)? 7) Can one human being control another human being? 8) Is it possible to control all of the variables in life?

For this mission task, reflect on a time during which you attempted to control your feelings in a particular way. This might have been a time when you told yourself how you should feel, or when someone else told you how you should feel, or simply when you felt a particular emotion and tried to control or change it into a different feeling. Pick an emotion or feeling you have tried to control, judge, or force in the past.

Completion Goal I:

Take careful notice of the next time you experience an emotion and you are inclined to change, ignore, criticize, or control the feeling, rather than just allowing it be. This time, instead of reacting to the emotion on an intellectual level, just allow yourself to feel the emotion as it arises. Instead of thinking about it, notice how it feels. There is no need to react, allow it to remain in awareness for a moment. What is this feeling communicating? Notice how it feels to listen to the deeper parts of your heart, rather than reacting with the intellectual mind. Reflect on how this practice could deepen your experience of consciousness at the emotional level.

Completion Goal II:

Reflect on whether aiming to control aspects of your reality has been effective in the past. Have you been able to control parts of yourself, including particular emotions? How about other people? Have you ever found that your efforts to control have backfired, resulting in the same outcome that you tried to prevent? Have you ever found that controlling other people (or parts of yourself) just causes rebellion and mischief? Reflect on the idea of control versus allowing. Are there particular situations or emotions that you could decide to relinquish control over? How difficult would this be? Which factors are relevant? What would happen if you just allow things to be, with no control agenda? Experiment with relinquishing control over one particular area of your life. It can be something quite small and trivial to start with (emotions, thoughts, beliefs, are all fine to work with here).

Completion Goal III:

After completing the above task, notice what happens as you allow this particular aspect to just be as-it-is without having an inclination or desire to control this aspect. Take a few moments to reflect on what this experience feels like.

EMBRACE RAW EMOTION

It is far more important to recognize and cultivate our own feelings and to allow our feelings to lead us in life, rather than expecting people to trigger our emotions on-demand. When we think in the latter terms, we tend to make judgments about the world as a singular construct. It appears, from that perspective, the world is not living up to our expectations. However, we could approach this from a different standpoint. Consider, in order to cultivate and expand our experience of feelings such as love, inspiration, excitement, and peace in life, we need not look to the external world, but within. As we look within, we allow these feelings to show us something new about ourselves, and then, our conception of the world and our self-concept changes as a direct result of these newfound feeling states.

To borrow a term from author Don Miguel Ruiz, the human being has been "tamed" in emotional experience. Social cues inform us about how we should feel in certain situations, and also restrict the number of emotions we can experience as human beings to an acceptable emotional spectrum. This is where the idea of emotional transcendence is perhaps most compelling.

Remember earlier on how we considered the limitations of language in encompassing our true emotions? There are particular emotions that have been reported in transcendence experiences in which the person describing the experience was lost for words. There exist no words in the English language to describe some of these states of consciousness. From childhood, we are given a definitive idea of which states exist on the acceptable spectrum of emotion, and we learn to recognize these within ourselves.

It can be noted that children who experience severe trauma during childhood often struggle with expressing particular emotions in adulthood. Often, these individuals do not even recognize their own capabilities for expressing these particular emotions, the degree of repression can be so deep. In another manner, we lock our inner doors to the full experience of certain emotions even without undergoing trauma. Societal imprints are sufficient to block the raw nature of these experiences. As a result, certain emotions become tamed and processed based on social rules, rather than experience via raw unadulterated emotional awareness.

> Judgment and criticism from those around us frequently results in parts splitting off. If a child is excited and enthusiastic about going somewhere, and is angrily told to calm down and be quiet, the part of him that is enthusiastic may shut down. As he matures, he may be unable to express or even feel enthusiasm.

> – Connirae Andreas and Tamara Andreas, 'Core Transformation'

In the previous mission task, I asked readers to connect with their emotions rather than formulating an intellectual response during emotionally-charged situations. Sometimes, we might believe that we are responding at an emotional level, all the while we still insist on responding within the intellectual scope of the beliefs and assumptions we hold about that certain emotion. It is important to remember that emotions cannot be grasped in mere societal or intellectual terms. An interpretation of emotion can be formulated intellectually, but the true emotional experience, the felt connection with ourselves, is never captured at that level.

Let's consider the feeling of love. In the earlier quote from Andreas and Andreas, we reflected on love as a force that transcends all definitions that we can assign it. The true state of love transcends words. However, most of us respond to the language we use about love, referring to its concept, rather than spending enough time on cultivating the feeling behind the words. 'I love you, I love cake, or I love basketball.' Are these all equal forms of love? How often do we use the word 'love' in general conversation without taking more than two seconds to feel the actual raw, complete state of love within?

One of the most memorable experiences in my life occurred when I was around 18 years old and said "I love you" to my mother. During this particular experience I felt the contrast between other times that I have mechanically said "I love you" and this particular instance, which seemed quite unique. I noticed that after I said the words my heart literally felt warm (it actually felt like it was afire). Since then, I have had similar experiences, sometimes to the point that the boundaries around my body felt like they were disappearing and the thoughts that I held in my mind seemed to vanish and quieten. Just the feeling of warmth remained and enveloped my entire being.

In the times that I have felt that sensation, a type of energy projected from my chest and seemed to connect me with the entire consciousness of the plant, almost as though I was being held in the embracing arms of the universe as I fell back into the sensation of warmth that continued to expand. In those moments, I could not feel hate or anger or resentment toward a single individual in the world, no matter how much I might have tried.

From time to time, I have had similar experiences with others, friends, my partner, and even sometimes those I barely knew who brought about a similar sensation in my heart. I noticed that I could bring this feeling on by focusing on the intention behind my words, rather than focusing on forming the words themselves. It is such an obvious truth, but one that we often miss. How do you tell someone that you love them or that you care about them? Instead of aiming to come up with the words, allow the feelings to arise within. The cultivation of the feeling can be infinitely more powerful than the mere construction of surface-level words. It is not the just words that those closest to you respond to as your consciousness touches their soul.

Experiences of raw emotional states such as these can come about when we connect with the inner world, rather than remaining trapped in the surface level intellectual musings in language. These being-states encompass a much broader field of consciousness than our finite emotional states. It is not sufficient to describe a state of pure love, or pure peace, or pure happiness, in mere societal terms, the feeling transcends these and originates from the soul. Experiences such as these show us how we often dull our emotions instead of embracing their full power throughout life. Is love conditional? Is happiness conditional? Asking these kind of questions helps foster states of being in which we experience our emotions in a raw, spontaneous, and generous fashion, without condition.

Once we clear those expectations that we have placed upon the world to deliver us particular emotional states, we create a new space for raw emotional experiences to arise within. Consider the number of emotions that we hold on to, memories and experiences from the past that we have carried into the present moment. Most people do not have a clear passage into the inner realm of emotion, and their passage is constricted via an intellectual wall of repeated feelings of anger, sadness, and regret that ring back to past events long gone. Transcendental emotion states (or core being states) arise once we let go of attachment to painful and traumatic experiences on our emotional timeline.

Let's consider an example of anger. Many people do not experience their anger as a raw emotion. The anger builds up from multiple occurrences of feeing anger in the past. And often, the experience of anger comes from this perpetual build-up rather than a natural response of this emotion to new situations or new experiences in the moment. It is not anger about the present moment that is then experienced, but rather anger from the past making itself heard in the present, when even small opportunities to become enraged arise. These emotional responses seem inauthentic and somehow geared in the past, rather than experienced here and now, in relation to present events.

How often do we see people becoming so angered over things that normally would not cause such great outrage, how often do their emotions appear out-of-proportion? The experience of anger in the present moment is natural and often feels cathartic. However a repressive viewpoint toward emotions causes us to continue holding on to past anger, sadness, and other emotional states, bringing them up again and again to the edge of our present frame of experience, but never quite processing them and moving on. This process of recycling emotional states rather than letting them go prevents us from creating a space for new feelings to arise within.

The term 'affect phobia' is sometimes used in psychological literature to describe the fear people have of experiencing emotion in general. In the Western world, most people have some degree of affect phobia, we are afraid of what would happen if we experience all of our emotions in their total essence. Yet, the truth is

133

that in experiencing negative emotions, we might find that these tend to pass, as we give them a voice. On the other hand, as we embrace core states and deeper-level emotional experiences that are enriching, we might find that these states can deepen and re-connect us with our core being.

There is something real and authentic about the experience of expressing our emotions in the present moment, rather than letting them build up over time. Others recognize this on an intuitive level, it speaks to their hearts. When we respond to previous emotional pain from long ago in our present moment interactions, we then fail to build a genuine, real connection in the present. We experience our ideas, thoughts, and conversations through the lens of the past, instead of being present in the here-and-now, emotionally available. Most importantly, by letting go of past pain on our emotional timeline, we free the space within to cultivate authentic compassion and love for others in the present.

EXPLORATION: RAW EXPERIENCE

In the mission tasks that follow, we'll explore the benefits of connecting with emotions for the sake of experiencing them in the present moment. This allows us to expand our emotional consciousness and to recognize some of the parts of ourselves that we have sublimated through previous painful life experiences.

MISSION TASK 49: YOUR TRUE VOICE

Completion Goal:

Next time you experience a rather strong emotion, take notice of whether the feeling arises from your own soul, or whether it is linked with past grievances, resentment, or pain, rather than to the present moment experience. You may ask yourself the question: 'Is this feeling congruent with the voice of my soul, or am I expressing someone else's voice (or a younger version of myself)?'

Side Note: Often, we experience emotions that are linked to past events. The problem is that sometimes we use the present moment as a means to resolve previous emotional pain, rather than engaging with the unique felt experience here and now. It is evident how many people embody the emotions of those close to them, or even of social groups, or broader cultures, in place of their own direct personal experience. For example, people valiantly defend their culture or religion, as though their culture is a representation of their soul. It might well be, but for most it's more of an unconscious conditioned response, rather than a true soul expression. Certain people express such emotion, such passion toward concepts such as patriotism, religion, and culture, constructs that could not be further from their true intimate experience of their individual soul that transcends those societal structures. In this exercise, rather than looking to external justifications for your inner experience, look within yourself, aim to understand how you are feeling and what you are experiencing in the present moment, regardless of past emotional associations.

MISSION TASK 50: IMMERSION

Completion Goal:

Next time you experience a rather strong emotion, allow yourself to embody the feeling completely. Take notice of what the emotion feels like, and rather than attempting to move on from it, ignore it, or analyze it, allow it to expand within your field of awareness.

Side Note: In which part of your body does the emotion manifest most strongly? What does the emotion feel like kinesthetically? This might be a warm, cold, heavy, light, textured, pulling, rising, expanding, or another feature that can be described in kinesthetic terms. Once you have described the emotion, allow yourself to fully embrace this feeling as it spreads throughout your entire body, rather than remaining in this localized area. What does it feel like to allow this particular feeling to flow through every muscle, every organ, and every part of your being? Allow the experience of embracing this emotion completely.

MISSION TASK 51: EMBODIED EMOTION

Sometimes people allow their emotions to take control of them. You may recall a time when, rather than being in control and expressing your emotions from a stance of empowerment, you felt a loss of control, as though your emotions reigned over your words and actions with little sense of authority on your part. Often, when we do not fully embody and understand our emotions, they can spin and spiral out of control in this fashion, and we become slaves to our emotions, rather than being capable of expressing them from a place of centeredness.

Completion Goal I:

Consider a time in your life during which you felt that you had no control over your emotions. For example, you may have been experiencing a sense of sadness or anger that you could not shake despite your best efforts, and all of your behaviors, actions, and thoughts were influenced by this emotion. Next, consider a time when you felt more in control and in balance with your emotions.

Completion Goal II:

Reflect on the benefits of letting go of certain emotions, while embracing others. Are there benefits of each approach? Does this depend on the emotion and context experienced? How so? Explore this further in your personal reflection time.

Side Note: Author David Hawkins illustrated that there is a distinct difference between the notion of power, and the notion of force. Power relates to a sense of inner freedom and strength, a stance of courage. On the other hand, force relates to domination, control, and manipulation. If we try to manipulate and force an emotion, we end up repressing that particular feeling, and people around us can tell that we are hiding something. From the stance of power, on the other hand, we endeavor to understand the feeling we are experiencing and to engage with it at a deeper level. This engagement may involve expressing the feeling, or perhaps simply acknowledging it. No force is required, yet we act from a place of balance and personal power.

Completion Goal III:

Reflect on the difference between control and power as it relates to emotional experiences.

Completion Goal IV:

In this final task, I'd like you to keep the above points in mind next time you find yourself experiencing an overwhelmingly powerful emotion that feels as though it is about to take you over and cause you to lose your center of balance. This time, instead of playing into the emotion and allowing it to control how you act and how you feel, engage with this feeling completely, by acknowledging it, understanding where it is coming from, and embodying the feeling as your own, rather than choosing to perceive it as an external force that might de-balance you.

CONGRUENCE

Disowning emotional experience has caused many people in our world to become incongruent with their true nature – many of their beliefs, emotions, and experiences are in conflict with one another, creating a dissonance within. Reclaiming our inner power, and returning to our center of balance can help resolve many of these incongruities, as we come to better understand ourselves and our core emotional states.

In the English language, we have many negative idioms, axioms, and adages, but we continue to use them without question. For example, consider a teenager that is speaking to her friend: "my mother will kill me if she finds out I went to this party." Is the teenager's mother going to kill her, in fact? Chances are, not so. Yet, how often do we use language in a loose manner just like this without feeling and embodying the words we are projecting forth? Lying, or being dishonest, or bending the truth is nowhere near as reprehensible on a moral compass as is being incongruent with oneself. Can you see how this is true? It is when we lie to ourselves about our true nature that we compromise the foundation of who we are. This is more diminishing than a thousand trivial lies.

Our self-talk offers insight into how loosely we use our words to express our inner world. Consider statements like 'I will do it tomorrow' – promises we make to ourselves that we never following through with. We can make a statement such as this with little conviction, with little embodied confidence. After a time, a person who does this will find it difficult to perform tasks, he will procrastinate and become disorganized because the unconscious mind has lost faith in his conscious directorate of promising to 'get it done tomorrow.' When we make promises to ourselves or others and then take them back, we lose congruence, we lose inner power. In the previous chapter we discussed the promise of limitation that language brings. To move from using language as a tool for limitation and embracing language as a method of infinite expression, we must first become authentic in the language that we use, infusing our words with what we feel within our hearts.

When a person is in congruence with themselves, their language reflects their inner world. So often, we attempt to shield others from being hurt by our words, so we fabricate an intention that is lesser than our true self-expression. Yet, in being honest and direct, we project a sense of congruence and authenticity, and that is much more important than saving face. For example, when you say to yourself 'I will do x tomorrow' or when you promise someone 'I promise I will do x,' make sure that you go to the effort of following through, no matter what it takes. You will find that when you do, your willpower becomes strengthened as your use of communication and intention move into congruence with each other.

Language that is infused with a strong emotion works as a powerful tool in this manner. For example, even though most people might be thrilled to win a million dollar lottery, at an unconscious level their thought-process will have some kind of justification for the reasons they need the money. 'I need a million dollars to avoid working,' 'I need a million dollars to feel secure,' and so forth, most of us have hidden reasons about what we do not want, rather than expressing the emotion corresponding to what we do want, what we feel with congruence and power in our hearts.

In that sense, it is important to learn how to be true to ourselves in order to experience our emotions from a place of inner balance. This process comes about when we respond to how we feel, rather than sublimating our emotional states and leaving them to later expressions. It is also important to delve deeper beneath the surface to recognize the wisdom and intelligence of certain emotions, rather than just perceiving them as erratic and irrational. As we delve a little deeper, we can find a great amount of wisdom behind specific emotions, as long as we are willing to listen to their true meaning.

EXPLORATION: EMOTIONAL CONGRUENCE

In the following tasks, let's consider how often our use of conscious language and expression captures our true emotional intention beneath the surface. These tasks encourage readers to develop a greater sense of congruence between their inner and outer world.

MISSION TASK 52: CONGRUENT COMMUNICATION

It is easy to hide ourselves behind our words in order to hide our true soul. Often, we might feel vulnerable for expressing these deeper aspects, but the truth is that sometimes expressing our true nature is the greatest stance of personal power, and leads to the most powerful points of self-growth in life. It is worthwhile at least experimenting with expressing our whole self to others and seeing which benefits this might bring.

Completion Goal:

Practice verbalizing exactly what you mean during conversations and notice how it feels to be congruent with yourself and 100% honest with others.

Side Note: Avoid skewing conversations in a particular light and aim to express your authentic self in each exchange.

MISSION TASK 53: ORIGINS

Whenever you feel a particular emotion that you do not understand, or are not sure about where it has come from, ask yourself: 'What is behind this emotion? Where is it stemming from? What is the energy behind it that moves it into my awareness? What is its reason for being here?' Sometimes, by practicing this technique we can come into contact with the deeper-level raw emotional experience beneath the surface.

For example, a person may save all of his money to buy a Ferrari, and adamantly explain to all of his friends that he needs a Ferrari and has always wanted one. Such a deep desire is often underlined by a particular emotional state. In this particular case, the individual in our scenario might believe that a Ferrari will make him happy, or increase the respect that his friends have for him. It is unfortunate to see that many of us go through life carried by the surface level emotional states that drive our behavior, rather than looking bit deeper. When the individual in this scenario performs an inquiry into his true reasons for wanting to purchase a Ferrari (by reflecting and introspecting on some of the questions above) he might find that he feels a needs to prove something to others, to make up for something that is insufficient within. In becoming aware of some of his meta-level intentions, he transcends his original self-construct and connects with a deeper emotional awareness.

Early on I suggested that when we long for a particular experience or emotion within, this often indicates that the particular emotion in question is already within us, it has just been hidden, fragmented. The individual in this case might find that his sense of confidence and respect has been lost somewhere along his life path due to a traumatic or painful experience. Interestingly, what he might find is that by re-connecting with and acknowledging the deeper level intention for respect and confidence, and working on rediscovering this within himself, his need to purchase external objects to validate that he is a confident, successful, respectable individual, to others, diminishes, or even disappears altogether.

Completion Goal:

Next time you feel a particular emotion that you do not understand, or are not sure about where it has come from, ask yourself: 'What is behind this emotion?' Reflect on the response that rises within.

MISSION TASK 54: FELT EMOTION

Another important aspect of congruence involves recognizing that we are not just intellectual beings, we also have strong emotional and spiritual dimensions within us, aspects that are seldom cultivated. Western societies pride themselves on intensive intellectual training from childhood to adulthood, while neglecting emotional and spiritual intelligence. Even when learning about emotions from an intellectual frame, we tend to conceptualize and categorize them based on our mental models – what is appropriate or not to express at a given time. But, at the core of it, connecting with emotional wisdom is not about construing our feelings with an intellectual lens, but rather feeling them in their true essence. This has nothing to do with how we conceptualize emotion. It is not about recognizing these parts through the intellectual lens, but rather recognizing that each one of us has a completely unique, new, means for perceiving and engaging with the world beyond the intellectual wall.

Author Robert Augustus Masters found that it is not even that important to recognize specific, individual emotions, in our experience. It is far more important, he suggested, to deepen our human emotional experience, regardless of the actual individual contents, or specific emotion, experienced. In deepening our field of emotional experience, we broader our capacity to intuit and sense aspects of our life experience rather than just operating through the lens of the intellectual wall; we recognize the value of relational-field knowing, a concept we will delve into in Chapter Six.

Completion Goal:

Reflect on what you have read in the previous two paragraphs. Re-read the above two paragraphs again, and this time instead of thinking about the words that you are reading, engage with their emotional content instead, feel the meaning behind the words, rather than discerning the language itself.

REIGNITE THE FLAME

One of the main blockades to experiencing transcendental emotional states can be noted in our melodrama with negative emotions. Often, people tend to embrace negative emotions for much longer periods of time than positive emotions. If we feel the raw experience of happiness or love, we might embrace this experience for a few seconds, and then return to our worrisome lives. In his book 'Happiness in Hard Times,' author Andrew Matthews noted that we tend to concern ourselves with negative emotional states, despite the actual magnitude of our external problems. Matthews noted that people seem to have a natural propensity for worrying.

For instance, if a person has just been diagnosed with cancer, he might be worried about his health and no longer worried at all about the little things, like whether he remembered to take the garbage out or to check the postal mail. However, should this individual recover from cancer, the previously lesser-prioritized worries will then re-fill the mental space of the cancer, and the individual in turn reneges to his same level of anxiousness, according to Matthews. The amount of worry hasn't changed, just the content. On the converse, even individuals who suffer from immense trauma or pain are capable of embracing happiness into their lives, despite the level at which pain occurs in the external world.

There is a predisposition in our mental health system with addressing our negative emotions, working through past pain, and acknowledging our trauma, but not enough of a focus on cultivating positive, enlightening, transcendental states of emotion and feeling. The inspiration that pulled me toward titling this chapter 'Reclaiming Disavowed Emotions' came from my observation that most people are thrilled about complaining, gossiping, whining, ranting, ruminating, and embracing their negative emotions, putting them on a thrown – misery's crown. It has become normalized in our world to feel 'bad.' We relish the chance. From such a mundane stance, higher states of consciousness and positive emotions are rare gems beneath a seabed of dark water currents, amidst poisonousness negativity. Part of the journey toward personal empowerment involves learning how to recognize all of our emotions and states of being, to embrace them and to feel comfortable with allowing these emotions. Thus, it is just as important to experience positive states as it is to work to understand and work with our negative emotional states.

Sometimes people feel a sense of guilt for allowing themselves to experience happiness or love, for instance. The truth is that these deeper states of feeling are within us right now, waiting to be rediscovered and brought to consciousness. Sometimes when people ask me whether I've had a very busy day or whether I've had a lot of work on, I reply "no, I've just been relaxing today and enjoying the experience of being," usually there will be some kind of response that this is unacceptable and that we must always be struggling with life, always immersed in work, always harnessing responsibility.

As one example, when I was marketing this book in a radio interview with Sheree and Chris Geo, Sheree spoke about an amazing state of losing her connection with the constructed self and experiencing a more expansive state of consciousness in which things around her just felt perfect, she experienced a sense of love rushing through her entire being. Yet, after 'coming back' from the experience, she felt a sense of guilt for not having had the feeling all along. Guilt is a major driving force in most people's lives in a similar fashion.

> Look, people in Africa are starving, what gives me the right to feel happiness right now?

> Are you kidding? My relationship is not where I envision it yet, I can't embrace a sense of deeper love right now, and it's too soon!

> Peace, yeah right … I am much too busy in my life to connect to a deep sense of inner peace.

It is our birth-right as human beings to experience deeper states of sincere love, connectedness with other people, and peace within. But, often we are held in the lower levels of emotional experience, we hold ourselves there. We are caught in past timelines that cheat us of a rich, filling, and vivid life experience. States of emotional transcendence thus give us just a glimpse into the full spectrum of our emotions and our broader conscious experience.

Consider a man who easily gets angered whenever he believes someone is speaking to him in an offensive tone. He reacts to the anger and thus he continues to respond in the same manner without examining the deeper raw emotions behind the experience of anger. What lies behind the anger, where did it originate from? Where was it born? Upon introspection, the man notices that he first started feeling this anger when he was rejected from his group of friends as a child. Upon being rejected by the group, he felt a great deal of sadness and isolation. Later, as his efforts at re-joining his group of friends became futile, his sadness transformed into a growing anger toward people and their seeming rejections of him.

Over time, the anger built and became difficult to overcome, as the real source of the anger had been long forgotten then. Once the deeper-level source of anger is identified, the original sadness and loneliness can be reflected on, thus the man can realize that what he wanted was a sense of love and acceptance from others, not to lash out at them, after all. Connecting with this deeper-level of emotional awareness allows us to recognize how often we prevent ourselves from connecting to the depth of our emotional experience. It also shows us an important truth: Our negative emotions are the faded voices, grown bitter over time, of lost parts of ourselves.

Engaging with our core emotional experiences connects us with the consciousness of our true self, the opposite of this is to become disengaged, and robotic, fleeting through life without purpose or meaning, and unaware of the depths of our soul. Rather than putting all of our faith into their external, imagine what would come of reigniting the flame within and putting faith within ourselves. We are taught from a young age that there is nothing special about us, until we acquire things from the external world. This is not true. Each person has within an immense potential to cultivate their unique wisdom, creative power, and self-expression.

Our emotions are the most powerful means we have with connecting to our authentic self-experience. In a world of concepts, we are instead often taught to attain generic markers of success, respect, and love in life, rather than trusting our own emotional understanding. It is here, in our emotional world, that we discover a unique felt life experience; it is our own sacred conscious experience, no-one else's, and herein lies immense power for personal transformation and spiritual growth.

In our world, emotional intelligence tends not to be taught at all. Instead, we pick up on maladaptive emotional reactions from others. Several emotional responses are socially inherited. Instead of evaluating other ways to respond emotionally, we tend to default to our preconditioned responses. Yet, if we look into the conscious soul, we recognize that there is so much more worth exploring within, rather than acquiring material wealth, possessions, and achievements that will just fade back into nothingness from which they originated. There are many more rewarding emotional experiences in human connection and understanding than could ever be found in the external world of material objects.

This mechanical, calculating method of engaging with the world has seeped into all facets of modern society, including the schooling system, including religious practice, including science and the spirit of inquiry, and including even the base discipline of self-inquiry: Psychology. Clinical approaches that are evidence-based (based on numbers), rather than grounded in soul-connection (in feeling), address thinking-based problems for a thinking culture. The intellectual mind can seldom calm the soul, because the soul precedes the intellectual mind, it espouses it. Materialists cannot fathom this, and thus it leads one to believe that the mind can cure itself of its own ails. Such approaches cannot pierce the intellectual wall because they exist within it.

Learning to trust in our intuition involves recognizing that there is a greater insight and intelligence in our hearts than what we can fathom within the boundaries of the intellectual wall. Emotional knowing can sometimes produce more powerful and convincing knowing than intellectual knowledge alone. Core states of feeling and deep-seated emotional wisdom can transcend rational, intellectual knowledge. As I mention in later chapters, the right-brain hemisphere is more receptive to transcendent consciousness experiences than the left-brain, as the latter aims to conceptualize and categorize exceptional states of consciousness into pre-existing mental frameworks. Women tend to have better cross-hemispheric communication, thus making them more prone to spontaneous experiences of deeper emotional, spiritual connectedness, as well as exceptional intuitive capacities. Women tend to report more intuitive experiences of 'just knowing' (through feeling) that something has happened hours prior to that particular event occurring, for example. Deeper knowing experiences such as these demonstrate that our emotional understanding can connect us with a much broader consciousness than the limited framework of the intellectual wall.

EXPLORATION: INNER SPACE

MISSION TASK 55: CREATE SPACE

It is common in our society to experience very briefly an emotional state, then to straightaway analyze it, comment on it, and move on. In this mission task, I would like to encourage you to practice creating an inner space in which you can dedicate a few moments of your complete attention and time on focusing the specific emotion you are experiencing and allowing it the presence it deserves. Avoid mentally categorizing the emotion as either negative or positive experience at first, you may be pleasantly surprised by the outcome as you acknowledge the feeling and allow it into your consciousness field without controlling it.

Completion Goal:

Next time that you experience a rather strong emotion, create the inner space to experience the emotion completely for a few moments. Reflect on the quality, or the nature, of this experience and what the content-free awareness of the emotion felt like. Remember, the purpose of this task is to focus on the feeling for the sake of it, without introducing any mental commentaries, content, controls, or judgments about the experience.

MISSION TASK 56: NOURISH EMOTIONS

Reflect on the potential benefits of nourishing emotions in the way described in the mission task above. In certain experiences, you may find that the quality of the emotion transforms. Reflect on this. In other instances, you may experience a transcendental state of emotion in which you engage with a core state, a deeper state that seems to enrapture your entire consciousness.

Completion Goal I:

Reflect on the benefits of nourishing our emotions and creating the space within to experience them.

Completion Goal II:

Next time you engage in a conversation with someone who is experiencing a very strong emotion, instead of attempting to engage with them on an intellectual level, consider how you might create the space in your conversation for them to experience the emotion fully and nourish it, rather than attempting to avoid or explain it with the intellectual mind.

MISSION TASK 57: EMRACE RAW STATES

Connirae Andreas suggested that if we follow each emotion that we experience to its core, we are bound to arrive at a core state of conscious experience. From a Core Transformation framework, all emotions originate from more powerful core experiences that we can learn to reconnect with once again, as we recognize the origin of our emotional experiences. Andreas and Andreas postulated that there are five core states: Being-ness, peace, love, OK-ness, and oneness. These core states differ from regular emotions that appear fleeting on the surface. It is from these core being states that surface-level emotions tend to emerge, like the bubbles flowing forth to the surface from an underwater spring.

Create space for your emotions to 'just be,' instead of attempting to force or control them. You may find that you begin to experience spontaneous deeper states that are not contingent upon societal programming or mental commentaries, they just arise out of the pure experience of being, from the direct experience of the present moment as it is. There is no special technique that can be carried out to bring about such transcendental states, they are our natural inheritance, a mirror of our truth being. You may find that moments such as these arise in your day to day experiences as you change your relationship with your emotions from one of reactivity to one of acceptance and understanding.

Completion Goal I:

In moments when you do find yourself experiencing a spontaneous sense of deep-seated inner happiness, love, or other peak emotional state that appears to arise from the depths of your being (rather than those triggered by an external cause), allow yourself to fully embrace this feeling. Nourish it and cultivate it. The more you practice this, the more often you may find these deeper blissful states begin to arise.

Side Note: Reflect on which factors brought about these more encompassing emotional states. What were you thinking about and doing (or not thinking about) during these moments?

Completion Goal II:

Whilst sadly it is beyond the scope of this book to explore core feeling-states in more depth, for those readers who are interested in venturing further into this area of their conscious experience, I recommend looking into the work of Connirae Andreas, in particular the 'Core Transformation' and 'Wholeness Process' workshops available from Andreas' publishing company, 'Real People Press.'

MISSION TASK 58: INNER KNOWING

Learning to value our felt experiences in life leads us to recognize that knowledge, wisdom, and understanding do not just arise in an intellectual frame, but can occur on a multitude of levels. This is an interesting notion to experiment with on a practical level, as it is not quite possible to explain within intellectual terms alone – this would defeat the purpose. Therefore, I encourage you to reflect on the questions below from a felt, emotional place of experience.

Completion Goal:

Have you ever felt that you just knew something for certain within, with no rational justification for this knowledge? Where did this knowing come from? Reflect on a few instances in which he might have had such an experience. If you cannot think of any instances, consider synchronicities and déjà vu experiences, and whether you believe these might somehow be significant consciousness experiences (in any way) or not.

MISSION TASK 59: SOURCE OF WISDOM

The notion that human beings are the sole source of intelligence and consciousness in the universe is grounded in materialist philosophies. On the converse, it is interesting to note that people who have experienced moments of transcending their self-construct come into awareness of a greater divine intelligence. Some have compared this universal intelligence to the natural processes occurring all around us that have existed and continue to exist regardless of human knowledge and intellect.

Consider the intelligence that causes rainclouds to form in certain regions, bees to pollinate flowers, and the subtle connectedness that all animals appear to have with the environment. There appears to be a deeper conscious process governing the universe – some have linked this to the idea of self-assembly and sacred geometry, which suggests that the universe is not only a densely material-based place, with human beings as the sole conscious beings who can interact with it. Rather, perhaps the entire universe is conscious, or at least operating on some level of consciousness. If that's the case, then what are the implications?

Completion Goal:

Reflect on whether you have experienced intuitive emotional knowing outside of the intellect alone. If so, what was the nature of this intuitive connection? This could be a connection to the environment, to other people, to animals, or to a source of general creative inspiration, for instance.

Alexander De Foe

MISSION TASK 60: SOUL CONNECTION

Reflect on your connection to a broader consciousness, whether that be a connection to God, to your higher self, or even to close friends or family members. What does it mean to have a connection with a source of consciousness beyond your constructed self? Throughout this book I have been challenging the notion that the sum of the human being can be captured in understanding one's personality. Beyond the personality, beyond our beliefs, our thoughts, and our entrained emotions, is a certain feeling of being conscious: The essential experience of 'I am' that exists regardless of our thoughts and opinions about it.

Completion Goal:

If we quiet our minds and look within, then what does it feel like to be conscious? Do you notice an essential feeling of 'I am' - a consistent stream of being that is always there despite our mental interruptions? Delve deeper into the nature of this feeling.

CHAPTER FIVE

TRANSFORMATIONAL MIND STATES

Our dreams are potential realities. Those realities await an imagination sharp enough to bring them to fruition, to birth their possibilities, and to bring to the foreground what we might term the background of infinite potential.

The source of all power comes from within the conscious soul. Too often we substitute what is in our hearts for lesser forms rather than sourcing our true sense of self from within. We give up our sovereign power and replace it with the lesser magic of the mind. In earlier reflections, we examined the difference between finding meaning in the external world and discovering meaning within the heart. In this chapter I explore the importance of cultivating the power we each hold within our hearts. The essence of all power comes from within – it is what projects meaning and sense to the external world around us. However, it is not difficult to fall into the habit of projecting the inner world onto the external canvas, and to forget the origin of our creative power. Once we become so disconnected from ourselves that we forget our true power, we mistake the external world for the authoritative force that rules our lives. It is not. It has never been.

If we reflect on this, consider that the external world cannot ever retain true power in and of itself. A hospital might house specialized million-dollar equipment, hire doctors who have studied 10 years or longer to gain advanced knowledge in medical procedures, but what is the bottom line? No healing can occur unless our bodies heal themselves. No doctor has ever healed someone. Rather, doctors apply the scientific method for diagnosis, treatment, and prevention. But, make no mistake: Doctors are scientists, not healers. Medicines can help the natural process of the body's healing. But, our bodies heal themselves.

Consider another example. Universities might house leading research labs, archive tens of thousands of scientific publications in a particular area of knowledge, and libraries with thousands of books about specialized topics. What is the bottom line? Learning and wisdom cannot arise unless we turn inward to make sense of knowledge and understanding within. Without the cultivation of understanding and wisdom, no transfer of knowledge can occur, and it never does. Text on a page is just text, until our inner consciousness touches it and brings it to life. Even with all of our technological advancement, endless wealth, and military power of our governments, these displays of strength are mere paper castles and cardboard soldiers, paling alongside the unlimited power the conscious soul. It is consciousness that brings the world to life, not societal, religious, or cultural constructs.

The power of consciousness feeds into societal constructs, it upholds them. It is a grave flaw to assume that the external world holds all of the answers, the full potential for healing, knowledge, trust, and progress. The power of the external is held with the consistent perpetuation of factors we assign our power to. The mass authoritarian structures (hospitals, universities, police, and courts) of our societies are all held in the consciousness that gives them power, and that consciousness arises from within each individual human being. Their perpetual strength is animated, on a moment-to-moment basis, via our collective consent. There is no power in the external, except where it is infused and perpetuated with a collective focus of consciousness.

Consider another example: Police officers who wear a uniform with a badge and a gun around their waist. Most people assign police a sense of great overarching power on an intellectual level. However, do police officers have power in and of themselves? Overall, police officers make up less than one percent of the overall population, so by pure physical means, the police does not hold more power than most other people combined. It would be more accurate to argue that the power we give police officers in fact holds their aura of justice, strength, and superiority. It is not the uniform itself, the gun, or the law that gives them all-encompassing power. These are constructs, reference points to a greater essence – and that essence arises from within each one of us. After all, we, as citizens of the world have an active role in political and law-making process, yet often we live as though we are disempowered. "Please, please do not give me a ticket, officer." We contribute to the mass structures that exist in our world on a moment-to-moment basis, but all the while we have come to fear those same structures that we uphold.

This is a ridiculous move on the chessboard of life. Yet we continue it, time and again, and often without question or reflection. How often do we stand for poor medical heath care, for unjust laws, for corruption and for a disregard of human rights, just because we feel that a doctor, a judge, a chief executive officer, or a police officer holds power over us? Though we perceive power outside ourselves, it arises as a result of our perpetual upholding of that power. No power can exist without collective conscious consent. Without it, that power fades into nothingness, into oblivion. It is a mere externalization of inner power, appearing (as an illusion) to exist of its own accord. It never does. In a literal sense, power that we perceive external from us corresponds to the same power that we have disavowed in our hearts and handed over to someone else. This process of disempowerment is the ultimate subjugation of the individual.

The above examples are all salient because these speak to each human being's inherent programming to surrender their inner power to the external world. In relation to consciousness studies, it is important to consider how often we look to the authorities, scientists, psychologists, religious groups, spiritual gurus, and others who act as authorities on consciousness. You would be able to find completely different definitions and explanations about consciousness states depending on whether you asked a medical practitioner, a priest, or a spiritual guru. However, none of these individuals would be able to point you toward your own personal experience of consciousness and what it means to expand your consciousness on a personal, intimate level. In this book, I have emphasized the importance of looking within for personal answers, rather than depending on specific religious, or spiritual groups that act as authorities about consciousness.

There is much wisdom in looking to the practice of Buddhist monks who separate themselves from modern civilization in order to meditate and reconnect with themselves. In one manner, however, escaping from society and living in seclusion is an extreme measure of separating our individual consciousness from the collective whole. Here, I suggest that, to a large degree, we can learn how to reclaim our personal source of power and consciousness from the external world by recognizing just how often we give our power to others with so little reservation. In order to go about this, there is no need to live in a monastery for several years in seclusion. Rather, we must leave behind the confines of the intellectual wall and to reclaim our ultimate power and purpose within our souls.

Thus, in this chapter we consider three main points: 1) Principles of self-empowerment and living a meaningful life, 2) transformational meditation and mind states and how these arise within, and 3) deepening our exploration of unconscious and super-conscious levels of experience. I will draw upon a broad range of techniques and examples to help illustrate the link between personal power and consciousness states throughout this chapter.

CULTIVATION OF INNER POWER

We depend on books as a source of knowledge and wisdom. We depend on doctors as a source of health. We depend on religions as a source of faith. Yet, true wisdom comes from within the heart. Our bodies heal themselves under the right conditions. Our source of faith and trust can be found within, rather than in the expertise of priests, spiritual leaders or gurus. Intelligence and wisdom are qualities of the soul rather than abilities that are imparted via education alone.

Instead of looking for happiness (an internal state) in consumerism (an external construct), faith (an internal state) in religion (an external construct), and confidence (an internal state) in other people's opinions of us (a language construct), a process of self-recognition calls for us to turn inward, to remember the wisdom and love that we hold within, recognizing that we do not need external structures to supplement it.

Franz Bardon offered an excellent example of this (9). His writing illustrated that in the past, human beings were forced to survive in environments of extreme cold temperatures. Now, in the modern Western world, most of us have ease of access to heating, air conditioning, food, and other comforts that do not require us to test our mental and physical endurance in order to sustain ourselves. Bardon noted that with proper mental training, we can learn how to generate our own heat in our bodies, according to this work, this is how we have survived in extreme temperatures in the past. Franz Bardon's observations are consistent with studies that have found physiology can be easily affected via visual stimuli (for example, those sitting in a movie theatre who are watching a scene of Antarctica have been measured to experience a drop in their physical body temperature during the scene).

Similar examples can be noted, such as when we look at images of fire, we begin to feel warm. When we look at images of food, we begin to feel hunger. When some people look at a person experiencing pain in their arm, their own arm begins to hurt as a direct consequence (empathic pain) (10). It is quite clear that our minds have an amazing amount of power in deciding upon some of our own physiological, mental, and emotional responses. The power of the mind, and of imagination, is tremendous. However, too often we lend power to the external triggers around us that pull our strings. Like puppets in a panoptic theatre governed by our masters, our elected authorities hold our power in an invisible bank, keeping us on a short leash.

For example, Researcher Dean Shrock noted that a person's will to live is far more important in the process of recovering from cancer than the actual treatment he or she is receiving. For example, it is the will to live, the motivation to fight for one's life, that is most paramount, and this source of motivation always come from within, not from a pill that a doctor prescribes, or a breakthrough treatment that a patient undergoes. Remember, all true power originates within. The power to heal comes from within. The power to learn and understand and empathize comes from within. The power to love comes from within. No amount of societal processes (no matter how complex) can replicate these authentic inner motivations of the soul.

In one of the conversations I had with Dean Shrock, we discussed how medical researchers discount the placebo effect when testing new treatments (3). The placebo effect does in fact illustrate the power of our own bodies to heal (and via mere suggestion, at that). It is not something we should make light of. Yet, often doctors disregard the placebo effect, stating that if someone's condition improves (not due to their medication) that this goes to show that the medication was not efficacious. However, the more important aspect is often negated. That is, that the placebo effect shows just how powerful the human mind is in the healing process.

People wonder about how after decades of research, no cures for diseases such as cancer or AIDS exist. However, first we must examine how we place our consciousness and our sense of power. There are hundreds of campaigns that speak out against these diseases, such as 'Cancer Awareness,' 'Stop Cancer,' and the 'Fight Cancer Campaign.' Most of these are fear-driven, focusing on what we wish to avoid, rather than painting a picture of health.

The outcome of the above campaigns is one in which we increase the amount of time that we spend worrying and fretting about cancer. In one manner, we mentally put the idea of the cancer outside of ourselves – we disempower ourselves and see it as an external force that cannot be stopped. It becomes out of our control. We lose control. We lose power. We make it society's problem. But, in this case, what is 'society' but a vague construct that we have externalized outside of ourselves? As we have demonstrated earlier, it is when we internalize the problem and take charge of it that we become empowered to create changes in our life, and by consequence, we shape the world around us. It is from within that we cultivate this power toward change, not from the external world. All true power is sourced within, from our deeper conscious experience.

Shrock devised interactive visualization exercises to help his patients connect with their bodies at a deeper level in order to promote the healing process. This is one example of recognizing our internal power for change. The opposite can be considered in a case such as where an individual takes no charge whatsoever of his own health and expects doctors, surgeons, and pharmacists to maintain his health and to fix his ailments, without considering how his lifestyle, diet or how he, himself, might have contributed to his own illness.

Similar examples can be drawn here with the eight-hour work schedule, as most people in the Western world work for 40 hours a week. This is fascinating, as we can observe the number of people who sit at work and do nothing at all just to fill the eight-hour requirement. It is astonishing. Yet, these same individuals remain at work for a dozen or more hours when their schedule becomes busier, but never receive the chance to leave earlier on less busier periods. It is one of the most ridiculous notions I've ever come across. The single explanation I can think of for this phenomena is that it would serve to tame the human being, to keep the human being regimented in a prison-like schedule.

For instance, when I work, I dedicate full awareness to the process, and if it takes four hours, then it takes four hours, if it takes a dozen, then it takes a dozen. I don't sit around from 9AM-5PM each day, every day, despite the actual quantity of work I have – what point does this serve? (Aside from conditioning?). Is it not more intelligent to work when there is work to be done, and to have fun and live life the other times? This process that most people in the world are subjected to is not just counterintuitive, but also illogical, as well as senseless. Nonetheless, we continue to maintain the social structure that enforces the 40-hour work week, despite recognizing that we are not machines in a factory, we are not conveyor belts that work for numbers and outputs, and we are most productive during spontaneous times throughout the week.

A friend of mine, Brandon Moreno, who spent over two decades working as an executive coach for Fortune 500 companies has highlighted on multiple occasions just how important it is for organizations to treat their people as, in fact, people (not as robots, as such a vast number of companies do) (3). Brandon has pointed out that when our talents, and our creative potential is cultivated, when we are respected by our peers, that is when we are most productive and contribute to the overall vision of an organization much more effectively. Yet, so many bosses treat people working with them as somehow inferior to them. Emotional abuse and sexual harassment cases in the workplace arise out of these ridiculous power dynamics that should not even exist in the first place. The power dynamic is perceived as an external construct, but this always arises within, even our acquiescence to the idea that we have to work from 9AM-5PM is supported within ourselves first, there is no external penultimate godlike figure that makes this true; it is us, our conscious acquiescence that supports it. And, we can change that, as soon as we re-empower ourselves.

Just as we demonstrated in the previous chapter, no other person can force you to feel a particular emotion. This directive comes from within you. It is important to clear our internal triggers that others believe they have established in order to walk all over us; to have us feel guilt, anger, shame, or regret at the push of a button. Likewise, it is important to withdraw the power that we have given others outside of ourselves and to reclaim it, to recognize that this power is sovereign, it is in our hands whether we choose to cultivate it or to give it to someone else. But, even if we choose to squander this inner power, it never really leaves us, it is always rising from within, and we just divert it into less-than-helpful avenues. Remember, the power of the conscious soul is never derived from societal constructs, it does not matter if someone is the president of the United States, or if someone has just been evicted from their home is now living on the street, the power of each soul is sovereign, and it transcends societal bounds.

In a manner of speaking, people support the perpetual disenfranchisement of their potential through their collective passive state. Someone (a human being, or a group of human beings, with the same rights as you and I) decided how the world should function (whether in a direct or indirect manner), and the remainder of people follow like sheep to the slaughter, without questioning the structure. The overdependence on the mind illusion and the fictitious idea that societies hold ultimate reign over its citizens is not sustainable. In the last few decades we have seen a massive growth in medical treatments, in technological advances, and in the diverse range of services and goods on an international scale. Yet, Western societies have some of the highest rates of physical and mental illness, and general unhappiness, despite endless entertainment outlets. This illustrates that it is paramount for us to recognize that core states of power, peace, happiness, love, consciousness, and healing arise from within, and the more we abandon our inner power and place that demand onto the external world, the more unhappiness we cause for ourselves.

In a philosophical sense, we move from ourselves and into the world, and in doing so, we forget ourselves in the truest sense. It is imperative that we renegotiate power from the small minorities who paint the face of the external world, and instead recognize that each individual person has equal power and potential to contribute to this world. To rediscover this is to become human, to become alive, and to become conscious, not a mindless robot. The external mirrors the internal. To begin, all that we are called upon to do is to acknowledge the true trajectories of our inner light.

EXPLORATION: EMPOWERMENT SCALE

In Chapter Two, we discussed the idea of sublimated consciousness and the constant dance between essence and existence – the flux between potential and actual. In this exploration, I encourage readers to consider their inner potential and how certain external authorities either serve to suppress or cultivate this inner power. Philosopher Neil Kramer posited the idea that if we do not become responsible for our own mind, then we in effect give up our power to other forces. Thus, to what degree is your mind truly your own? To what extent do you surrender your mind to external ideas from others? Often our minds mimic the ideas that others give us, rather than reflecting our inner nature. The original mind is rare.

In his work, Neil Kramer discussed the idea of an individual consciousness field that each person emanates. Yet, according to Kramer, we each also connect with

157

a global consciousness field. This collective field is subject to the channels of media, cultural programming, and societal convention. If we do not individuate and become sovereign over our own minds, then we default to the cultural norms of the world and the collective field (3, 11).

> The field can be talked about in many different ways. When Zen Master Shunryu Suzuki spoke of little mind and big mind, he was proposing a clear distinction between the conditioned individual mental sphere and what, perhaps, we might call 'field knowing.'

> – Neil Kramer, 'The Unfoldment'

Instead of drawing upon our authentic connection to ourselves as a source of power, we so often supplement our power with false idols and impossible dreams. Oscar Wilde is often quoted for the passage: "Be yourself; everyone else is already taken." Yet, so often we aim to attain a standard outside of ourselves. A basketball player aims to be as good as Michael Jordon. A computer programmer tries to reach the same success as Bill Gates. A Christian aims to be more like Jesus Christ. These are all impossible pursuits. In fact, unattainable. We can be ourselves, nothing else, nothing less, nothing more.

My partner, Izabel, introduced me to an excellent metaphor for this concept. Izabel stated that pursuing some else's dream is a bit like a flower in a field looking upward to a nearby tree and wishing 'I wish I could be as tall as that tree.' It makes no sense for a flower to want to be as tall as a tree, because it is not a flower's nature to become a tree. It is a flower. In the same manner, it is far more empowering to embrace our own true nature rather than to aspire to external standards of attainment and success. In recognizing and nourishing our individual nature, we can then become the best versions of ourselves, rather than attempting to replicate someone else's experience.

> Most people are other people. Their thoughts are someone else's opinions, their lives a mimicry, their passions a quotation.

> – Oscar Wilde

When we embrace our own inner light, we bring something new into the world, we allow our soul to shine outward. If movie star Arnold Schwarzenegger, for instance, felt ashamed of his accent and was embarrassed to appear in motion pictures, then he would not have become a famous actor. Yet, because he embraced his accent and decided to frame it as a personal strength rather than a weakness, his accent became a strong asset in his acting career. Likewise, Steve Jobs did not aim to design computers to meet the design trends of the 1990s. Instead, Jobs developed new and innovative designs for computers that challenged the norm. The designs could almost be considered as weird and bizarre at first. Yet, it is Apple's unique designs that often draw popularity from the mass public.

It is not when we acquiesce to other people's markers of success that we flourish, but it is when we embrace our own uniqueness and let it shine that we are flourish. This is the origin and manifestation of our ultimate creative power. Yet, how few people recognize this? How few people practice cultivating their essential power, their personal gifts?

MISSION TASK 61: PERSONAL EMPOWERMENT

Refer to Appendix C, 'Empowerment Scale,' and consider times in your life when you feel inclined to compare yourself to an external standard and make an excuse for why your life is not turning out the way you would like it to as a result of this unmet goal. Consider how you could turn this statement around to take responsibility for this aspect of your life instead.

Is the second statement you wrote down more empowering? How does it help you change perspective, from making excuses about your life, and toward becoming accountable and becoming an active author of your own life?

Remind yourself that you have the power to create new realities irrespective of what is occurring in the external world. Others have rethought the world through their own imaginative eyes before, and the world transformed before the eyes of all. It was not their intelligence or fame that allowed them to do this, but rather a sense of personal empowerment – recognizing that they could become a part of the co-creation of the world as we see it from moment-to-moment.

Refer to the worksheet in Appendix C, 'Empowerment Scale.'

Disempowering statements: Disempowering statements are those that we use to discount our own control over our lives and instead blame someone else, or society in general. 'If only I had more money, I could then live the life I wanted; if only I was more attractive, I could then find true love; if only things turned out different ... if only, if only, I would be happy right now ...' Do you ever qualify your life results in this fashion? Disempowered thinking occurs when we place our focus upon the world as having a source of power over our lives.

Empowering statements: Empowering statements take the power back from the external world and promote personal autonomy and empowerment. Each time you blame someone else or discount your own ability, you give up a piece of your inner power. The adage 'where there is a will, there is a way' is a good example of an empowered attitude. In this way, you focus instead on new possibilities and opportunities rather than on limitations and restrictions that prevent a particular goal or inner state from being achieved. For someone in an empowered state, there are no limitations, just opportunities; no failures, just lessons for improvement; and no boundaries, just growing pains.

Completion Goal:

Fill out the left side of the worksheet with as many disempowering statements you can think of that you tend to make about yourself or other people on a common basis (also refer to examples in the appendix). Reflect: 'How could I rephrase each statement to be more empowering'? Then, re-phrase each of these statements by writing a new statement on the right-hand side of the worksheet that would bring the power back into your own hands. How could you make a proactive and positive choice about each statement instead?

MISSION TASK 62: EMPOWERING BEHAVIOURS

Discuss your transformed statements with your partner or a close friend, someone you are comfortable sharing this information with. Brainstorm other empowering statements that you could come up with for each disempowering statement on the sheet. Discuss with your friend how you could go about adopting the new, empowering, statement into your life. Does each statement change how you perceive the world or life in general? How? Think about practical action steps to take toward enacting this new statement.

Completion Goal:

For each transformed statement, decide upon at least three new behaviors, goals, or actions that you can take toward enacting this new empowered perspective.

MISSION TASK 63: FINDING STRENGTH

I have found that most people living in modern societies act in a disempowered manner. They adopt a disempowered position to such an extent that they do not even realize how much power they surrender to others: To their partner's requirements, to their boss's expectations, to their friend's opinions, for instance.

In this mission task, consider how often you act in an empowered manner in your life, pursuing your own dreams and goals regardless of what family, friends, superiors at work, or the general public have to say about it. It is rare to see someone act so confidently and in such an empowered way in our society, isn't it? So often we look to others for guidance and direction instead of taking a stand.

Refer to the 'Life Scribing Sample' worksheet in Appendix C. The individual in this example gives all of his power to those in his workplace. He allows others to make him feel upset and disrespected. He feels as though he will never experience happiness until others start treating him in a different manner.

How could the individual in this example change his attitude and adopt a more empowering frame of mind? For example, a basic change could be that from 'others must treat me a certain way in order for me to feel respected and happy' to 'I am in charge of my own happiness and sense of respect.' Can you see how the latter statement puts the power back in his hands to make a decision about how to act in the situation (whether that be to change how he interacts with his co-workers, to change his attitude toward them, or to build the confidence to find another job altogether)? Yet, until this man stops complaining about the external situation and disempowering himself, he is unable to become accountable for his own life to make the changes required and to move out of a negative situation.

Which hidden strengths might the individual in the example not see in himself? The fact that he cares about how others treat him at work implies that this individual is quite a caring person and is aware when he might make others feel uncomfortable. It is this aspect of himself that makes him notice when others are treating him in an unfair manner. Embracing this strength rather than seeing himself as 'vulnerable, weak and always picked on by others' could be helpful in developing friends outside of the workplace who share similar qualities of respect for others. Rather than perceiving the situation as an issue of not fitting in to the group, the man in the example might take the situation as a cue that the sorts of people he is involved with at work do not match his own personal attributes and core principles in life. Here, he moves from seeing himself as disempowered (giving power to his co-workers), to reclaiming his power (reclaiming a sense of confidence).

Completion Goal I:

Make a list of the parts of yourself that you do not like, or parts that you see as weaknesses. What is it the reason for those parts being present? Reflect on the points in the previous chapter about embracing lost parts of ourselves. Consider how you could adopt a more empowered attitude toward these parts of yourself. Do they offer you some benefit, or a secondary gain? How could you see these aspects of yourself as potential strengths or learning points rather than as weaknesses?

Completion Goal II:

Can you think of a situation in your life, or in someone else's life (either someone you know or someone you have heard about), in which that person has changed an external situation around from being disempowered, to empowering themselves and making a change for the better? Think of at least one other case example that is similar to the Life Scribing example provided above. Reflect upon the value of an empowered approach in life in general.

Completion Goal III:

Reflect on at least one time that you have formed a disempowering self-image because of what you assumed others think or feel about you.

Side Note: It is so important to be kind toward ourselves, far too often we are too critical toward ourselves. We also tend to believe that others are more critical toward us than they actually are. Consider how kind and compassionate you would be toward your partner or your best friend if he or she was in danger or had a major life dilemma. Consider how much you may empathize with a stranger who sincerely needs your help. Often, we are much more compassionate and understanding toward others than we are toward ourselves, yet we work under the false pretense that others are somehow critical and judgmental of us.

PEAK MEDITATION EXPERIENCES

On the morning of December 10, 1996, a woman named Jill Bolte Taylor woke up in her home to find that she was experiencing a stroke in the left side of her brain. In recalling her experience, Taylor spoke about her left-brain hemisphere systematically shutting down as she began to lose all logical and intellectual thinking ability (11). Even as Taylor attempted to dial the telephone for help, she could not cognize the numbers on the phone, she perceived them as different squiggles and shapes with no logical meaning.

Taylor's experience illustrates a spontaneous process of having the left-brain neurological processes disabled temporarily, while the functioning of the right-brain hemisphere remains. Interestingly, Taylor noted that although the experience was considered by most a medical emergency, for her, the experience was also a profound spiritual awakening during which she was able to connect to a state of love, compassion and "deep inner peace."

Taylor's account also astutely captures an experience that many meditation practitioners and adept monks strive to achieve their entire lives as part of their meditation practice. This is a state of consciousness that we have been moving toward considering throughout this book, illustrating that the left brain hemisphere processes the world in a very limited, finite manner, while the right brain hemisphere is far more receptive to creative, abstract realities.

Meditation practice has an observable effect in cultivating transcendent experiences in which we expand our self-consciousness, just as Taylor did in her account. There are a large number of studies available on transcendental meditation, for instance, which illustrate just how powerful meditation practice is in terms of mind potential transformation. It does not matter whether we consider Zen meditation, transcendental meditation, mantra-based meditation, chakra-based meditation, or even more basic mindfulness-based practice. The constructed self begins to dissolve in each of these states to reveal the greater consciousness and sense of being-ness.

The left-brain impulse, as Neil Kramer put it, keeps us confined to inflexible and conditioned intellectual notions about the world, and the intellectual wall magnetizes our conscious experience to false ideas about how we should live our lives (12). The secret of meditation is thus not just about basic relaxation techniques, it is about re-wiring the mechanisms of the brain, and the perception of the mind, in order to recognize our broader self-experience for what it is. In spontaneous instances, this expansion of consciousness can be brought on via meditation, neurological damage (see Alexander Eben's account, for instance), spiritual dedication, or through the use of entheogens such as psilocybin mushrooms or ayahuasca, for example. In this book I rather propose that we can engage with this process of awakening to the broader mind from a place of deeper empowerment, re-recognizing our sovereign

reign over our true unique conscious experience, rather than leaving this to external forces.

> Nevertheless, the more it becomes clear that to be is to quarrel and to pursue self-interest, the more you are compelled to recognize your needs for enemies to support you. In the same way, the more resolutely you plumb the question 'Who or what am I'–the more unavoidable is the realization that you are nothing at all apart from everything else. Yet again, the more you strive for some kind of perfection or mastery–the more you see that you are playing a rarified and lofty form of the old ego-game, and that your attainment of any height is apparent to yourself and to others only by contrast with someone else's depth or failure.

– Alan Watts, 'The Book'

Philosopher Alan Watts pointed out that all intellectual deductions about ourselves are subject to comparison and contrast. When we consider power and consciousness from a personality perspective, we can only be 'more compassionate than someone else' or 'less compassionate than someone else.' It remains a matter of contrast. This is the ego's game, the ploy of the constructed self. The intellectual mind compares and contrasts, which is its role, to make logical deductions. The inner heart does not compare, it just experiences in wholesome reception. Have you ever heard a couple having an argument when one of the partners suggested the other that she does not 'love him as much' as he loves her. Only the constructed self recognizes such a distinction. In terms of consciousness, states such as compassion and love are not quantifiable. It would be preposterous to consider love in gradations from a felt-level experience. Yet, within the cold and calculating intellectual wall, we do.

People attempt to make these transcendent experiences, such as love and compassion, somehow quantifiable with the tools of the intellectual mind, and in doing so diminish their power. Treating states like love as mechanical currencies that we can somehow define and separate into clusters does a grave disservice to the true nature of such immensely empowering emotional experiences.

In his most acclaimed work, 'The Book,' Alan Watts stated that: "No one who has been hoaxed into the belief that he is nothing but his ego, or nothing but his individual organism, can be chivalrous, let alone a civilized, sensitive, and intelligent member of the cosmos." This statement highlights the difference between an individual who grounds himself in the constructed self, turning to his intoxicated mind illusion when searching for higher states, and the individual who embraces the no-self perspective in his meditation, abstaining from attachment to a given self-image. This individual embraces all-potential to find that these peak states of consciousness exist within (there is no need to look for them outside). These transcendent states are not contingent upon the construction of an intellectual or social self-image. From that point, one recognizes that the intellectual wall does not bear fruit, it so often rescinds our access to what lies in our hearts.

In this book, I have purposely avoided discussing meditation techniques at great length, as at the core of it, meditation is a tool for mediating between different realities, and different states of consciousness. It is not something that can be taught as an intellectual concept, but rather something that must be experienced firsthand. Therefore, while I have included some basic techniques in this chapter, my foremost intention is to point out that many people disempower themselves in most facets of life, including spiritual and meditation practice. Thus, personal empowerment in our physical, emotional, and spiritual lives is far more important than memorizing techniques. It is atrocious to see the number of spiritual groups and communities around the world who create trademarks and specific be-all end-all approaches to meditation that serve to segregate our understanding of this process, rather than liberating its power for all to benefit from.

People look to gurus and spiritual teachers instead of looking within their own hearts. They rely on the power of external drugs to transform their consciousness, rather than recognizing that drugs serve as a trigger for an inner process, rather than a cause. They rely on a book or a class to learn meditation. They rely on others to show them a path that has been within their hearts all along, awaiting their awareness and recognition.

Thus, there are no techniques that could ever be as valuable as your own personal experience. By putting all of your trust into a certain meditation teacher, or into a guided meditation disc, you take away from your own power to search within – without external tools or guidance. Surrendering our external tools and trusting in our inner experience might seem a difficult task, but this is what we are required to do to in order to witness the deepest and most transformative consciousness experiences firsthand.

Real meditation is a courageous process. It is a process of intuitively questioning the basis of our reality, to temporarily break the foundation of self that we have constructed. This is done in order to broaden our experience of consciousness. No-one can teach you or show you how to do that. It is in your own hands. This is the essence of true meditation. It is never the practice of aiming to conceptualize meditation within one's safe intellectual wall. It is the practice of on surrendering the self and entering into the infinite chaos of unbound potential.

> Still there are moments when one feels free from one's own identification with human limitations and inadequacies. At such moments, one imagines that one stands on some spot of a small planet, gazing in amazement at the cold yet profoundly moving beauty of the eternal, the unfathomable: life and death flow into one, and there is neither evolution nor destiny; only being.

– Albert Einstein

In meditation, we can observe that the constructed self is a container for consciousness. It contains a small fragment of all we are and fails to acknowledge all we could become. It is a falsely enveloped prison around consciousness, a prison which aims to delude one's perception into believing that it is fixed and restricted, that it can live and die, that it can gain and lose, and that it is subject to the laws of the social world.

Consider the previous examples we have drawn upon throughout this book. The daughter who learns about the defining characteristics of the world from her mother. The mother who forgets her capabilities and talents because she focuses her entire attention on parenting her children. The depressed man who has forgotten how not to be depressed, or rather, how to find happiness again, because he has become so caught up in the mental construct that has been assigned to him and reinforced throughout his life. Through true meditation practice, he renegotiates the terms of his experience and takes back his sovereign power. Once he acknowledges his broader conscious experience, his attitude might change to a more empowering one. 'I am in control of how I feel and how I choose to see myself.' He reimagines himself in a new light.

In meditation, the aim is to let go of the constructed self, however we do not need to figure out which new experiences will arise to fill the emptiness we have allowed within. In fact, the intelligence of the soul is so divine that we can never dream to grasp it with the intellectual mind, nor should we. It is far more important to trust in the process and open to the new possibilities that arise within meditation. Just as an artist cannot force a brushstroke with the intellectual mind, we ought to open ourselves to the inspiration that arises from the higher aspect of ourselves.

In some Gnostics traditions, when we embrace the no-self state, the true nature of consciousness, the soul, begins to arise as we create the space within for this to occur. The divine being within each of us recognizes that we have made space for its appearance. Thus arises the appearance of our unique soul, beyond the constructed self.

In her work on kundalini awakening experiences, Jana Dixon has mentioned that the loss of the self is not just common, but paramount on the road to spiritual awakening. The sense of self we hold begins to expand and broaden to connect with the universe (as pointed out in the Einstein quote earlier) to reconnect us with a much broader range of experience. Sometimes, first we must embrace the emptiness of the abyss within, as we clear out all about negative programming, we might find deep sense of loneliness arises. 'What is the meaning of 'being me' if all that I am is made up of social programming, language, and external constructs?' It is important during these dark nights of the soul to embrace the emptiness, rather than contesting it. For when we embrace it, our true soul begins to arise from the depths of our being.

Here we can note the importance of connecting with our life experience based on our heartfelt connection with the world, with others, and with ourselves. Instead of expecting something more from our partner when we do not feel enough love, it is important to turn inward to discover our source of love independent of what's going on in the external world or with other people. Instead of expecting religions, philosophies, and political movements to offer a sense of security about life, it is important to search for a deep-seated sense of security within that persists regardless of the external climate. Instead of depending on books or college programs to give us knowledge and job prospects, it is far more important to discover our inner talents and to cultivate creative potential within first.

EXPLORATION: MEDITATION PRACTICE

In this exploration, let's consider some basic meditation techniques. These techniques center on the idea of focus, the concept that where we place our attention, our consciousness follows in that direction. These mission tasks are intended to illustrate the link between broadening our self-consciousness and meditation.

MISSION TASK 64: OUTER FOCUS

Begin to concentrate on each one of your five senses and notice which input you can pick up on. What can you see in front of you right now? Notice as many objects as you can in as much detail as possible. Do the same with your sense of hearing. What do you hear right now? Give attention to even the slightest detail. Birds chirping, the sound of the wind blowing, the hum of a washing machine in the background, perhaps? Continue with each of the other senses. What do you smell? Is there a particular taste and texture in your mouth that you notice? How does it feel to be sitting where you are right now? Give attention to even the slightest sensations such as the pressure of your feet on the ground.

Completion Goal I:

Practice this meditation approach, incorporating awareness of each of the five senses for at least 30 seconds.

Completion Goal II:

Did you lose awareness of the details of the prior sense when you moved on to each of the following senses? I would like to encourage you to practice this exercise again later in the day and to notice whether you can become aware of the sensory input coming through each of the five senses, all at once. Instead of moving attention from one sense to the next, incorporate the next sense into your existing awareness of the environment. Is that possible to move from sense to sense in this cumulative fashion, progressively broadening our awareness, rather than merely relocating it?

Side Notes:

You will soon find that it is in fact possible to expand our consciousness in a very direct way. This is a form of meditation that allows one to tune into their reality at a greater level of depth, in more detail. Certain professionals, such as detectives, have to maintain a clear awareness of their environment at all times, giving attention to even the slightest details or changes in a room. It is essential for their job. However, detectives are not just born with this awareness about distinct details through each of the five senses. This skill can be taught and learned, and this demonstrates that our external awareness is not static. In fact, it is possible to expand our consciousness to new parameters and to make this process more permanent, so that whenever we enter another room or go outside, we notice more of the environment saturate our senses more than ever before – this process then becomes second nature.

One of the benefits of this process is that we are then able to engage with life more and experience the environment around us in more richness, in more depth. However, we can also choose to hone our awareness and direct all of our consciousness on one particular object, or person of focus. When we do, our focus becomes more magnetized than it was prior to practicing. The process also builds personal willpower. It shows us that we can decide what we choose to focus on at a given moment. This seems trivial, but is in fact profound. How we perceive the world is learned throughout childhood. Even our perception is a form of behavior. When two people walk into a room, these people experience different things and act in different manners. Their perception is directed to different elements of the room. Each person's interpretation differs. There are substantial differences in experience. As we learn how to hone our perception and direct it in a conscious manner, we begin to engage with life on a whole new level.

MISSION TASK 65: INNER FOCUS

It is also possible to expand your inner experience, to turn to a deeper awareness of the realm of thought and emotion. How often is your awareness consumed in one single thought or idea? In meditation practice, it is often suggested that people get caught up in repetitive thought patterns that serve no real function aside from rumination. In conversation, we do not repeat the same sentence to our friends three times. Likewise, we just need to think about each original idea or concept once, not 1,000 times. Yet, we often do the opposite. We ruminate, ponder, and despair over the same thoughts over and over again. One of the benefits of learning how to expand our consciousness through meditation is that we can quieten the mind and decide where to place our focus at a given time – this is a common aim of meditation techniques.

Although a woman might state that she wants to leave her abusive partner, this expression of confidence and willpower is just one thought in her mind, among myriad thoughts that dispute or contrast with her split-second decision of strength. It is counteracted in moments – "what will I do without him?" Thoughts stack upon one another in patterns – "my mother would not approve if I left, she thinks it is my fault for not being a good wife to him." Our mind is filled with a constant barrage of thoughts, an influx of self-contradicting decisions: Cognitive dissonance, with ideas and mental commentaries opposing other mental commentaries within the same mind.

Some psychologists believe that the average human being thinks of between 20,000-100,000 thoughts per day. These thoughts can often be in conflict with one another and cause a great deal of neurosis. Meditation and mindfulness practice shows us just how often we get swept up in our thoughts and carried with them. The thoughts have power over us. Yet, shouldn't the situation be reversed? The idea behind meditation is that a mind that is ever-thinking and caught up in mental chatter is an untrained mind. It requires discipline and willpower to stop thinking and to decide which thoughts are worth the time to focus on and to cultivate. The untrained mind can often run wild, dominating our consciousness and taking us on a ride.

This goes right to the heart of true empowerment. Meditation can help us gain a clearer, more empowered view on life. Earlier on I gave the example of a woman who was pondering leaving her partner. If this particular woman decided to quieten her mind and focus for 10-20 minutes, and then to affirm with confidence "I am leaving right now," that statement would hold much more power and conviction (when contrast with the barrage of conflicting thought responses she had experienced earlier). Her mind was in chaos, unfocused, but with the power of conscious intention this can be changed. We can, in fact, alter the mind with the power of our consciousness, and herein transcendence experiences of meta-thinking become quite powerful.

An adept meditator who sits in quiet meditation for three hours with almost no thoughts and then makes a firm, willful decision, has a great degree of conviction and willpower. If we do have around 20,000 or more thoughts per day, then imagine how dispersed our attention is. About 10% of thoughts might be about work, 10% about our partner, 20% about what we have to get done tomorrow, 10% of worries and doubts about life in general, and so the list goes on. How dispersed does our attention become? It is as though our consciousness becomes fragmented into a thousand different directions, all pulling us in different trajectories.

What is the result? We are left with no true power or conviction remaining within. Powerless, we surrender to the confusion of the intellectual wall. A singular moment of clear focus and will is more powerful than a million dispersed thoughts. Imagine drawing an arrow back in order to shoot a target far in the distance. You could either choose to draw a bow 100 times and put one percent of your strength into each attempt at hitting the target, or you could put 100% of your strength into hitting one single target, with great precision and power. This metaphor demonstrates the power of meditation for developing mental discipline.

Completion Goal I:

Pick any object in front of you, such as a teapot, or a pencil, or even something outside such as a tree to focus on. Place all of your attention on this one particular object. Set a timer and aim to place all of your attention on this object and hold it in your mind's awareness for 60 seconds. If your attention becomes distracted before the 60 seconds finish, start over.

Completion Goal II:

Did you get distracted? If you managed to finish the entire 60 second exercise, this time repeat it again, but also monitor your thinking process – become aware of each thought that runs into your mental awareness while looking at this object. If your attention becomes distracted (either looking away or thinking random thoughts, rather than just experiencing and reflecting on the object in front of you) before the 60 seconds finish, start over.

Completion Goal III:

Complete the above task again, but this time set the timer for five minutes.

MISSION TASK 66: INNER PATTERNS

The above exercise is intended to demonstrate just how little control we can have over our minds unless we learn how to develop mental discipline. How many attempts did the task require in order for you to hold your concentration on a single object for 60 seconds? It took me about two dozen attempts when I first practiced a similar task. If you were able to do it straight away, then this indicates a high level of mental discipline. Most people find that they can hardly hold their attention on one single point for longer than a few seconds, let alone an entire minute without interruption. Yet, it is easier to hold one's attention for an entire hour after first learning how to hold one's attention for even a couple of minutes, and likewise, it is easier to hold one's attention for a couple of minutes after learning how to hold one's attention for even a few seconds. The first few seconds are the most challenging.

Completion Goal I:

Reflect on the notion of mental discipline and how this concept relates to our previous discussion on power and consciousness. Meditation techniques such as this help to illustrate just how much power we have within. Often, mental commentaries cling together to form patterns. You might find yourself thinking about the same sort of things – reflect on how often your thoughts take you on a ride.

Completion Goal II:

Over the next hour, take notice of the trajectories that your thoughts take. Do your thoughts generally react to one another, leading you to think about something else, in a pattern-like fashion?

Completion Goal III:

Next time that you find yourself lost in your thoughts, or thinking about a particular topic randomly, bring your attention and your focus back to your center of being and take a deep breath. Then, reflect on the idea of reactive and proactive attitudes discussed in the 'Empowerment Scale' handout in Appendix C. Are your thoughts reactive (random patterns), or proactive (driven by your conscious intention)? Practicing this exercise helps us recognize that there is a place of stillness within each of us that does not get swept up in the constant flux of thoughts and emotions.

MISSION TASK 67: TRIAD

In his work 'The Three Mountains,' Gnostic Master Samael Aun Weor noted that meditation calls for us to become aware of the 'three brains' of human experience: 1) The intellectual, 2) the emotional, and 3) our motor reflexes. Interestingly, Weor proposed that true inner peace cannot be achieved until one becomes aware of their motives at each of the three levels of being. Consider, for example, a person who feels quite angry for no apparent reason (emotional manifestations). She cannot seem to shake this feeling of anger, and then she thinks to herself, "why am I so angry for no reason?" Soon, she recognizes that there is a distinct reason for the anger (mental manifestations). Her partner said something that offended her earlier on and triggered a feeling of anger, but she forgot what he said up until she thought about it again. All the while, she may have been walking home with her arms swinging vigorously from side to side (physical manifestations). This is an example of how we become unsettled at all three levels, the emotional, the intellectual, and the physical. The mirror of the constructed self manifests at each level.

Have you ever seen someone agree that they are no longer upset about a particular situation, only to find that they are fidgeting their leg or clenching their fists? Sometimes much of this behavior is unconscious. Often, we might feel that we are aware of the reactive patterns behind our thoughts, but might still have a chaotic emotional state, or a physical manifestation of our unsettledness. Thus, in this practice, the aim is not just to focus our thoughts, but to consider all three centers of being and the benefits of centering ourselves during times of emotional flux.

Completion Goal I:

Reflect on the three different centers, or three brains – physical, emotional, and intellectual. In particular, reflect on the parts of yourself that manifest in each of these three centers. Sometimes, when a person is irritated, he might suppress his irritation, and instead start tapping his foot. He sublimates the irritating thoughts, ignoring them, but instead channels the irritation into his foot. Have you ever done this with your own thoughts or emotions? Or, have you perhaps sometimes noticed yourself brushing your hair, biting your fingernails, tapping your foot or doing other actions, and then later noticing that these relate to particular feelings such as being anxious, upset, or irritated, for example?

Completion Goal II:

Reflect on how the idea of the three centers relates to the notion of congruence discussed throughout this book.

Side Note: Have you ever experienced moments of genuine inner congruence, when you've had a strong sense of alignment with your true self, and all of your behaviors, emotions, and thoughts moved into congruence as a single unified force?

MISSION TASK 68: MINDFULNESS

Remember the detective example from earlier on? It is possible to teach ourselves how to lower our threshold of awareness to tune into more of what is going on within (and outside) of us. Most people are generally aware of only their thoughts, or only their emotions at any given time, not both. We become overly engaged in the thought or emotion that is most prominent, and all else becomes somehow tuned out of awareness, it fades out of our subjective awareness, however it is still present just below the surface of focus.

Neuro-Linguistic Programming (NLP) trainer Tom Best pointed out a relevant example of this process, suggesting that sailors often become so attuned to the currents of the ocean that some are able to determine the direction of sail without a compass, tuning into the natural ebb and flow of the tides. This intricate power to tune in to our surroundings does not require special training or education. It is no more than a conscious direction of focus. Meditation teaches us that this process comes about as we let go of the mental chatter of the thinking mind and to reconnect with our environment and ourselves at a deeper level.

Completion Goal I:

Bring awareness to your thinking mind and notice the thoughts running through your consciousness now. Do not become involved with the thoughts. Just observe them. Then, bring your awareness to your emotions. What are you feeling right now? Observe your feelings without reacting to them or thinking about them, just observe and notice what it feels like to feel the emotions in your awareness right now. Next, bring your focus to your body. What does it feel like to be in your body? Do some of your muscles feel tired or fatigued, or relaxed, perhaps? What do your feet feel like pressed upon the ground? Are you doing anything with your arms or legs, or is your body still? Notice the pace of your breathing.

Completion Goal II:

Repeat the practice above, but this time maintain your awareness on each of the three centers, physical, emotional, and mental at the same time. You may find that parts of your experience float in and out of peripheral awareness, this is okay, however the overall aim is to maintain a clear awareness of what is going on within us as best possible – with practice this techniques becomes easier.

MISSION TASK 69: MINDSET

Has this subchapter changed your perspective on meditation? The true purpose of meditation practice is to empower ourselves and to understand ourselves in the grand scheme of the universe, rather than just to relax or de-clutter our mental place. Do you agree or disagree with this statement?

Completion Goal I:

I encourage you to find a number of articles about meditation techniques (at least 10, these can be found online). Rather than reading the articles with particular expectations, instead approach each article from the perspective we have been discussing so far: The use of meditation as a method for expanding self-awareness and inner power. Does this perspective change how you approach meditation techniques?

Completion Goal II:

Your task for this action step is to describe the purpose of meditation to someone else. Aim to utilize the same concepts that we have been discussing in this chapter (expansion of external and internal awareness, empowerment, and broadening our consciousness).

CONSCIOUS AND UNCONSCIOUS UNION

In a 2011-2012 series on BBC, a group of scientists were asked to draw a visual representation of the unconscious mind. The interviewer gave each scientist a pen and piece of blank paper and prompted them with the question: "Imagine this sheet of paper represents everything the brain can do. How much do you think is conscious and how much do you think is unconscious?" Each scientist filled in a small portion of the paper, indicating that the conscious mind represents just a few percent of our entire consciousness. Some drew a miniscule circle in the top corner of the paper, while others shaded in a narrow horizontal line toward the top of the paper. The narrator concluded the short segment with the question: "Are you in control of your unconscious, or is it in control of you?"

Perhaps an apt reframe of the above question would be: The unconscious is in control of us 'until' we learn to control it (or rather, learn how to foster a deeper understanding of and connection with the unconscious). Potential at the unconscious level can never be forgotten, instead it is transmuted, transformed. As we've discussed throughout this book, some believe that at the deepest reaches of the unconscious we connect with the realm of the super-conscious mind, making distinctions between unconscious and super-conscious somewhat limiting. On one level, all is connected at the deepest level, the all-mind which encompasses conscious, unconscious, and super-conscious realms. Yet, in order to gain more of an understanding of how the unconscious and super-conscious awareness can be cultivated, it can be useful to consider some of the features of different methods of processing the world. Once we familiarize ourselves with the features, it becomes easier to strive toward congruence between both minds.

Common phrases that describe the characteristics of conscious language: Thought-based communication; knowing through reasoning, commands and linear progress, direct, explicit, decisive, deterministic and ordered; logic, rigid specifics and clear-cut concepts, contained laws, set structures, forces of control, dichotomies

175

arise through segregation and distinction, limited with clear edges, concrete and measurable.

Common phrases that describe the characteristics of unconscious language, and super-conscious awareness: Feeling-based communication, intuitive knowing, metaphor, symbolism, archetypes; indirect, implicit, abstract, creative, imagination; transcendental possibilities and ideas; expansive, natural flow; patterns arising within chaos; oneness; limitless, ethereal and divine.

As we touched upon in Chapter Two, the power of the unconscious can rule over our conscious experience in life, that is, until we bring awareness to the deeper more encompassing parts of ourselves.

Therapist Danie Beaulieu published a book titled 'Impact Techniques for Therapists' which includes techniques that aim to bypass the conscious mind and work with the unconscious mind. That book provides some great examples of kinesthetic metaphors that bring about powerful change through dialoging with the unconscious. One example of a technique used in the book is that of the $20 note. Beaulieu recommended using this approach when working with self-esteem. In the example, the therapist takes out a $20 note and asks the client how much it is worth. Then, the therapist scrunches up the $20 note and stomps on it with his shoe, then picks it up, and asks his client again: "How much is it worth?" The use of imagery and the concept of money (linked to value) is quite powerful in creating change at both the unconscious and conscious levels. On the contrary, if a therapist had simply said to a client "each human has intrinsic value even if he has been through difficult times and felt like he has been trampled on by life, therefore you have just as much reason to be confident as anyone else," a client might not necessarily feel better or more confident at the unconscious level (even though he might feel better on a conscious level for a few moments).

For example, even a simple act of replacing a statement such as "I must go to the mall later today" to "I 'may' go to the mall later today" acts as a simple reframe from finite rules toward possibilities and opportunities. In most human communication people's unconscious motivations and processes are in conflict with their conscious communication. It is crucial to learn how to recognize both forms of language and to utilize them effectively. In doing so, we become masters of both minds.

Our world and its functioning is dominated by a highly-strung, highly focused, surface-level emphasis on the intellectual wall; there is no place for metaphor, magic, or explorations into the depths beneath the surface. It is all about direct, surface-level, interaction. The power structures force us to follow the rules of clearly determined laws, dogmas, and linear paths to progression. The unconscious and super-conscious potential within does not follow these strict lines, it breaks the rules that serve to constrict it and makes paradigmatic leaps, it is more free-flowing and abstract. In that sense, our experience of the super-conscious mind can be much more powerful than our restricted conscious experience of the world that has been contrived through social programming. The unconscious is not restricted to the same rules and language as the constructed self. Here we can emphasize once more the balance between certainties and possibilities, between control and flow. And, as we learn to reconnect with the deeper parts of ourselves, these new experiences come into conscious light once more.

> Most leaders agree that success comes from decisiveness and course correction, not long delays and procrastination to attempt making only flawless choices. Few successes are achieved via a straight line, from point A to point B, from idea to fruition. Most successes are achieved in a zig-zag manner.

> – Maxwell Maltz, 'Psycho-Cybernetics'

When we focus our thoughts on the same situations, on the same patterns, reinforcing the same ideas over and over, then we subvert our greater soul power and transmute it in accordance with the intellectual wall. Often, these thoughts lead to negative outcomes in our lives, because they do not mirror our true intentions, our true purpose. As illustrated in the earlier examples, the unconscious mind magnetizes those concepts which we feed most often. For example, a woman who is worried about finding herself in an abusive relationship might notice that she continuously embarks on relationships that have a destructive dynamic. What is the reason for this? The constant thoughts and aversions to what she does not want magnetize at the unconscious level, leading to an inversed outcome. "Do not think of a pink elephant," the hypnotist proclaimed.

Despite how we see our connection with the deeper more encompassing levels of mind, it's important to recognize that this intuitive understanding is not limited to constructs we might have formed on a surface level. There are no absolutes in that sense, just variations that we perceive with the intellectual mind, shades and contours. It is relative happiness, relative love, or relative success that we come to know at that level. There is always possibility for contrast, for less, or for more to come into our existence. This is how the constructed mind works. However, the heart does not discriminate. While the mind works at categorizing the world before us into dualities and contrasts, the heart unifies and expands.

> The trick to freedom is not to get caught sticking to either side. Notions of praise or goodness or rightness can't be attained to remedy life's dilemmas, because they automatically affirm their polar opposites and bring them along to the party. The light and the dark are simply manifestations of the core contraction that gives birth to the entire dualistic display in all its variations.

– Jack Elias, 'Finding True Magic'

Connecting with the unconscious mind can allow us to open a dialogue with the deeper parts of ourselves. As mentioned in Chapter Two, this could involve working with dream states, or more subtle states of self-consciousness. For example, Paul Schenk's work, 'The Hypnotic Use of Waking Dreams,' suggests that images in our dreams represent aspects of our unconscious selves. Schenk provided one example in his book in which a woman experienced a strong connection to a nun in one of her waking dreams. She later realized that the nun represented a part of herself, a connection with her sense of religion and spirituality. On a conscious level, that connection was lacking, and yet it still existed, it just lacked essence. The essence of spiritual connectedness that the woman once felt was sublimated, and she experienced it in an external dream character, the nun. This woman recognized the nun as a part of herself and achieved a congruence between both minds, therefore she re-empowered herself to take charge of the spiritual dimension in her life that she had once neglected.

Once we recognize that these supposed divisions of mind are essential qualities of the Self, it becomes possible to arrive at a place of inner union, a balance of mental energies. There is no longer division or separation between the two (conscious and unconscious minds), and the processes of sublimation that we have used in the past come to conscious awareness. This is a re-empowering road, as we recognize our deeper potential and power. And, so we re-recognize the essential parts of ourselves, beneath the surface that we have once forgotten, and bring these to conscious awareness again, in turn expanding our threshold of experience to new bounds.

EXPLORATION: INTERNALIZING OUR EXPERIENCES

In this exploration, I will introduce a number of techniques for working with the unconscious mind and for reconnecting with our greater human potential. These techniques are intended to illustrate that the constructed self limits our consciousness threshold with particular barriers that we have enforced at the intellectual level. Our aim here is to traverse the part of our mind that we are conscious of and enter the realm of deeper experiences just below the surface. A number of our self-characteristics at the unconscious level represent parts of ourselves that we have sublimated, and in recognizing these parts once again, we are then able to bring them to consciousness, and work with these aspects on a tangible level.

MISSION TASK 70: SUBLIMATED POTENTIALS

Throughout this book we have been considering the notion of the constructed self in contrast with the broader self. Meditation and other techniques to expand consciousness can help us mediate between our local awareness, and our broader awareness in this manner.

Completion Goal:

Recollect at least three experiences during which you had a unique perspective that challenged your existing self-understanding. Did you notice that these experiences showed you a broader experience of self and expanded your previous understanding of the world? Reflect on this now.

MISSION TASK 71: ONE MIND

Reflect on whether different categories of mind states are real divisions, or rather just divisions that we have made up. For example, can we discuss a distinct representation of the conscious mind, pre-conscious mind, subconscious mind, unconscious mind, and super-conscious mind? Or, is it beneficial to instead consider the idea of 'one mind,' with differing levels of conscious awareness; differing shades of essence and existence, depending on which vantage point we take?

Completion Goal:

Reflect on how the notion of 'one mind' contrasts with the idea of the constructed self that we have been discussing throughout this book.

MISSION TASK 72: KILL THE BUDDHA

Sheldon Kopp's book 'If You Meet Buddha on the Road, Kill Him,' suggests that human beings tend to elevate inspirational leaders to 'guru status,' thus setting a massive division between themselves and their external leader of higher status. Kopp argued that it is important to see such proclaimed leaders as individuals like ourselves, human beings also struggling on the path of life. Instead, most people build a metaphorical temple around individuals who have demonstrated exceptional spiritual, artistic, athletic skill, or talent in a given life area.

Each human being, on a soul-level, has equal value and potential for unimaginable creative expression. Therefore, instead of looking to our heroes as gods, it is important to recognize our own inner potential. If we fail to do so, then we engage in an act of externalization, striving to act just like our religious leaders, to dress like a favorite celebrities, and to follow in the shoes of our idols. It's far more important to make own path, to recognize our uniqueness and creative potential within, and to cultivate this, to bring it to the surface of conscious awareness, to contribute our uniqueness to the world, rather than mimicking someone else's ideals, no matter how perfect or divine we perceive these.

Completion Goal:

Take note of particular individuals that you have elevated to 'guru status' on a mental level. Is it possible to recognize that these individuals are just human beings like you and me, capable of tapping the same reservoir of inner potential within? What are the implications of this perspective?

Side Notes:

The notion of 'killing the buddha' is not intended to disrespect Buddhist tradition. If we look to the Gautama Buddha's teachings and writings, his spiritual message suggests that each human being is capable of attaining spiritual enlightenment. Yet, in most countries with a large population of self-proclaimed Buddhists, we still see extreme statures of externalization amongst people living there.

For example, when arriving at Bangkok Airport, there are signs stating that it is disrespectful to purchase golden Buddha figures. Yet, in the same frame, these self-proclaimed Buddhists have built massive golden temples, multilevel supermarkets, and their lives around materialism and capitalism, rather than following a sincere inner path. Therefore, the true meaning of killing the Buddha suggests we kill the mental representation of the Buddha as a supreme guru that we should bow down to and look up to. Instead, we can learn to recognize that spiritual and inspirational leaders have much to teach us, that is, if we treat these individuals as real human beings, rather than enshrining them in metaphorical and tangible gold.

MISSION TASK 73: PERCEPTUAL POSITIONS PART I

Let's explore the above mission task in a bit more depth. When we place a particular person or idea on a pedestal, we disempower ourselves. In doing this, on an unconscious level we externalize our personal potential onto an external figure or idea, rather than internalizing this potential and recognizing it as part of ourselves.

Remember in the previous chapter how we discussed the idea that certain emotions can become disavowed, as we perceive them outside of our self-awareness? For instance, a person might place all of the demands on their partner for love, rather than recognizing the emotion of love within themselves first, and cultivating self-love. This process of externalization is also applicable in this chapter, as we consider personal power. Most people give their power to external constructs, ideas, and particular people. Yet, that power arises within first and foremost.

It's amusing that atheists makes proclamations such as 'I do not believe in God,' first conjuring God into conscious language, and then arguing against God's existence. Negating something suggests that on some level this force exists, but it has been externalized, disavowed. Likewise, when a basketball player states that he could never be as good as Michael Jordan, he first recognizes the skill level of Michael Jordan, and then externalizes this rather than cultivating this skill within. Once we recognize something outside of ourselves (a skill, talent, or characteristic), this suggests that it exists within ourselves, for we have seen it through our local lens of consciousness. Whether we choose to externalize or internalize that potential is the choice that follows.

An aspiring writer who believes that he could never write as well as Charles Dickens externalizes his potential to write onto the external construct of Dickens. A Buddhist who believes he could never reach the same state of consciousness and spiritual awakening as the Buddha externalizes his potential onto the construct

181

of the Buddha. Recognitions of outer potential occur all the time, but whether we decide to externalize or internalize our conscious experience of these potentials is a choice in our hands.

All perceptions arise in the one mind, and we cast certain perceptions upon the external world, while recognizing others as intrinsic aspects of ourselves that can be cultivated and brought forth. Perhaps certain individuals are born with predispositions or talents toward succeeding in a particular area of life. Yet, this reservoir of potential, of unimaginable creative power, arises from the same place, from the universal mind. On some level, each of us recognizes this, but we often fail to act upon it, thus disempowering ourselves and believing that particular people, organizations, religions, groups, cultures, and so forth to hold much more power than we could ever attain as an individual. Yet, as we recognize that power within our grasp, we see that it is possible to act upon, right here, right now, we reclaim this potential into our personal awareness rather than perceiving it resting just on the fringe of our consciousness threshold.

To explore this process of internalizing inner power, I would like to introduce a technique from NLP practice based on the idea of perceptual positions – the notion that our consciousness can experience realities from multiple vantage points, not just from the local self-perspective.

Our perspective of the world is centered on the five senses – we see, hear, smell, taste, and touch. This informs our experience of the world. There is something interesting about the visual sense in particular, in that our eyes have a certain magnetism about them. When we look into someone else's eyes, we can gain a glimpse into their soul. Our eyes also penetrate reality and define it, as each person looks upon the world from a slightly different perspective. Each of us also has the capacity to mentally 'see' by closing our eyes and visualizing. This process of mental perception will be explored in the following tasks.

Completion Goal I:

Next time you meditate, I would like you to experiment with moving your mental visual perspective from your eyes to a different space, such as slightly above your head, or to your chest area, or even outside of your body altogether. What does it feel like to mentally change your center of visual perception to this different space?

Side Note: The mental visual perspective we experience differs from our physical sight, it refers to the area that we place our consciousness. Most of us place our consciousness on our eyes as this is the main sense through which we experience the world. Do you notice this in yourself? Upon practicing the above task, you may notice that you are capable of moving around your mental visual perspective to practically anywhere you choose, within the limits of your imagination. You could even imagine that you have taken on the visual perspective of a particular object, an animal such as a pet, or another person.

Completion Goal II:

How would it feel to observe the world from the vantage point of someone else? Close your eyes and imagine taking on the visual perspective of another person, as though you had embodied their body, and looked through their eyes upon the world. What do you notice?

Completion Goal III:

Can a visual perspective exist without an observer? That is, what would reality look like without anyone around to perceive it? In order to practice this task you may like to repeat the original mission task, but this time imagine taking on a visual perspective of overlooking your house from above (with no sense of body or personhood attached to the perceiver).

MISSION TASK 74: PERCEPTUAL POSITIONS PART II

Completion Goal I:

How would it feel to observe the world from the vantage point of one of the people you look up to most in life, your role model, or inspiration? Close your eyes and imagine taking on the visual perspective of that person, as though you had embodied their body, and looked through their eyes upon the world. What do you notice?

Completion Goal II:

In taking on the visual perspective of someone you admire or someone whose personal qualities you look up to, you may recognize that those qualities are in fact also mirrored within yourself. Can you see how this exercise may illustrate moments in which you foster those qualities within, as well is moments in which you project those qualities onto others? What does this process tell you?

Completion Goal III:

Recall some of the main characteristics and qualities that you noticed when taking on the perspective of the person who you admire. What is it about their self-experience that appeared most memorable? Which core principles do you believe the qualities these people embody relate to?

MISSION TASK 75: MIRRORS

Our inner frame of the world tends to be mirrored outward, and we perceive similar characteristics in others that we perceive within ourselves. Someone who takes the role of an abusive person tends to abuse themselves the most. Likewise, someone who has a lot of positive and empowering things to speak about when talking to others, tends to recognize a great deal of positive things about herself as well.

Completion Goal I:

Next time you speak to someone who seems to have either quite a negative attitude, or quite a positive attitude about life, reflect on what that might have to do with their own self-image, and how they perceive themselves. Which qualities and characteristics do you believe that person has internalized, and which characteristics might they have externalized onto others?

Completion Goal II:

Consider your own experience of the above. Do you find that you notice many of the characteristics and qualities that you perceive in others within yourself as well? Or, are there some disparities? Do you externalize certain attributes onto others, disowning them within yourself? How could you utilize these observations in life?

Completion Goal III:

List 10 qualities that you admire within others that you also perceive within yourself somewhat, but have yet to fully cultivate. Brainstorm action steps that you could take to cultivate these characteristics within yourself. Do you believe you once had these characteristics and have since disowned them? Or, do you believe you have yet to develop these characteristics, and feel as though there is something holding you back, an internal obstacle that prevents you from embracing these aspects of yourself?

CHAPTER SIX

RELATIONAL DEPTH

The impressions others leave on us can mirror our understanding of ourselves.

Each individual contributes to the collective unfoldment of consciousness through their mere existence, their conscious being. As I mentioned in the previous chapter, without consciousness, without human beings, there can be no enlivened reality. All of the social structures, all of the beliefs, ideas, and creations that we witness in our world have arisen from conscious creation. Yet, so often we tend to instead assume the perception that we are feeble, humble, and weak, that the only true objective reality is the one that exists 'out-there' somewhere, that we are just interacting temporarily with the external world. In fact, reality arises within each one of our souls, we collectively contribute to its ongoing unfoldment. The soul is an immensely powerful creative force.

In the thinking experiments demonstrated throughout Chapter Three, we noted that we tend to believe the world we see before us is a true representation. However, the perceived external world arises from the sum of perceptions projected forth by each individual being. We contribute to, and support, a consensus global reality. In infusing certain paradigms, cultures, and ideas with power, we solidify them into tangible existence, each conscious being has an intrinsic connection with the entire conscious universe. Through each act and deed, we contribute to the collective unfoldment of life. Just as we have the imaginative power to perceive ourselves in a new light, so too, the observations that we impress upon the external serve not as mere passive perceptions, but rather acts of creation, acts of defining and solidifying essence into distinct form. This creative unfoldment process occurs in the mediation of two forces, the force of potential essence, and the force of solidified existence: Shiva and Shakti in their perpetual dance.

In our modern world, men tend to embody the force of tangible and solid existence (represented in Hinduism by Shiva, the masculine side of duality). In its pathological form, this force serves the intellectual wall and turns itself into stone, unwilling to accept and allow alternative realities. In its creative form, however, this force can help shape potential essence into clear, tangible realities, it grounds and centers undifferentiated potential and makes clear patterns, tapestries of new realities, all the while, recognizing that these forms are temporal and are not meant to last forever.

On the other hand, women tend to embody the force of potential essence in our world (represented by Shakti in Hinduism). In its pathological form, this force is destructive and reigns chaos, incapable of being tamed. Yet, in its creative form, this deep potential allows new realities to emerge and unique expressions of consciousness to come forward. The archetypal man and woman in union are capable of balancing these forces of perpetual flux, through mediating, together, the perpetual flow of essence and existence.

This process of conscious creation arises from a union of masculine and feminine energies. Yet, note that there is no hard and fast rule to state that men must embody only masculine energies, and that women only feminine, at all times. In fact, these energies do tend to fluctuate quite a bit; men can embody traditionally feminine experiences of raw emotion and creativity, while women can also embody more hard-headed and definitive qualities at the persona-level.

It's sad to observe that in our society we tend to define woman and men in quite strong and harsh terms that do not allow for these more subtle expressions. This is quite problematic. Further, it is troubling to see that throughout human history, these forces of creation have been corrupted through social programming and the abuse of our essential conscious power. This seeming feminine creative energy has been suppressed, criticized, and disenfranchised in the past. Now, on the other hand, we can see the opposite occurring in our world: Feminist groups who fight for equal rights and power. The sentiment behind these groups might be sincere, however, the expression is often damaging, as women attempt to increase their masculine energies as a source of strength and empowerment (trying to act more like men), rather than drawing upon the deep reservoir of the divine feminine and re-aligning with their true nature (the feminine archetype).

Beneath the mask, the constructed self, lies a deeper reservoir of intuition and wisdom that arises from within the heart; it balances and infuses these once polarized energies. Yet, when we attempt to regulate and control these forces, to attempt to shape them with the intellectual mind, we come out of balance with ourselves at a fundamental level.

The essential feminine (Anima) and masculine (Animus) energies that Jung spoke about have a unique role in the spirit of creation. This role extends to a deeper level than the intellectual mind, it must be felt and embodied. From a dualistic vantage point, we can consider these two forces as representations of the Tao in balance. In their union, emerges balanced creative force. It is here that the true meaning of union, becoming 'one,' becomes know, from an experiential, not an intellectual, perspective.

As soon as we open a line of communication with another individual, we form an emotional and empathic association. We merge consciousness with that person, if even for slight a moment. It would not be accurate to state that this sense of mutual connection just resides within ourselves and within others as separate feelings. Rather, a common feeling of connectedness resides in a new relational consciousness field which comes about when we connect with another individual. The two selves blur into one common presence, a shared intuitive understanding that arises in the field of consciousness between the once separated 'two.'

In conscious experiences at the relational level, we feel empathized with, cared about, and loved within the depths of our soul. It is a feeling, a direct experience, rather than a belief or concept. Often, people intellectualize the communication process instead of fostering such a connection. That being said, transcendence experiences are perhaps more relevant in relationships than in all other aspects of life. After all, much literature about the nature of love has pointed to love as an inexplicable quality, something that can be equated with beauty, magic, and surrender. Perhaps to experience pure undifferentiated love at the relational level is the ultimate transcendental state of consciousness.

As this chapter will explore, the nature of love is often misinterpreted as something that just arises within intimate relationships. For the purpose of this chapter, we will consider the deeper meaning of love and connection. In its pure form, this connection can give rise to some of the most profound consciousness experiences, whether shared with a lover, friend, child, parent, or even a stranger. This chapter will explore the idea of the relational consciousness field, the experience of presence in relationships, and the value of connecting at a consciousness level.

In this chapter I will continue the tradition of this book in 1) questioning the societal beliefs that reinforce a superficial understanding of self, while also 2) illustrating the potential of our broader conscious experience. The practical focus here is placed on the nature of love and relational experiences with consciousness. I will also delve into the idea of transcendence of the constructed self in relationships, and letting go of our surface-level constructs in order to experience sincere conscious connections with others. Toward the end of this chapter, I will also introduce some techniques for exploring core energetics; the essential qualities of experience that come about from connecting with our personal consciousness field.

DEEPER CONNECTIONS

In modern times, people use the intellectual mind to find love, rather than the heart, and often fail in their pursuit. In terms of intimate love, millions of people join dating sites to find the ideal partner, someone who matches their particular characteristics or idealized expectations. This is a multi-million dollar industry based around people's desire to find love. The problem is, most people forget their core principle for finding love and instead strive, with arrogance, to find someone who embodies the same persona-level beliefs they have formed about love; beliefs as trivial as good looks, wealth, power and status, none of which have to do with love in themselves.

Through a constant barrage of media, we look for images that represent love rather than pursuing direct felt experience, direct relational connection. It is more beneficial to look for deeper qualities, such as one's values, ideas, dreams, passions, than just to the surface. Just evaluating how compatible we are with others in terms of the constructed self prevents an experience of genuine, transcendental love that has nothing to do with those constructs in the first place.

To delve into this idea of essential human connection further, let's consider the question, how does it feel to be around a particular person? It is not the definitions, not the roles that make meaning in themselves – it is the essence of a person that is important to look at – we must search their hearts. Taoist Master Mantak Chia stated "it is said it takes seven years to know the rhythms of a woman's body, seven years to learn her mind, and seven years to understand her spirit." In order to achieve that depth we ought to understanding the human spirit beneath the mask, not just via our own expectations, impressions, understandings and past recollections. Assuming that we can know someone based on a few interactions prevents us the chance of knowing that individual at a deeper level. This is not just applicable in intimate relationships, but in all human connections.

All the while, the pursuit of real human connection is not prioritized in modern societies. The emphasis, rather, seems to be on forming superficial connections based on surface level interests. Furthermore, the growing emphasis on constantly moving through life, finding a societally appropriate partner, buying into the idea of a mortgage, getting married, having children, having friends at the same social status, pressures us in modern life, in particular in the Western world. Pursuits of raw emotional connection are rare and often take a seat to societal and cultural pressures. Yet, nothing else matters in this life more than real human connection. In a manner, this is ironic. Such a vast number of people acquiesce to the false notion that nothing else matters except for the latter: Maintaining the status quo.

It doesn't help that the mythos of fairy tales alike to 'Cinderella' creep into our collective understanding of true love. These stereotypical images magnetize our attention and pervade direct our conscious experience. These images seem to lure us into aligning with idealistic stereotypes of love, paining an alluring and picturesque, false portrait. Hence, millions forsake a true experience of love for these false, unattainable ideals. We reimagine ourselves in a false light, not a reflection of our hearts, but a made up fictional tale that someone else has invented. It is the illusory love of actors in a film, of characters in a fairy tale, of stories that were never our own. In understanding another person, we set them free, and in doing so, we see them for all they are and can be. Here, we can discover the true authentic potential of love in relationships.

Throughout this book I have been asking you to consider your essential nature behind the constructed personality-level mask. This is an important consideration in relationships, too. It's important to recognize that each individual has a unique energy, a unique field of consciousness that they bring to the world.

On that point, I believe that violence and war occur in our world because we reduce human beings to mere flesh and blood. We do not recognize their deeper soul aspect, the consciousness within. If we did, we could never truly wish to kill another conscious being. It is beneficial to begin noticing how each human has a unique consciousness vibration, a soul, or energetic field. None are worse or better than another. Each is unique in its own right, and each individual's experience is worth cherishing and exploring. This sacred energetic connection is worth engaging with at a subtle level. Yet, all of this has little to do with our megalomaniac affair with the constructed self that demands we reduce human beings to their name, age, status, gender, race, occupation, and affiliation on a perpetual basis.

What then, is the true value of authentic human connection? In order to answer this question, we must step beyond the constructed self, and into another's essential world of experience. In this chapter, I would like to take a unique approach by focusing on the essential consciousness field, or unique soul energy, that each individual contains within. This energy can be said to relate to their essential soul essence, it cannot be replicated by another.

Throughout millennia, the concept of a consciousness field has appeared in myriad esoteric texts. Some have referred to this field as the human aura, or the conscious energy surrounding each human being. Emotions and thoughts are said to arise within this field, not just within our local minds. The consciousness field is a concept worth exploring at a practical level, as this helps us understand how human beings can share a subtle energetic connection that transcends the intellectual mind. At the touch of two consciousness fields coming together, a new relational field arises, as these two fields merge into one collective experience.

Alexander De Foe

Once we recognize that each human being resonates a particular energetic vibration, then we can also see that all interactions occur on a consciousness level, not just at the intellectual level. From a field-consciousness perspective, relationships serve the purpose of soul-connection between two beings. On the other hand, the constructed self is alone in relationships. When we pursue relationships to serve the constructed self, then we do so at our peril. We merely project all of our personal baggage, programming, and expectations onto the other. We see them in a false light, a light born from our own projections. Yet, in connecting at the consciousness level, we experience real connection with others, 'as they are,' not as they exist within our conception. If we imagine that a person's self-image, beliefs, and ideas about themselves all disappear for a moment, what remains is the true essence – their consciousness. Moments in which we connect with another person's direct consciousness often have a powerful, memorable impact. There is something quite special about such experiences indeed. These are transcendental states of relating.

Consciousness field experiences allow us to emerge from the constructed self and into a shared experience with another human being. There is a certain blurring of barriers and a point at which 'my' experience and 'your' experience transcend into one shared experience. Individuals who are in-tune with the movement of subtle energies can have a strong sense of this process. Those who are less sensitive to subtle energies at first might recognize this as a confusion between their own thoughts emotions and another person's. These field consciousness experiences challenge the common idea that the self is an island, and rather reinforce the idea that each human being is connected at the most profound level.

Sometimes, people speak about being able to connect with the true essence of a Guru or spiritual teacher, or even a priest; it is easier to sense and connect with certain individual's direct consciousness. A number of spiritual teachers have done inner work to remove the barriers of their constructed self. Their consciousness shines through as a result, and it is easier to sense something special and profound about these souls. It is easier for people around them to notice that there is something special about that individual that seems to stand out, even if most can't quite put their finger on what it is. We can get a sense for what it feels like to be around their 'essential being.' In some instances, this is what certain people mean when they say that someone is a good person, or a caring person, or an intelligent person, as they have sensed their essential being at the experiential level, rather than just making logical observations based on their behavior. There is the distinct difference between referring to the direct conscious experience of relating, and making intellectual judgments about an experience of interacting with a particular person.

A diffusion of human consciousness occurs when a person interacts with their intellectual wall, rather than with the real, felt experience in front of them right now. Thus, deepening our relational awareness can help us to connect with the true essence of others. This process can also help recognize when someone is not interested in fostering an authentic relationship and is instead just projecting elements of their constructed self forth onto the world, in a 'feedback loop' of sorts. Once we attune to relational dynamics at a subtle level, we can often avoid hurt and disappointment by others, as we recognize that certain people supplement direct real human connection with an idea, belief, or a concept about that connection. Thus, we recognize that these individuals are merely causing self-harm, rather than attempting to cause us direct harm in their negligence.

On the other hand, once we connect with a person's true essence, we recognize a unique aspect of their soul, we then connect with a conscious being, rather than just a sequence of repeated beliefs and traits that a person has amalgamated. Such heart-to-heart connections serve as powerful moments of transcending the constructed self, these experiences show us a new means of connecting with others.

Too often people use relationships for selfish reasons, rather than embarking upon a relationship for the purpose of introspection, a deeper connection, and authentic life experience. In fact, in our world, few people practice developing heart-to-heart connections with those closest to them. Instead, their connections are constructed, serving just the constructed self and its immediate needs. In a transactional analysis sense, we simply pat each other on the back when one party carries out the desired or expected behavior in a relationship. No transcendence nor expansion of self occurs in those instances, instead only the needs of the constructed self are fed over and over.

Emotional vampires thrive upon relationships that are sustained at a constructed level in this fashion. The constructed self is always looking for something, always lacking, always desiring, always empty. Yet, the inner heart is infinite, replete with omnipresent love. Thus, vampiric connections are unsustainable on a heart-to-heart level. When we form a relationship or a connection to serve the needs of the constructed self (whether doing so consciously or not), we subject ourselves to an exchange of give and take, constantly measuring and evaluating expectations, rather than recognizing that love does not limit, nor does it discriminate at its purest level and raw expression. Constructed relationships thus take the infinite conscious soul within another and makes it something less than its true infinite expression.

Individuals who are not attuned with the source of their own consciousness often attempt to source their power from other fields, due to the false perception that their personal connection to the collective field is somehow lacking. This explains the prominence of vampiric connections in our world, as certain people attempt to steal energetic power from external fields. In recognizing our deeper soul aspect, we can then reclaim our creative inheritance and begin to develop a sincere connection with our deeper self, and the deeper nature of others. Once we begin to see our true nature, we recognize that the reservoir of creative potential beneath the surface is infinite, and to purport that we could somehow become depleted, permanently disconnected from the primordial collective field, is preposterous.

In that sense, some therapists use techniques such as cutting cords in order to break apart destructive relationship dynamics that are maintained due to vampiric energetic dependencies. The metaphor of the cord is a good one when we consider intimate and close relationships. We tend to establish cords with others and we then begin to feel as though we owe them something, or as though they have some kind of supernatural power to make us feel bad. In fact, some believe that when we form a destructive connection with another person, if that person even thinks a negative thought about us, we will be able to feel it on a subtle level. I believe that this is true based on my own experiences. I have found that over time we can tend to strengthen negative cords (leading to energetic dependence) that connect us to others. However, we can also learn to cut cords to abolish these energetic dependencies (see Rose Rosetree's work on emotional healing, for example).

It is also possible to work toward strengthening authentic heart-to-heart connections with those close to us, instead of, or in tandem with, abolishing the negative connections that we might have formed. In deepening our conscious connection with others, the toxic links that we have formed tend to vanish in time, of their own accord. Connections born from sincere presence in the eternal moment exceed the seeming power of dependencies born from the poisonous fear of past constructs.

EXPLORATION: RELATIONSHIPS AS SPIRITUAL CONNECTIONS

In order to begin connecting with another's consciousness field, some basic somatic awareness is required. It's a good idea to start noticing what is happening in your body when you interact with certain people. For example, what does it feel like when you connect with a specific individual? Notice in particular, the sensations that arise in the field of awareness of your entire body.

Usually, when we communicate with certain people, we might begin to feel quite negative talking with them. Someone's harsh words might feel as though they have just punched us in the stomach, and indeed this often feels like real physical pain when a person maliciously targets us with an insult or a personal attack. Yet, in other conversations, when someone tells you that they love you, or shares some kind words with you, you may literally feel a sense of warmth or elation in your heart.

These subtle sensations arise at both a physiological and at a consciousness level. Taking notice of these sensations helps to appraise the quality of particular connections, while also helping to increases our discernment about whether a relationship is grounded in a particular construct (based on beliefs and expectations), or rather in love, genuine care, and acceptance from a state of engaged presence.

MISSION TASK 76: RELATIONAL AWARENESS

Sometimes when we spend time with particular people, we feel a certain way around them. This feeling does not just relate to how they communicate to us or how they act around us. It is more of a presence. Have you noticed this sense of presence around certain people, and that this overall sense differs with each individual you encounter? You might feel motivated and energized around a particular person, and then suddenly begin to feel drained and very pessimistic around someone who walks into the same room the next moment. Each individual embodies a unique expression of consciousness, and thus generates a unique presence. Yet, what most people don't realize, is that, like antennas, we constantly interact with, and partly merge with, other people's presence when they are in close proximity to our personal consciousness field.

Completion Goal I:

Take notice of how you feel around particular people. Is this sense of unique presence easier to connect with around certain individuals? Do you find this sense of overall presence easier to notice with family members or close friends, as opposed to strangers, for instance?

Completion Goal II:

Reflect on the general feeling of being in the presence of three of the people closest to you in your life. How is the essential experience of each of those individuals unique? Do not attempt to describe it, just notice the unique presence of each individual as an intuitive felt experience.

MISSION TASK 77: RELATIONAL IMPACT

Completion Goal I:

In each of your interactions over the next few days, take notice of the experience of being in each person's presence that you interact with. What is the essential feeling associated with being in the presence of each of these individuals? Take notice of whether their presence has a predominantly positive or a predominantly negative impact on you. Do you suddenly feel drained or exhausted around certain people? On the other hand, do you feel uplifted and energetic around others, as soon as you enter their field of presence? Reflect on how these experiences are relevant to our discussion so far.

Completion Goal II:

So far, we have discussed the idea that each individual emanates a unique field of consciousness, a unique presence, and that we can begin to sense this field with our own awareness. Do you believe that this might also be true of particular objects, or even specific places and spaces? Have you ever felt a strong sensation when entering a particular room, such as an instantaneous feeling of excitement, hesitation, peace, angst, or anger, or another distinct emotion that seemed to be associated with that particular location?

Side Notes:

It's important to distinguish between feelings that we generate within our own local field of consciousness, and feelings that we acquire from other people, objects, or environments. For example, when some people visit the concentration camps in Auschwitz, they notice an immediate effect on their consciousness, as they feel a sense of dread and an empathic connection to the suffering faced there long ago. This sense does not just arise from their local awareness, but it is rather gleaned from the external environment and the energetic imprint that has been made there.

On a relational level, we integrate and experience certain energies as soon as we emerge in their presence. This bears a distinct difference to an intellectual awareness that comes about from ruminating and reflecting on the events that happened at a particular place. Similar contrasts can be made when we consider sacred places such as churches, places of burial, and other designated locations that serve a specific purpose for cultivating a focused collective field of presence. These concentrated fields are sometimes easier to glean than core energies that might be more dispersed and less focused, for instance.

Note that a relational awareness comes from direct conscious experience, while an intellectual response arises from our subjective interpretations of (and mental commentaries about) a particular event or connection.

Completion Goal III:

Reflect on which factors you believe make it easier to form a relational connection with other people, or even certain objects or places. What is it about certain energies that makes us more susceptible to their presence, while repelling others?

Completion Goal IV:

Spend at least half a day in complete solitude without interacting with anyone else. Can you get a sense for your own personal field of consciousness? What does this experience feel like in the absence of others?

Side Note: Usually, our consciousness is exposed to a vast number of fields on a relational level, and we can lose ourselves in this flux of interacting with dozens or even hundreds of people each day. We are susceptible to merging with external fields and confusing these for our authentic soul essence. This is the reason that sometimes it can be so difficult to encounter human beings who have a strong sense of connectedness to their true self. Authentic conscious experience is of paramount value (as this book has been suggesting all along). Take time to connect with and learn about what your core essence, your core being, feels like at this subtle energetic level.

MISSION TASK 78: SOUL WEAVING

Individuals who practice deepening their consciousness are able to expand their field of awareness, and their expanded presence begins to touch others around them to a greater degree. However, most of us remain caught in our intellectual walls, rather than connecting with this felt experience, that is, until we learn how to form, and expand, this deeper connection to our consciousness.

Completion Goal:

Recall at least five individuals that come to mind who have a profound sense of presence, a presence that has touched and transformed the lives of others. Some examples might include spiritual or religious leaders, individuals who have displayed transcendent qualities of altruism, or even those with a powerful motivational or inspirational energy, such as speakers who seem to be able to transform the emotional state of thousands in an audience within seconds. Reflect on five (personal or historical) examples of individuals who have a strong sense of presence, and impact on others with their mere being.

CREATIVE POTENTIAL

The meaning and understanding that we hold about the world is derived via our felt connections with others. Yet, we often perceive the world as a singular construct of ultimate importance. Relational processes run much deeper beneath the surface, and our connections with others literally contribute to our perceived consensus reality. The constructs 'out-there' wouldn't exist without the relational connections that support them. In order to understand this process, it's important to get a feel for how core energetics work at the relational level. For example, you may admire the qualities of a particular person on a constructed-self level, that is, their personality, but all the while you may feel uncomfortable in their field of their presence. This can be observed in many circumstances in which people seem to get along very well (have the same interests and similar personality on the surface), but argue often and find it uncomfortable in each other's field of awareness.

These subtle processes affect the quality of relationships, business interactions, and even politics at a broader scale. In that sense, resistance between two people can be perceived as a failure to connect at the consciousness level. There arise disparities between two fields – a failure to embrace the person's awareness, and vice versa. The lack of resonance between fields runs much deeper than surface-level conflicts that might manifest. At the intellectual level, we might form a tangible conflict. 'I hate him,' or 'he is my best friend,' serve as labels about how we relate. Yet, it's pointless to view human relationships (or human beings for that matter) in gradations of good or bad, worthy of love or hate, friendly or unfriendly, and so forth. Beneath the surface, each individual generates a unique conscious essence that cannot be boiled down to particular language constructs, nor definitions.

These same principles are applicable to monogamous relationships, in which we might pursue a partner who seems to have our ideal characteristics or preferred qualities at the personality-level. These don't matter so much in the end, however. Surface-level characteristics are just temporal manifestations of one's eternal soul consciousness, and connecting with one's deeper soul beneath the surface is far more rewarding. Likewise, intellectual definitions such as race, culture, religion, gender, and so forth, serve little purpose, as these point to the surface-level experience of a person, not to their true essence. It's very sad to see many societies emphasize the former to extremes, all the while, disenfranchising the latter. This process contributes to a world out-of-sync with essential conscious connection.

Indeed, each individual projects an entire unique world of awareness from their consciousness field. Remember how in earlier chapters we considered the notion that there is a certain degree of objectivity and neutrality in reality? Despite this, our view of the world is shaded with particular ideas, contexts, and cultural frameworks. At the deepest level, this process of making meaning in the world occurs through an unfoldment of relational dynamics, as we merge and expand certain realities while negating and resisting others via our relational understanding. Our entire conception of the world was born from relational negotiations about 'how the world is.'

Collective consciousness at the relational level can also account for social dynamics that allow tyrants to rise and suppress millions of people without challenge nor contention (13). Such dynamics, too, account for the display of amazing feats of human potential such as exceptional intellectual, emotional, and spiritual expressions, and even accounts of psychic abilities. When these amazing feats are attempted within a new collective field (such as under rigorous scientific testing), the abilities no longer seem possible, however (14). We literally limit and define our scope of reality via relational dynamics that permit and expand certain potentials, while negating and rejecting other realities. Relationship and group dynamics appear to only thrive when there is a certain cohesiveness in the collective field that perpetuates a given construct or idea.

To offer some examples, we can consider the main paradigms prevalent in our world at present: Promoting environmentalism, protecting ourselves from terrorism, preventing overpopulation, reducing the effect of climate change, and so forth. These all seem to be globally accepted aspects of our reality. Yet, they might not have been relevant at all 50 years ago, or so. How come this is the case? Consider that any aspect or characteristically-defined feature that is accepted and approved of, however vaguely, by at least 50% of our populace seems to gain dominance at the collective consciousness threshold – it then defines the scope of our perception. These dominant ideas thus negotiate and define the limits of our perceived reality and the scope of human potential. The collective field perpetuates what is societally appropriate, popular, and approved upon in terms of behavior, values, and modes of expression.

Yet, we make a grievous error of believing this collective field is somehow absolute, when in fact the macro-expressions of consciousness never exist independently of their collective 'consensus' (which is given by each individual human at the micro-level). Most of us acquiesce to the global reality paradigm unconsciously, rather than recognizing that we are actually helping to generate it with our inaction. The impact of each human being's energy field is insurmountably powerful, whether they decide to act on this or not. If we begin to understand the power of our inner world and learn the value of connecting with others on this deeper spiritual level, together, we can move mountains. But we choose to drink beer and watch television instead, serving the megalomania of the constructed self, rather than creating new potentialities, new realities. Millions of people assimilate and regurgitate the collective paradigm of the world as it is, rather than challenging and working to create a better world for all.

On a global level, we each hold a vaguely defined general reality model. Yet, at micro-levels of perception, particular cultures, groups, and individual relationships encompass their own parameters for reality, which may coincide, contrast, or even exist independently of broader systems. Macro fields and micro fields have a certain symbiotic energy relationship. One influences the other. As the ancient Emerald Tablet goes, "as above, so below." No conscious being is separate from the macro field that connects all as a collective consciousness. Yet, we can influence our individual consciousness dynamics by working with our personal field of awareness, which in turn, propagates and sustains broader energetic constructs at the macro level. In doing so, we can change the world. But, it all begins with examining the dynamics in our personal relationships.

As we can see, this collective construction of reality has major implications for human consciousness, as we define ourselves through the lens of such subtle relational dynamics. In the last couple of chapters, I have been building to the idea that each individual is, in part, responsible for expanding the scope of reality so that conscious human potential can flourish, rather than being limited to specific ideological or societal paradigms. Throughout the remainder of this chapter, I would like to explore how this idea applies to personal and intimate relationships. And, in the chapter that follows, we will consider how relational dynamics play a role in human potential, free will, and our greater conscious creative expression at the macro level.

EXPLORATION: RE-FRAME RESISTANCE

Each time a person expresses themselves, a certain energy is infused into their words. That energetic expression impacts upon the reality they are sharing, whether they are expressing themselves to another person, or a group. And, often, this energy is more powerful than their words on the surface. That subtle power behind their words constructs a new world and invites others to join in their unique reality. For our purpose here, it's important to note that we can either acquiesce to someone else's reality, or redefined the scope of expression in our own terms. One technique that is often used to facilitate this process is called reframing. Reframing can change the relational dynamics in a given situation and alter the collective experience of reality in a given circumstance.

Putting aside macro dynamics for now, let's consider the metaphor of communication as a process of 50-50 contribution. You bring 50% of your world to the table, and the other person brings 50% of their world experience, and you both meet somewhere in the middle to form a consensus perception. On a consciousness level, your two fields of awareness merge to some degree. But, on a surface intellectual level, you might attempt to negotiate the terms of your reality using verbal communication and tangible concepts.

Consider an example. During altered reality experiences, such as lucid dreams or out-of-body experiences (OBEs), environment dynamics are much more fluid, as we deal with the dimension of emotion, rather than time-space. When one person has a particular feeling or a thought, the other automatically recognizes this and responds in turn. In shared lucid dreams, for instance, if your partner imagines travelling out into space to explore the Milky Way just for a brief second, you may find yourself automatically flying out into space to join him just a split-second later. The process of transferring intention into reality is much, much faster within these subtle dimensions of consciousness.

These shared consciousness experiences also occur more rapidly with the aid of certain entheogens such as LSD or psilocybin mushrooms that alter brain functioning. The left-brain, intellectual part of ourselves, tunes out for a moment and we begin to directly perceive intention, as it flows from another's field into our awareness and vice versa. Field dynamics are much less stable during these experiences (or, a better way of putting it may be, more fluid), and telepathic and empathic connections within the conscious relational field become seamless. In these states, we can recognize that unique realities do indeed arise from an interplay of relational consciousness.

Yet, in our everyday normal life, this seems less apparent, as the external world seems persistent, solid, and immovable. In our normal waking state, this process of reality-framing is much less noticeable, yet it does occur on a social level, and probably occurs to some degree on a mind-over-matter level (though far less noticeably than in dream-states, for instance). In all relationships, we accept a consensus reality whether we notice this process occurring or not. Yet, we can learn to renegotiate the terms of our reality-model in order to foster intimate and expensive connections with others, rather than limiting ourselves to singular societal constructs.

MISSION TASK 79: REALITIES REDEFINED

Completion Goal:

Reflect further on the notion that each individual is a unique expression of consciousness, rather than just an embodiment of their constructed self. Next, reflect on how learning to become more empathic and compassionate toward other people's unique experience can benefit in understanding their underlying reality experience.

MISSION TASK 80: REFRAME CONSTRUCTS

Recall how in Chapter Three I spoke about Neuro-Linguistic Programming (NLP) techniques and their role in reframing our perception of certain circumstances. In Chapter Three I gave Paul McKenna's example of a controlling boss, and how we could begin to see our 'superiors' as just people who sometimes have an authority-complex – not to take them all too seriously.

Completion Goal I:

Re-read the 'side notes' in mission task 33, (refer to the exploration, 'Testing Truth,' in Chapter Three). Imagine three other examples of how you could mentally re-frame your perspective on certain circumstances to place them back into a neutral frame, and to perceive them less seriously for a moment.

Completion Goal II:

Do you believe reframing techniques can also work in real-life (rather than just mentally imagined) circumstances? Next time you are faced with a difficult or uncomfortable circumstance in life, consider a creative approach to reframe the situation in a new light. You could do this by either 1) saying something that would produce a new perspective on the shared reality, 2) doing something completely different that would alter the terms of the conversation, or 3) simply noticing how you could perceive or interact with the person or situation slightly differently. Can you see how much of reality is socially-constructed, and that we can either agree with these constructs, or alter them with the slightest twist of words and perceptions?

Side Note: Reframing techniques are often used in business and sales for unethical purposes (such as displaying an item on a 50% discount sale from the original price, when in fact the original price was just made up out of the blue for the sole purpose of advertising item as cheaper than before). Business people qualify reality in this way often, it is part of the selling process. Yet, we all qualify reality based on our personal beliefs about the world every day, too. I can't really say that this is an unethical process, as it is more so unconscious. However, you might like to ask the question: Which realities have I been sold into believing? Remember that once we learn how to re-frame our realities, we take back the conscious power to shape, or rather co-shape, the world in a new light.

MISSION TASK 81: NEUTRAL FRAME OF EXPERIENCE

You might notice that conflict and disagreement arises due to a mismatch between two people's unique soul expressions, rather than at a surface-level. This is useful to consider in terms of conflict and disagreement. For now, consider the benefits of adopting a more neutral frame of perspective in conflicts. Is it possible to see reality through a clearer lens in this manner?

Completion Goal I:

Next time that you find yourself in an emotionally-charged situation (such as a conflict), I would like you to reflect on the experience from a more consciously-neutral perspective. For the first part of this mission task, imagine that you are perceiving the situation from above your body, high above the ground, or standing on a balcony several floors above and looking down. Can you notice that from this objective perspective, the particular situation or conversation has a certain neutrality to it? Are the perceptions and judgments you made during the experience still present from this objective perspective that you have taken on for now? What can you learn from this practice, in terms of how you shape and frame certain realities?

Completion Goal II:

Next, imagine that you are standing in the other person's frame of perspective in this particular situation. Does this slight shift in awareness have an impact on your perspective?

Side Note: This practice can be somewhat difficult to complete during an emotionally intensive experience or conversation. If this is the case, then you may like to complete this exercise after the event, when you have a quiet moment to yourself. Simply imagine yourself mentally going back into this emotionally charged experience, but this time perceive it from a different vantage point: 1) From outside of your own body, and 2) from the other person's perspective who was involved in the exchange.

MISSION TASK 82: EMPATHIC CONNECTION

The idea of normal perception in our world implies sharing a common relational experience with a large proportion of people, whether those people belong to a religion, culture, social class, or even a particular specialist group. To an outsider, that group's collective experience might not make sense, and those who are not part of the group might not understand the group's reality model. 'Normality,' then, is a relationally-enforced concept, it is contextual for the most part. At a global level, we each hold a consensus model of reality, and that model defines which expressions of consciousness are legitimate and which are not permitted. Indeed, people who attempt to cultivate experiences outside of this norm tend to be harshly judged, criticized, or even called insane. Yet, judging another's sacred inner experience and reacting in a negative light is tantamount to creating a divide between their experience of consciousness and our own.

This does not mean that by empathizing with and connecting with someone's consciousness field you automatically agree to accept their reality in place of your own, it simply implies that you are willing to extend the empathy and understanding to them that each human being deserves. Co-founder of NLP, Richard Bandler, has offered many examples of this process in his work. One of the popular examples that comes to mind relates to those who have been diagnosed with schizophrenia or psychosis who reported having visions of different realities. Bandler suggested that instead of attempting to convince an individual that his reality is somehow unreal or that he is crazy, it is far more valuable to empathize with another's experience, no matter how bizarre or deviant from perceived 'normality.' Bandler, in his book 'Using Your Brain for a Change,' suggests that we ought to enter another's reality, in order to understand it. This process of 'entering another's reality' is central to our discussion on relational fields so far; we must traverse the consciousness divide between ourselves and others to recognize that value of true human connection and the creative potential of the soul.

People tend to cling to their reality model very strongly, and believe that opening their mind to alternatives is somehow a threat to their understanding of the world. For instance, people will often defend their meat-eating habits if someone claims that they are actually a vegetarian. The same observations can be made with other ideologies that people cling to, such as religious or political inclinations. What is the reason to so vehemently defend our position in these cases? Is it so difficult to be vulnerable for a moment, and to allow both positions to exist as equally valid expressions of consciousness? I have observed that people seem to think as though they have to either accept or reject other people's reality, it is difficult for most to just empathize with and experience it.

Completion Goal:

Do you notice a difference between accepting someone's reality as true, and simply extending your empathy to understand their experience (without necessarily agreeing with it)? Reflect on the ideas discussed in this mission task.

MISSION TASK 83: RE-FRAME POTENTIAL

Each human being is capable of achieving anything, as the nature of the soul is infinite in potential. Yet, at the language level, at the intellectual level, we create boundaries and limitations. Many use language such as 'I can't, I won't, it's impossible, I could never,' and so forth throughout their lives. Yet, these are just surface level constructs that they have placed on their infinite potential. Surface-level language does not permanently limit one's full potential, only temporarily. Can you see how this is true?

Completion Goal I:

Refer to the example in the 'Life Scribing' worksheet (see Appendix C). Brainstorm some of the limiting language and beliefs that the individual in that example might have enforced that kept him trapped in his negative workplace.

Completion Goal II:

Consider how in everyday conversations you could reframe other people's use of language. For example, you may challenge someone's use of the phrase 'I can't' by asking 'what if you could?' Reframing can help change language patterns from impossibilities to possibilities in this manner. Notice whether this slight change at the surface level can create a profound change at a deeper level.

MISSION TASK 84: INDIVIDUATION IN RELATIONSHIPS

People have a tendency to lose themselves in their relationships, as the external influence of a particular person's energy field may be overpowering. For example, bosses at work, or a family members, or even persistent friends or acquaintances can have a strong presence over our lives. They may overtake our own identity to some extent. A part of ourselves blurs into the other's reality. Yet, by getting to know ourselves at a deeper level, as we ground ourselves in our true sense of self, it becomes possible to extend empathy to others and to comprehend their total experience without necessarily losing ourselves in relationships.

From the vantage point of the constructed self, we tend to be in a constant war in relationships, attempting to win the power struggle, as one person aims to dominate and reign over the relationship. Yet, on a consciousness level, heart-to-heart relationships serve the greater purpose of expanding self-awareness.

Completion Goal:

Refer to the 'Overlapped Consciousness I' and 'Overlapped Consciousness II' figures in Appendix C. Notice how relational dynamics occur in a shared consciousness space, yet we also have a private conscious experience. There are two ways to approach these dynamics. The first, to assume that a part of ourselves is lost in the 'other,' and second, that our unique conscious experience contributes to the relationship. Reflect on how it is possible to co-create a new reality in relationships from a stance of recognizing your unique potential within the relationship. Ask yourself the question: 'Who am I in (certain relationships)?' Again, search for a felt understanding within rather than looking for an intellectual answer here.

CONSTRUCT-FREE CONSCIOUSNESS

In the previous mission tasks we considered the idea that it can be worthwhile to step back from certain situations in order to observe how we frame and shape realities. At first, it might seem that stepping back is a disempowering process. After all, in responding to certain situations with passion and emotion, we assert our perspective. However, by recognizing that we can also step back and notice the neutrality of certain experiences, we can begin to see that we are so much more than just our personality playing out a particular role. In fact, we are not the constructed self, but the consciousness behind it all. In taking a step back, we recognize the source of the energy from which our emotions rise. And in doing so, we actually re-empower ourselves. We are then able to decide whether we still wish to act the same way, or to slightly, or even drastically, change our interactions with others and with the world at large.

In relationships, people tend to react to past pain and expectations, rather than perceiving others in the present moment, without judgments or perceptions. In the same manner, if a particular person from a specific group, race, culture, or religion has wronged us in the past, we may be more likely to hold judgments about that entire group of people. A common example that comes to mind relates to those who have been hurt in a relationship and hold negative judgments and expectations about all men or all women (yes, indeed, all three-and-a-half billion). This is harmful, as it disenfranchises our ability to see reality clearly, as it is.

Our experience of the past is only based on our own mental estimations, and yet often we trust in the accuracy of those estimations so supremely. There is no absolute way that we can know for certain that what occurred 2,000 years ago, or even 20 minutes ago, did actually occur as we remember it. However, I am not stating this out of cynicism, rather, I believe that there is something magical about embracing the present moment and all that it presents right here and right now. Often, the present moment transcends our plans, expectations, and assumptions about the world. This process of engaging with others in the here-and-now can transform our lives for the better, if we do not resist our felt experiences in the moment.

In the exploration in this subchapter it's worth considering again a notion that we touched upon in Chapter Three; that we tend to build a particular image and expectation of others. There is a distinct difference between experiencing our connections through the filters of the past, and connecting with the direct felt experience of our present moment interactions. The constructs that we form in relationships create a sort of 'ground' for communication, but it's important to recognize that although human beings meet in the middle, their soul essence extends to a far greater source than their appearance at the ego-self level. Then, we can ask, would we rather recreate the woven past, re-conjure our idealized versions (whether positive or negative) of certain people? Or, would we rather create a new ground for experience, and open to new possibilities for conscious engagement?

Here we can note the value of cherishing human relationships for the sake of deepening our connection with, and understanding of, others. In this process, we can form some of the most enriching connections, as these are not founded on expectations or assumptions. Can you envision how liberating and powerful it is to let go of these previous grievances, and to begin to see others as they are right now, in the present moment; the filters of your assumptions and limiting ideals, now gone?

EXPLORATION: IDEATION OR CREATION

In this exploration, let's consider how forming connections in the here-and-now can bring about transcendent relationships. Letting go of our false 'images' of others can also facilitate the healing process in past relationships in which distrust or pain has festered into the present moment. Once we liberate our false images of others, our source of creative power becomes refreshed, and we are able to then free those energies toward creating new enriching connections. This process calls for us to move from the intellectual mind and into direct felt experience: The direct felt connection we share with others. The mission tasks below can be useful for intimate relationships, but are also just as applicable in broader human relationships.

MISSION TASK 85: AFTER THE APOCALYPSE

Establishing and nourishing a felt connection is the most important element of relationships. Many of the demands and expectations that we place on other people, especially those closest to us, are often not that important in the grand scheme of things. By placing expectations on others, we actually push them further away, yet by learning to understand others on a deeper level, we open a felt conscious connection with them that brings us closer.

Completion Goal:

Imagine that the world ended, and only the five people closest to you survived the apocalypse. Would your core principles and priorities change in those relationships? How so?

Side Note: This imaginative exercise is intended to dramatize how often our demands and expectations of others arise at the surface level, from societal pressures. Rather than deepening the meaning of our relationships at the soul-level, we often supplement them for societal roles and concepts. Imagining that the world ends, or that society collapses, can help put things back into perspective when it comes to connecting with others, and realizing how important relationships are for their own sake, above social etiquette, societal roles, gender expectations, and so forth.

MISSION TASK 86: SHADOWS AMID LIGHT

In most societies, there is a presumption that by age 18 or 21, most adults have ultimate responsibility, and this promotes the false perception that people are somehow complete or fully matured by this age. In fact, our emotional and spiritual maturation is a lifelong process.

Recollect some of the mission tasks that we considered in Chapter Four on disavowed emotions. In your interactions with others, can you notice that sometimes these individuals might be communicating from a place of inner certainty and congruence, and at other times they could be expressing a part of themselves has not yet fully matured or integrated? In our world there is a tendency to react to people on the surface level in communication, rather than recognizing that most people are far from complete in their self-realization and that we are all on a learning path. The latter view promotes a compassionate perspective on human connections, in which we can then aim to understand others, rather than judging them for their perceived limitations. Although each individual's soul shines bright, we each have shadows to work through.

Completion Goal:

Reflect on the false assumption that human development is complete by age 21, and consider how perceiving people on a lifelong process of personal and spiritual development can help in building connections with others. You may also like to reflect on some of the mission tasks in Chapter Four in this exercise, as these could be beneficial in considering the particular 'parts,' and sub-parts that people might be expressing in relationships, as they endeavor on the process of discovering and reconnecting with their true self.

MISSION TASK 87: LIBERATE IMAGES

Rather than perceiving others through the magnetizing eyes we saw them when we first met them, we can allow others to express their full potential. In doing so, we liberate our mental images of others in our mind and allow them to emerge as their true selves.

Completion Goal:

Reflect on the overall mental concept that you have of certain people who are close to you. Just as most of us have a self-image (an overall conceptualization of ourselves), so too, we perceive others in a certain light. Reflect on how releasing some of these false images could be beneficial for strengthening the quality of your connections and relationships with these individuals.

Side Note: This process can be healing for both ourselves, and those close to us in relationships. Relational dynamics change as soon as our perceived images of others are adjusted, and the lens of perception is cleansed.

NEW REALITIES

Practices such as 'tantra' can show us that when two individuals share a common energetic connection, their consciousness fields move into congruence, their heartbeats and breathing can align, and they can even begin to exhibit similar brainwave patterns. Higher experiences of creative expression become possible in these states of authentic union. It is also common to experience new energies, or sensations, throughout the consciousness field when we learn to connect at a deeper level. Although those who are adept at meditation can achieve deeper field consciousness experiences, these experiences are most profound when shared with others. As you might have noted from our discussion earlier on in this chapter, this openness at the subtle energetic level can also facilitate profound, authentic, transcendent connections. This process of deepening our field awareness can make us more susceptible and sensitive to people's energies.

There is a discourse for discussing these field experiences in Eastern philosophies and language, such as Sanskrit. For example in, Sanskrit, the greeting, 'namaste' captures this soul-level connection between two individuals at a deep profound level. In the West, we often fail to place this much emphasis on human connection. Often, we sublimate our direct experiences at the field level – we intellectualize them, or disregard them altogether.

For instance, when someone attacks us with harmful, negative remarks, we might sense a feeling of anxiousness without our stomach, our anger coming from the chest area, but we tend to ignore these sensations and focus on the surface-level interaction. Yet, these sensations, in effect, relate to field-awareness. Often, we might disregard somatic sensations as just physiological markers of anxiety or stress, but it's important to keep in mind that the physical body and the energy body are inextricably linked, and cannot be considered in isolation. It is worthwhile to become attuned to the subtle feelings in our bodies, as these can indicate imbalances at the field-level, as well as potential opportunities (or invitations) to connect at a deeper level. You might feel a warm, embracing sensation in your heart around certain people, for example. It's worthwhile to give our attention to these somatic experiences.

Perhaps a more obvious example of this sublimation process is that of sex. Some people seem to believe that sex leads to pleasurable sensations due to physiological factors alone. This is not the case. In fact, when we connect at a deeper relational level, we can are capable of experiencing a sexual union at all levels, not just within a particular point of our bodies. This is what is referred to in tantric teachings, in regard to heart and mind connections in intimate relationships.

Some people believe that these tantric teachings are abstract spiritual notions with no practical significance, however if we pinpoint the pleasurable sensations in our bodies during sex, it does indeed become possible to move (with our intention) those energies, to expand and transmit them, rather than just expending them. For those not trained in tantra, the experience of sex is short lived. Yet, in learning tantric practices, it is possible to raise these pleasurable sensations to the heart level, or to the mind level to experience whole-body (and mind, and heart) bliss.

This is not a process limited to relationships, as a number of gurus and spiritual teachers are able to experience blissful sensations within the mind, and within the heart through meditation.

This life-force flowing through our consciousness field is termed 'prana' or 'chi' in some traditions, this is what animates our consciousness and infuses it with particular energies. We can in fact learn how to infuse certain connections, and even objects and places with particular energies when we master our awareness at the consciousness field level. A number of Eastern healing traditions incorporate energy principles into their techniques. In the past I have worked with a number of these techniques including Pranic Healing and Quantum-Touch methods in order to explore the subtle energies that arise during meditation and their potential for expanding the consciousness field.

In this subchapter, I would like to draw upon some of these basic techniques to encourage you to experiment with core energies during meditation. Indeed, some of the most powerful transcendent experiences feature a strong energetic component, in which a person reports their entire heart opening up, or their entire being expanding beyond the physical body. These sensations are more noticeable in meditation, as the intellectual mind is quiet; however, this awareness is possible to connect with in all life interactions. Again, it's useful to remember that these unique energetic sensations are not just hallucinations, nor just physiological responses, but are in fact distinct experiences with the human consciousness field.

At the relational level, the deeper level intention that we experience is far more impactful than surface language communication. This idea is central to how we express ourselves at the field level. For example, when we smile, we can project a deep sense of the warmth and happiness; this is much more powerful than proclaiming "I am happy." How often do we smile toward someone, or hug someone, and spend a moment cultivating the feelings associated with the experience? It is quite beneficial to do this as it allows us a moment to connect with others, rather than just reacting in responding to social cues in a fast-paced manner. The former approach relates to cultivating field-awareness, and conscious connection, while the latter represents a more surface-level, superficial connection.

Does a movie star with a photo-shopped smile project this deep sense of warmth from their soul, from their consciousness field, when being photographed? Often, just by looking at magazine photos, despite how big a celebrity's smile is, can you sometimes just tell, that the smile is not authentic, that it doesn't project sincere happiness? Often, we can tell, intuitively, that these individuals smile just to have their photograph in a magazine, not because they have cultivated the essential feeling of joy within and projected it outward.

It is likewise possible to recognize authentic expressions of emotion at the field level. These expressions are so powerful that they literally imbue our field of consciousness, drawing us in to an empathic understanding in which we have a unified experience, a shared emotional or spiritual connection. An individual who takes the time to express this energy from within more powerfully impacts others in their relational field. Their intention is a direct expression of felt conscious experience, rather than just a passing thought or sporadic emotion. It is worthwhile to cultivate the core essential energy behind our words, deeds, and emotions, in order to express our true nature, and in doing so, to create powerful transformations at the field level.

The realities we experience before us are not as solid as these appear. In fact, all realities are infused with the human touch, a particular energetic essence. There appears to be an active passage between the spiritual realm and the material realm in that regard, as our consciousness shapes our experience. Therefore, learning how to connect with our essence and project this into the world can have quite a powerful impact on those around us, and in turn, on our collective human experience.

EXPLORATION: CORE ENERGETICS

In the workshops I teach about energy dynamics, one of the approaches I focus on the most is the healing power of human touch. Heartfelt human touch can give us an example of direction connection at the field-level. When someone coincidently touches your shoulder or hugs you briefly in passing, you may notice that the quality of the human connection is minimum in comparison to a meaningful heartfelt touch. Advanced energy healers and practitioners are able to sense this field connection even without physically touching someone, as the human consciousness field extends far beyond just their physical body.

You might not read much into someone accidently touching your shoulder while walking past you, for instance. Yet, we integrate energies from our external environment all the time. Someone who is in a positive, bubbly mood, imprints their energetic patterns onto everyone they encounter throughout their day, and especially so if the interactions involve physical touch. Have you ever suddenly felt angry, or upset, or another distinct emotion when someone hugged you, shook your hand, or touched your shoulder? Can you compare this with other instances, with different emotional qualities after someone physically touched you? Notice just how powerful relational connections are in terms of transferring certain emotional and spiritual states across consciousness fields.

In turn, it's important to become mindful of how we assimilate certain energies and states from our encounters with others, as well as noting the intention and 'quality' of consciousness we project forth in our interactions.

MISSION TASK 88: SUBTLE SENSATIONS

Completion Goal I:

Next time that you have an opportunity to practice meditation, notice any particular subtle sensations that arise in your field of consciousness. These might be a sense of buzzing, a sense of warmth, heat, cold, tingling, or numerous other core energetic sensations that are common in deeper states of meditation.

Side Note: If you do not notice any sensations specific to the meditation experience, you may like to instead focus on a particular part of your body during your practice. Focus on your heart, for instance. What does the sensation around your heart area feel like? Do you notice any of the sensations mentioned above, or others? These can be quite subtle, and these sensations expand in time as we become more attuned to them.

Completion Goal II:

Repeat the above task. This time, use your conscious intention to expand any of the pleasant, positive sensations that you noticed in the previous task. Expand the sensation(s) throughout your entire body. For example, if you felt a warm sensation along your spine, you could imagine the sensation spreading throughout your entire body, permeating your entire being. It does not matter where these sensations arise at first, as we can learn to expand and focus them with practice.

Completion Goal III:

During the next three conversations you have, notice whether you can sense the deeper-level energetic imprint behind the words a person is using. What is the overall sense of the connection you are experiencing with them? Can you get a feel for the energy that person is projecting forth? Does it have a particular quality, or texture, that you can notice behind the surface-level words?

MISSION TASK 89: INFUSION

Completion Goal I:

Throughout the next three days, decide on the core energy and intention that you would like to project in each of your connections with others. Notice the core energy that arises within before you communicate using certain words. Is this the energetic intention that you wish to send forth, or would you rather project a different intention? Notice whether others react to you in a different way, as you adjust your communication and expression based on the intention and overall feeling that you put forth in each connection.

Side Note: If you have trouble getting a sense for the core energy, focus instead on the core emotional state, the essential feeling behind the words. This intention does not have to be the same with each conversation or connection, the aim is to become aware of your intention and its subtle impact in certain relationships.

Completion Goal II:

Practice the above task with non-verbal communication. For example, practice smiling wholeheartedly, by truly capturing the emotion of joy and happiness and expanding it throughout all of the muscles in your body.

Side Note: This technique also relates to the idea of congruence that we have been discussing throughout this book. When we feel happy, it is important to allow this happiness to permeate our entire emotional state, our whole somatic awareness, and our entire field of consciousness completely, so that we can more deeply and more completely express this feeling in the moment. Practicing embodying our core emotional and energetic state thus allows us to form authentic connections with others.

Completion Goal III:

Close your eyes and imagine that you are holding an imaginary basketball in front of you. Now, choose a particular intention, an energy, or emotion that you would like to embody in this present moment. Now, allow this energy to move through your hands and into this imaginary basketball. For example, you might imagine joyful, loving, compassionate, or peaceful energy flowing down through your arms and hands and into this mentally-constructed basketball. Next, imagine mentally passing this basketball to a particular person who you wish to send these positive intentions toward.

Side Note: Practicing this mission task can replicate what occurs on a field consciousness level in each of our interactions. Often, our consciousness influences others in this manner, but because we might not be projecting our intentions in such a focused manner, these might be more dispersed, and thus less powerful in our relationships. Practicing this basketball technique (projecting particular energies forth in a direct, conscious fashion) can have much faster results in relationships, as we will explore in the following mission task.

MISSION TASK 90: SOULFULNESS

Completion Goal I:

Reflect on the connection between consciousness and emotion. For example, reflect on where you sense the overall feeling of love in your body, when you express love to others. How about confidence? How about sadness? How about anger? What is the overall consciousness field experience of connecting with these states?

Completion Goal II:

Practice infusing your focused energy into the external world. For example, next time you experience a heartfelt sense of love or compassion, aim to project this energy forth (either via direct physical contact or mental intention). This process allows us to transcend surface-level constructs as we allow our direct conscious experience to flow; our core feelings in the here-and-now emerge in the collective field.

Side Note: Some examples of infusing our core intention into the external world include smiling (and projecting forth authentic happiness and joy), hugging (and experiencing a deep-seated sense of love), using particular words (and embodying their deeper energetic intention), and myriad other potential avenues for expressing our core energetic intention.

Completion Goal III:

In this final mission goal, consider five other applications of infusing our energy into particular behaviors in the external world.

Side Notes:

As suggested above, there are numerous advanced applications of these techniques. For example, next time you are required to conduct a presentation about a particular topic, or to speak at an event, you might aim to cultivate an emotional state of confidence and enthusiasm, rather than merely relying on an intellectually-rehearsed speech. Aim to place all of your energy into external tasks in this manner in order to fully express your true self.

At the field level, our intention and energy has quite a powerful effect. A sincere smile can transform someone's day in a powerful manner, not just because of a surface-level interpretation of your smile, but because a person can genuinely, directly, connect with the presence, the energy behind the smile. A core part of your soul is embedded in your conscious expression in this manner.

This is applicable in all life areas, and this is worth considering in much more depth than can be afforded here due to the word constraints of this chapter. You may notice, for example, that food tastes better when someone has cooked it whilst in positive state of being, rather maintaining a negative, upsetting vibe. You might notice that certain conversations have a particular feeling or energetic quality behind them. Or, you may note that particular environments and spaces have a deeper energetic sense that permeates throughout. As we connect with more subtle fields of consciousness, these qualities become quite apparent.

CHAPTER SEVEN

ULTIMATE FREEDOM

Freedom and choice are not at all alike. Choice is a selection from a finite palate. Freedom is the embodiment of original creation. Choice is: Should I go left or right along this well-outlined path? Freedom is: Abandon the path. I will make a new direction, I will move forth through the wilderness.

In the collective herd, people live as a passive agents, never quite cultivating their unique soul essence. As we wake to our essential conscious experience, we then individuate and become aware of our true nature; we recognize consciousness as the driving force of all life experience. From this frame, we are no longer people in a herd mentality that reflect their cultural and societal programming, but rather we become soul-centered individuals who weave unique realities in the world. There is a distinction between the robotic nature of the person in the herd and the conscious individual who is aware of their inner creative potential, as well as the ecological (energetic) impact of their consciousness field on others.

This process of awakening to our true nature involves coming to a deeper understanding of what it means to be human, and what it means to be a conscious being. At the intellectual level, there are vast distractions in our world that prevent most from taking even a brief moment to consider these major questions. Yet, these questions are at the heart of why the world exists as it does – our realities are generated from collective conscious experience. The suffering in the world is in fact not sustained by political, economic, or technological factors, but through a disconnection with essential conscious experience – a misidentification with the constructed self in place of our authentic soul nature.

Of course, it is fine to embody certain cultural principles, if these are in line with our true nature. Yet, such a vast number of people wander through life, as zombies, asleep; slaves to their programming, rather than conscious on a moment-to-moment basis. Even the most brilliant minds throughout history have struggled traversing these facets of societal programming, despite their successes in various areas. For instance, many prominent authors in the 20th century used language biased toward men in their written work, as women were marginalized in society to a great degree during that era. These individual's intelligence and material progress in life did not necessarily allow them to transcend the societal and cultural indoctrination at the time (such as gender bias). The same observations can be made of discrimination toward a particular race or group of people. No matter how much intelligence or material success one achieves in life, this cannot be considered a substitute for the recognition of one's essential nature outside of the constructed self. To recognize that our true nature exists outside of the cultural and social paradigm of our time is the ultimate meaning of transcendence.

Transcendence experiences involve stepping out of the intellectual models we have formed, and acquiring a clear perception. However, we tend to intellectualize our perceptions rather than focusing on becoming more conscious, more self-aware, and more mindful of the essence of our life experiences. We perceive the essence of goodness in another, and then feel obliged to intellectualize it into a religion; we perceive the essence of moral acts, and intellectualize them into policies, laws, and rules; we perceive the essence of love, and intellectualize it into the institution of marriage. The diffusion of consciousness into an immutable intellectual construct is a common practice in our world – we take the magic of the conscious present moment and aim to condense it, we aim to capture and make it permanent. This process is not so problematic in itself, however it is problematic once we begin value the object of our creations to extremes, all the while forgetting their soul essence altogether.

"To be is to be perceived," as George Berkeley put it. To use Plotinus' wording, we 'ensoul' the world with our consciousness, we are not just passive observers responding to our social environment. We are the watchers in the panopticon that is reality. Yet, in our watching, we shape, inform, and create new realities through the act of active observation. That source of consciousness is much more powerful than the freedoms afforded to us that were born in this world, as the freedoms we acquire here are constructed, whilst the freedom of the unlimited mind has no intrinsic boundaries.

Laws and rules born in this world have no meaning at the consciousness level. Their meaning is restricted to the constructed self, and these rules make no sense outside of their self-confirming logic. Even the rights that we are granted in this life are superimposed via social constructs, such as the right to vote, for instance. How is this even an intrinsic right? On the other hand, the essential rights of the soul, such as creative and emotional expression, are meanwhile sublimated.

From birth, most people are assigned a life mission task along the lines of: 1) There is only one purpose, to procreate and continue the species, and in order to do that you must 2) find a suitable partner and make a living to support a family, and that requires that you 3) learn specific skills to spend most of your time working in order to fulfil these first two goals. This common narrative is reinforced throughout schooling and in the workforce, even though it might be inferred rather than explicit. Few people pause, stop for a second, and ask themselves, 'why am I spending most of my days doing this?', 'what ultimate value does it really have?' The answers mentioned at the start of this paragraph might comfort the constructed self, but do little to nourish the soul.

The 'human paradigm' presupposes that we are just flesh, blood, and bone, and nothing more. Yet, we are not just human beings, we are not just personalities walking around in bodies. We are so much more. We have chosen to identify with our material existence. In that sense, moments of transcendence illustrate our broader conscious potential beyond this identification with the constructed self. Professions and careers are a poor supplement for expressing our broader gifts and talents in boundless possibilities. Likewise, religion is a poor substitute for individual spiritual exploration. And, social class is a poor replacement for authentic human connection across gender, race, religion, and occupation. We acquiesce to these collective constructs in place of an authentic experience of consciousness far too often.

> Every morning, billions of people get up to start their daily chores. A large percentage hate their jobs, they hate their boss, they have to travel to their lousy jobs for hours, on the bus, or train, or bicycle, or walk, in the rain, the snow, the heat, or sit in bumper-to-bumper traffic for hours.

> Why do all these people repeat this insanity every day? To earn money – so that they can buy bread and milk and clothing; to pay electricity and send their children to school and somehow make it to the end of the month – and then start the madness all over again.

> On a planet of seven billion people the majority of us live in poverty and in a state of quiet desperation, waiting for some kind of miracle to deliver us from the harsh economic times. Millions dream of fame and fortune, which can be seen in the endless number of reality television shows offering exactly that. People are searching for any kind of salvation, often choosing the wrong kind that only leads to more misery.

> – Excerpts from Michael Tellinger's book, 'Ubuntu Contributionism'

Michael Tellinger's remarks above capture the difference between choice and essential freedom quite well. Most people chase the dreams portrayed on their television screens, all the while failing to perceive their personal inner power, their inner creativity, and their inner potential, which far exceeds that of those self-professed idols in the external world. Indeed, most people believe they are free, but they are not. They live life from choice to choice, immersed in the illusion of free will. The truth is, choice has nothing to do with free will. In our world we are presented with myriad choices, tapestries of variation. From our dress, to our diet, to our career, we choose. Yet, even complex decisions such as being able to choose one's religion or political alignment have nothing to do with free will at an essential level. Freedom to choose is a poor replacement for true empowerment.

Having the chance to pluck choices from vast varieties of options does not amount to essential freedom at all.

What is it to be free, after all? In terms of religious affiliation, for example, a great proportion of people choose to follow a particular religious tradition because their parents followed the same customs growing up. Most of the varieties in choice that we experience in life, in fact, have been indoctrinated into our mindset by parents, teachers, and other influential figures in our life. Still, we present these as expressions of our true self. But, are they?

Is your country, your political group, your religion, and so forth, intrinsic to who you are at the core? Are these not merely temporal constructs that have been contrived by someone else? The pursuit of true freedom involves first recognizing that this process of entrainment and cultural indoctrination has occurred. Much of our behaviors, thinking, attitudes, and ideas about the world seem autonomous at the surface level, but these are in actual fact driven by someone else's conceptualization, born from someone else's truth. Most people believe these choices are based on their own decisions, but the process is one of a mere assimilation of ideas from an external source, and claiming those ideas as our own. Consider, then, what is free will?

Timothy Leary's famous words capture the essence of independent self-exploration and personal freedom quite well; "to think for yourself you must question authority and learn how to put yourself in a state of vulnerable open-mindedness, chaotic, confused vulnerability to inform yourself." In our world, no-one knows for certain the definitive answers about who we are, what we are, and how we came to be on this planet. Scientific leaders look to theories, while religious leaders look to scripture and faith for answers to these questions. However, it is honorable to admit that we do not know for certain the potentials of our true nature – much more honorable than to settle for an inferior concept, or theoretical idea about the human being.

In examining self-transcendence experiences, we can see that emotional and spiritual experiences are more powerful than the intellectual beliefs we hold about the world. These experiences connect us to a deeper understanding that no singular model or intellectual idea could capture in full. Therefore, it is important to listen to our intuition and to explore the depths of our hearts from a curious, open perspective.

In this chapter, I will aim to bring together the ideas from the previous three chapters on the power of emotional connections, relational consciousness, and the ultimate potential of the conscious individual. As I suggested in Chapter Six, we can consider that each individual carries within them an entire world of perspectives, possibilities, and ideas. There is no objective social truth in that regard, as each person's mind and heart contributes to a common field experience. As we interact with others on this deeper empathic level, our heart reaches out and touches theirs. Social narrative and meaning overlaps, collides, and unites on a perpetual basis. Our experience of life itself thus varies between resistance and acceptance of other people's worlds. If we accept certain worlds, these become integrated into our experience. Yet, those that we reject (unconsciously) are excluded from our map of reality and what believe to possible and true. This is the process of making meaning from conscious experience. In this process, it's important to become mindful of our essential creative freedom.

In the first part of this chapter, I will explore the distinction between free will and choice, with reference to a few case examples, including an exploration of religious beliefs compared with spiritual experience. Next, I believe it would be worthwhile for us to explore how our level of consciousness in life predetermines our ultimate freedom. And, toward the end of the chapter I would like to conclude with a discussion on the existence of consciousness outside of the constructed self, and transcendence experiences of altruism. This will pave the path for the final chapter that deals with exceptional consciousness states and higher mind potential.

MOTIONLESS SHAPE

All constructs coax us into believing that certain realities would be static, immutable, and frozen-in-frame: A motionless shape. Yet, even at the atomic level, particles move in constant motion. Despite how much we attempt to freeze, or capture, or confine our conscious experience, a fixed and limited construct can never encompass the full spectrum of the conscious universe.

The more faith that we place in scientific authorities, religious doctrine, societal expectations, and so forth, the less faith we hold in our direct conscious experience. There are many acting authorities in our world: Social, cultural, political, religious, scientific, and so on. All of these present static, immutable, standards for us to reach toward. All the while, few people recognize their innate conscious experience as an authority in itself. We have a tendency to externalize our ultimate power onto static objects outside ourselves, whether these consist of our conception of other people, certain groups, organizations, or even particular symbols.

For instance, throughout history, our dependence on religion has been one of the major roadblocks that has prevented us from knowing our true conscious nature. In fact, religious authorities have defined the scope of acceptable conscious experience throughout the ages. It is only recently (in the grand scheme of history) that scientific authorities have taken this role.

Individuals who report transcendence experiences often find themselves faced with various skeptics attempting to dismiss their experience. Religious figures tend to pose that only those who have been blessed with the divine grace of God, or those who have been elevated to sainthood status, could ever experience such mystical states of transcendence. At the other end of the spectrum, scholars and scientists often assume that transcendent experiences are just hallucinations or figments of one's imagination.

Often, we devalue the power of conscious experience, we turn to experts and authorities, rather than trusting our direct conscious understanding in the here-and-now. From this perspective of subjugation, the object is then seen as more valuable than the subjective experience. Hard data and objective truths appear much more important in our world than the pursuit of the direct, personal, subjective, experience of the human being. But, in fact, it is personal experience, personal consciousness, that provides the meaning and narrative of all objective interpretations in the first place. Therefore, conscious experience should be cherished, not considered second rate.

The problem here is that people tend to confuse their static mental interpretations of the world for direct conscious experience. There is a distinct difference between experiencing the world through the filters of the mind illusion, and opening our consciousness to direct connection with life here-and-now, the present moment as it presents itself, without filter nor shade. The latter is the supreme knowing that gurus and enlightened beings have spoken about throughout the ages. These direct conscious knowing experiences illustrate a relational connection to the broader consciousness field. It is the deep-seated knowing that arises from being here now, rather than attempting to shape the present moment to a static model or standard in our minds.

The 'object,' whether a social standard, a scientific model, a religious doctrine, or any static truth, can impede our direct consciousness experience; it filters this direct conscious knowing and diminishes its power. The university is perceived as the authority on knowledge and wisdom, the hospital as the authority on health and healing, the police station as the authority on security and safety. The actual source essence of these powers arises from consciousness in the first place, however, and can never be self-sustained in these constructs alone. Wisdom always arises from within the mind, not within universities as such, healing occurs within our bodies, not at the hands of doctors as such, and security comes from personal confidence and power – all qualities of the conscious mind, rather than an external construct. I am not suggesting that we do not need these mass structures in our societies, but we need not diminish our power in place ultimate faith in those external constructs. In our world, we do this to extremes, and have forgotten the wisdom, healing potential, and confidence of the individual soul.

Here we can consider another example: Religion. Jean-Paul Sartre's 'Existentialism Is a Humanism' considers how human beings use religion as a means of dispelling their ultimate responsibility. Just as with religion, we often align with many other social constructs, and in doing so, we surrender our inner power and freedom. Sartre's work highlights the hopeless dependence people have on religions as a crutch; an avoidance mechanism that ensures we never have to ask ourselves the hard existential and spiritual questions about life.

Too often, people tend to rely on the idea of God as a substitute for their sense of personal morality or ethics. In fact, most people seem far fonder of the idea of God, rather than the process of fostering a transpersonal, conscious connection with God. It is far more comfortable to remain oblivious, hiding behind an intellectual wall that conjures ideas about the nature of God, rather than connecting with the truth of the experience. What is your personal experience of God? Few people ask themselves this question, and instead prefer to rely on the doctrines within their religion of choice. This is problematic, as anyone can choose to join a particular religion. The choice does not require much insight or courage. A more difficult decision involves surrendering the mental idea of religion altogether and pursuing the direct personal experience of connecting with a higher source of wisdom and consciousness, whether we call that the super-conscious mind, God, or whatever else we hold most true, most sacred within.

Similar analogies can be drawn in the sciences. Scientist often fall into a trap of perceiving the world through the lens of their theories. Yet, even the best theoretical model, even the best religious doctrine, even the best social standard, is nonetheless a poor supplement for direct conscious experience. As soon as we become fused with these constructs, we negate our direct conscious experience, we forget our essential unlimited potential to perceive new realities.

Most people are slaves to their own beliefs, mental commentaries, and intellectual ideas, all the while believing that their free will is their own. So, what is ultimate freedom then? Sartre argued that if we allow, for a moment, the notion that God does not exist, this then places an almost insurmountable burden upon our shoulders. It is the ultimate accountability. If we are absolutely free as conscious beings, with no divine ruler or moral guide, then by consequence, we are ultimately responsible for each decision and action that we take and its effect on others, our planet and, even the cosmos. Most people are not prepared to take on this level of freedom and the responsibility assumed here.

In modern culture, an emerging trend can be noted in which people place as much responsibility onto others as possible, there is an avoidance of being courageous and standing behind their own personal truth, their direct conscious experience. Just consider the 40 page copyright agreements that lawyers draft for major organizations such as software companies to cover their own vulnerabilities. There is little care for human beings in these contracts, it is all about the bottom line, supporting a given construct or immutable procedure.

This fixation with procedure is also obvious in medical systems around the world, which would charge patients in the six figure range for a single operation. Doing this makes sense within their demented closed-logic, but makes no sense whatsoever from an empathic, conscious, perspective. If we see a fellow human being in pain and suffering, then the only reason we would ever not feel an empathic connection and immediate desire to help them, is if we placed the construct above the conscious experience (the construct relating to hospital procedure, and the conscious experience relating to a person suffering right in front of us, with no other qualifiers attached to this direct firsthand perception). The decisions regarding the human being are boiled down to policies in our world, rather than being grounded in genuine, conscious care for our fellow beings.

Perhaps a less abstract (and I admit, somewhat off-tangent) example that can be considered here is that of the modern internet. In the late twentieth century, the internet was perceived as a symbol of open collaboration and sharing, offering instant access to all information for all, for free. This was perhaps one of our biggest accomplishments as a human race. Yet, over the previous decade, we have taken a few steps backward. We have superimposed our social and cultural norms onto the internet. A place that was once open and free to use is now commercialized, certain content is limited to certain countries, particular websites are censored outright, and copyright infringements are placed on content without the creator's consent. The internet has been transformed from an information-sharing platform to a mass-media platform, a platform that reflects the values of our Westernized capitalist worldview.

The internet has become a reflection of our societal values, even though it started out transcending those values and serving as an open platform. The development of the internet offers empirical proof that we can create, and have created, a medium in which open connection and sharing is available to all, without the need to capitalize, nationalize, and monopolize the platform.

Indeed, no-one controls the internet. Yet, through our content-engagement, we persist on creating a pyramidal structure in which the illusion of control is maintained. It is the mindset of the herd, rather than the awakened mind that maintains this illusion. The top 500 websites appear to generate more traffic combined than the remainder of the world-wide-web. Critical and valuable spiritual teachings tend to receive thousands of YouTube views, whilst videos of people illustrating the worst characteristics of the human race accumulate millions of views within hours of broadcasting.

In fact, the word-wide-web has now become a superimposed construct, rather than a neutral platform. In the past, websites gained popularity based on the quality of their content. Now, the internet is no longer open and no longer provides equal creative opportunities for each individual. The fact that it once did accomplish this aim is a travesty, as we have literally had endless opportunities for human expression that we have now constricted and regulated to shape this platform in line with our cultural values. Lawmakers intend to regulate all websites across the entire internet. Such a plan would have been perceived as nonsense a couple of decades ago, but it's common to hear people talk about this as though it as common sense in the present decade. The internet was fine as it was for the previous 20 years. It was never broken. But, like so much in this world, we feel the need to correct it with our societal ideologies and prejudices that we adore so much.

The development of the internet is analogous with our potential for conscious creation. Boundaries such as racial, religious, cultural, and sometimes even regional, restrictions are human-imposed rather than absolute. These restrictions are part of the mind illusion that separates us from authentic conscious connection and free creation. It's important to develop faith in ourselves, in our conscious experience, rather than placing all of our faith in an external object. In the earlier incarnations of the internet, we almost achieved this via our technological advancement. But, in fact, we took one step forward and two steps backward. Rather than transcending constructed boundaries and recognizing our infinite potential, we tend to regulate and control the human being through finite filters of perception.

Consider this example. Leo Babauta's blog, 'Zen Habits,' includes an 'uncopyright agreement' that is entitled 'Do with me as you please,' allowing his content to be shared and contributed to openly. Likewise, you can create websites, language, art, and much more online with almost no restrictions and in boundless creative potential (or at least, you could, in the past, as those freedoms now appear to vanish from week to week). The conscious soul neither becomes more liberated nor more enslaved as a result of certain technologies. It is rather a case that certain technological advancements create a temporal disruption in our false illusion of free will. In these moments we recognize that our freedom is supreme, not limited to superimposed structures.

The illusion that certain authorities set the parameters of our free will is broken when we recognize the ultimate creative power of the soul. In the example of the internet, it was never governed, and now, governments are beginning to reach their fingers into the infrastructure of the world-wide-web to grab hold of it with their fists of control. And, we allow them to do so, we remain passive, discounting our own freedom and surrendering it to another authoritative power that we will never meet, never see, and never connect with firsthand.

In that sense, cherishing our conscious experience and having conviction in our decisions are two qualities that people so often lack in our world. It is far easier to place the burden on governments to make global decisions. It is easier to place the responsibility on schools to teach children wisdom. It is far easier to place responsibility on hospitals to maintain our health. Thus, discovering the true meaning of essential freedom is not easy, as most of us would prefer to live within a conceptual illusion of free will instead.

In order to develop a strong sense of conviction, it is essential that we embrace this deep-seated sense of freedom that most people seem to fear so much. In mind, in emotion, and in soul, we are sovereign. Yet, how frightening would it be to sit in a room for three hours just with your own thoughts and emotions, completely alone and in perfect quiet? Most people cannot do this, their distraction in the world is their salvation. However, when we face ourselves, we discover that the sovereign mind is not subjected to its social limitations, its freedom is ultimate and its creative potential unlimited.

Our deepest fear is not that we are inadequate. Our deepest fear is that we are powerful beyond measure. It is our light, not our darkness that most frightens us. We ask ourselves, Who am I to be brilliant, gorgeous, talented, fabulous? Actually, who are you not to be? You are a child of God. Your playing small does not serve the world. There is nothing enlightened about shrinking so that other people won't feel insecure around you. We are all meant to shine, as children do. We were born to make manifest the glory of God that is within us. It's not just in some of us; it's in everyone. And as we let our own light shine, we unconsciously give other people permission to do the same. As we are liberated from our own fear, our presence automatically liberates others.

– Marianne Williamson

From childhood, we are taught that the individual has little power and that it is governments and large organizations that shape the world. This is either done on a conscious level (following all governance without question) or at an unconscious level (forming assumptions and beliefs, such as all knowledge learned in schools is true). The belief that the object is more powerful than the individual is in fact a lie perpetuated to keep people asleep, unconscious, and oblivious to the broader consciousness spectrum. It creates the illusion of free will, albeit free will dictated to us from an external source. We remain in a prison of consciousness, to use Graham Hancock's words.

All high-control societies tend to enforce the illusion of freedom in their perpetual disenfranchisement of the individual's conscious experience. It is acceptable in most modern societies to follow the predominant governing structures, such as a religion, a political group, or a social class, but it is often discouraged to trust in our own direct conscious experience, to take the road less travelled. There are a number of controls in place to ensure that we do not pursue the inward path toward spiritual and emotional freedom.

First, religions demand absolute faith without question. This abolishes critical thought and our connection to personal intuition. Second, any practice, substance, or method that cultivates inner wisdom and conscious awakening is discouraged, or categorized as esoteric, weird, or New Age nonsense. Substances and techniques to open the door ways of consciousness, such as entheogens or spiritual meditation practices, are either made illegal or deemed socially unacceptable. And, finally, it appears that any legitimate investigation into transcendent consciousness states, such as the study of parapsychology, is violently attacked by mainstream scientists in order to undermine its validity. Transcendent and altered states of consciousness are often diagnosed by psychiatrists as reminiscent of delusions and pathologies; thus labelling someone's experience as 'crazy' or 'insane' is often enough to dismiss and ignore it altogether in our world (even though this is a weak argument in terms of explaining certain phenomena).

As people who live in the herd, we never quite set the scope of the game of life, as we surrender the meaning of our conscious experience to an external construct. The freedom we experience is never our own. If we allow external authorities to control the parameters of conscious experience, then we will never rediscover our inherent power to set the scope for the game. In order to re-define our realities and the scope of our conscious experience, we must surrender all fixed notions, all meaningless shapes that would aim to capture and hold the world in a single light.

There is something liberating in the recognition that our conscious experience is important and relevant in making moral, ecological, and creative decisions in this world, rather than just depending on the voice and command of our authorities. The experience of the conscious human being cannot be replicated, it is not subject to procedure, or control, or a particular model. No matter how much we map our anatomy, our neurology, and our biology, we will always have a transpersonal connection to something greater than these models – a soul spark of conscious experience that traverses all constructed limitations.

We ought to become more courageous in our consciousness exploration; not to just remain docile, walking through life without questioning the nature of our experience, and our purpose for being here. Once we ask these questions, we begin to learn that what we see in front of us is just a miniscule fragment of all potential realities, and our conscious experience is much vaster than the collective herd believes. Here, we recognize the true value of transcendence. Transcendence experiences connect us with our broader self, with the creative and spiritual inheritance of the eternal soul. This process of reconnection with sacred conscious experience is not in the hands of the draconian structures in our world, it could never be. Rather, the decision is, and always was, within our reach.

It is distressing to note that most modern societies either ignore or sublimate avenues for exploring the nature of consciousness in this manner. Spiritual exploration is sublimated in the hundreds of different religions that exist around the world, most of these seem to form models and ideas about transcendent experiences, without teaching how to cultivate transcendent states and a more genuine connection with the cosmic mind.

In that sense, it's important to become mindful of falling for intricate and cunning illusions of freedom within particular spiritual and religious structures. For example, even so-called holistic and spiritual groups that are based around teachings from a particular guru can serve as control mechanisms. Particular rituals and dogmatic thinking is often prevalent within these groups. Again, critical thought, and forming an intuitive connection with ourselves is dissuaded in these cult-like traditions. In truth, what we need in this world is not another construct, group, or control mechanism, but rather a better understanding of the sovereign power of the individual conscious being. Instead of incorporating more control mechanisms in our world, we should rather incorporate more channels for conscious expression and exploration of the vast encompassing consciousness spectrum.

Thus, based on our discussion so far, it might be worth our while to consider freedom in two distinct forms of expression. The first form of freedom is limited to the control structures that exists in our world. People explore alternative consciousness experiences only to the degree that their exploration is approved by the external structures they serve – their religion, government, and their social affiliations. This 'discursive freedom' can be distinguished from 'ultimate freedom,' which transcends external structures.

Ultimate freedom is the freedom of the soul, not the freedom of the construct. In essence, ultimate freedom is about recognizing that consciousness is a spectrum of experience, not an intellectual model. Consciousness has no container. From a stance of discursive freedom, the common discourse sets the potentialities of the conscious self. The social parameters in our world define the basis of self, mind, and consciousness. But, from a stance of ultimate freedom, it is rather we ourselves, as conscious individuals, who set the parameters for mind exploration, emotional scope, and the depths of our spiritual connection that we endeavor toward.

EXPLORATION: TRANSCENDENCE OF RELIGION

In this exploration, let's consider transcendence experiences associated with mystical or religious states of consciousness. Experiences in which a person has a direct encounter with God, or a higher force, are interesting to consider for a number of reasons. Perhaps the most interesting factor is that people who have transcendence experience often seek for an explanation, rather than recognizing the essential experience as a natural aspect of broader consciousness. As such, a powerful consciousness experience is encountered in a direct manner at first, but later tends to become sublimated as a construct, a mere memory. Religions tend to form around enlightened individuals who had encountered a broader spectrum of consciousness, however, rather than cherishing the experience, religious discourse tends to cherish the myth – their discourse is doctrine-based rather than experience-based.

Thus, often the most profound encounters with the divine start as undifferentiated experiences of self-transcendence, but then later become sublimated into mythos and religious narrative, and finally turn into an immutable construct, an unattainable standard for others. This is common in all profound consciousness experiences that fall outside of our collective mainstream experience of consciousness – we sublimate them rather than recognizing their intrinsic value and the potential to share them with others close to us.

For example, when people speak about having a near-death experience (NDE) and coming into contact with hell or heaven, these individuals report encounters with different levels of consciousness, rather than travelling to a different spatial location as such. The threshold of consciousness is more important to consider than whether an actual place called 'heaven' or 'hell' exists. All that is possible, was possible, and will be possible, exists within the scope of consciousness. Consciousness can experience it all in endless bounds. Yet, the intellectual self constricts these experiences to its preconceived constructs. It makes religions, philosophies, and sciences from these vast indescribable encounters with the consciousness spectrum. These can be useful to an extent, but seldom capture the full depth of transcendent experiences.

In this exploration, I'd like to draw upon some examples from religion. Religions, like other control structures (governments, cultural ideologies, and political-legal frameworks, for instance), tend to sublimate rather than accentuate our ultimate human potential. One of the most dangerous acts that we can ever take is to surrender our faith in ourselves and to acquiesce to an external power. Yet, we happen to do this all the time. During a given moment, a person has ultimate power to develop her sense of faith and connection to God, and the next moment she gives it all to an external force, such as a religious or spiritual group, and surrenders her ultimate freedom. In this manner, we surrender our moral compass for ethics and regulations, we give up our spiritual center for blind belief in religious doctrines, and we expel our freedoms and acquiesce to foolish laws.

In our world, mainstream religions tend to set the scope of discursive freedom when it comes to spiritual exploration. In Catholic traditions, experiences with the transverberation of the heart are considered unique to saints and sacred beings, non-Catholics who claim to have them are often dismissed or ignored outright. In some Gnostic traditions, kundalini experiences are reserved for those who are celibate. And, in Hinduism, there is often a 'holier-than-thou' attitude adopted toward people who claim to have 'samadhi' (spiritual enlightenment) experiences, it is often believed that these states are reserved for master gurus who have practiced meditation for decades. Each of these discursive freedoms are false illusions, as each human being is capable of having each of these transcendent experiences, without having to follow a particular ritual or practice. Indeed, at the core, the consciousness spectrum is within our reach, and there are no qualifiers or boundaries to our consciousness potential. Isn't this an amazing and awesome realization?

There is a particular discourse of learning on an intellectual and theoretical level that persists in religions, rather than encouraging people to explore their boundless potential of emotional and spiritual depth. Hence, people often approach religion from within the confines of the intellectual wall rather than from their direct soul experience. This is not to suggest that Catholics, for instance, do not practice what they preach, but rather that religions such as Catholicism often involve more theorizing than practice, reading the Bible, attending service, attending communion, confirmation, and so forth, rather than developing an understanding of moral and spiritual connection via direct practice.

Most religions concern themselves with what it is to be a good person. From the golden rule referred to in the Christian Bible to the Noble Eightfold Path referred to in Buddhist teachings, we can see a common thread here toward wholeness, congruence, and essential human goodness. Basic principles such as 'know thyself' and 'love thy neighbor' appear throughout various texts, but these are often misinterpreted for their theoretical, rather than practical value. In Catholicism, for instance, volunteering in the community and doing good deeds is considered an essential part of being a good Catholic. Yet, a small percentage of Catholics actually engage in these activities, and an even smaller percentage do so from pure intentions (for instance, they might believe that their passage into Heaven will be secured by doing these tasks – again, the pursuit of a construct rather than a direct experience in the present moment).

MISSION TASK 91: PERCEPTUAL POSITIONS IN RELIGION

In Chapter Five, we considered the notion that the each of our experiences arise within our field of consciousness, but we often externalize them. For example, when we recognize particular qualities, skills, or characteristics within another, it is important to also recognize that we, in doing so, also perceive a mirror of ourselves in others.

Nothing can exist as an island. Therefore, when Christians recognize particular qualities in their interpretations of Jesus Christ, for instance, or when Buddhists recognize particular virtues in the Buddha, this externalization process should be noted. When we commend someone for their altruism, for their wisdom, for their courage, we are, in part recognizing these qualities within ourselves. Unless we contained these qualities within on some conscious level, whether unconscious, or not, we would not be capable of perceiving their value in others.

I believe that a number of prominent spiritual gurus have attempted to illustrate this throughout their teachings. Their acts were intended as a means of showing us our greater potential. Yet, people too often build a religion or a model around these remarkable individuals, elevating them on a pedestal, constructing and interpreting their teachings, instead of learning from them at the direct consciousness level.

Completion Goal I:

Reflect on three of the main spiritual or religious teachings (or philosophies) that you follow in life. Consider how you externalise your inner potential into these teachings, rather than recognizing these qualities within yourself. Is it easier to expel your responsibility by aiming to live up to particular teachings throughout your life, rather than integrating those teachings within and living your personal version of them right here and now?

Completion Goal II:

Are there particular gurus of leaders that you look up to and admire? Is there something about these individuals or figures that you can also see reflected within yourself, on some level?

MISSION TASK 92: HEAVEN AND HELL

Completion Goal:

Reflect on your conceptualization of heaven or hell, if you have any mental concepts or ideas about these constructs. Consider how representations of heaven and hell could relate to states of experience on the consciousness spectrum, rather than specific places or locations. You might like to also reflect on the ideas we discussed in Chapter Four on the nature of emotional timelines. Could heaven or hell be considered in terms that relate to emotional or spiritual states of being? Reflect.

MISSION TASK 93: GOD CONNECTION

Completion Goal I:

What is your understanding of forming a connection with God? Do you have a mental construct or idea about what it means to connect with God? Do you have an intuitive connection with God (through prayer or meditation, for instance)?

Completion Goal II:

Do you believe that you may only form a connection with higher states of consciousness under the guidance of a guru, priest, spiritual leader, or other authority? Consider whether this belief is true, in light of our discussion so far.

Completion Goal III:

Consider five examples of symbolism in religion(s) that you are aware of. How do these symbols serve as metaphors for direct experiences of a spiritual, or transcendent, state of consciousness?

THE FINAL REVOLUTION

Each human being is sovereign over their own mind and soul, despite their inclination to externalize their power. Therefore, humankind's final revolution will not be in the form of a civil war, nor will it rise from a global conflict, nor will it center on political ideologies. Rather, humankind's last revolution will be a revolution of self. As we break from the shores of the mind illusion, and traverse the vast oceans of consciousness, we will rediscover our broader true nature. The final revolution, the final conflict, is a conflict within ourselves. It is a conflict that resolves in the recognition that the temporal self is just a small drop in the ocean of infinite consciousness.

> What is important is not a philosophy of life but to observe what is actually
> taking place in our daily life, inwardly and outwardly. If you observe very

closely what is taking place and examine it, you will see that it is based on an intellectual conception, and the intellect is not the whole field of existence; it is a fragment, and a fragment, however cleverly put together, however ancient and traditional, is still a small part of existence whereas we have to deal with the totality of life.

– Jiddu Krishnamurti

This process of deliberate self-transcendence involves developing an active association with a part of ourselves that existed long before we were even born in this world, a part that exists outside of the scope of space and time: Our soul aspect. The deepest depression can often precede such a revolution of self, as we are forced to consider that the self we have built in this lifetime is not a true reflection of our ultimate nature, or at least, not in whole. The constructed self, like an intricate sand castle, is fated to be washed into the ocean when the tide comes to shore. However, the sand, the sandcastle, and the shore, and the ocean, were never in separation, these are parts of a ubiquitous gestalt. Although we might at first experience sadness about surrendering our investment in the constructed self, this is in fact a process of opening to our broader conscious experience and greater human potentials.

Most of what we have come to know as real, tangible, and solid in the external world, is tied to a constructed language reference. However, transcendence experiences tend to traverse language and all constructed forms, which can make these experiences frightening for the constructed self. Remember that the language we use to contextualize our world arises from direct conscious experience in the first place. Thus, for example, the phrase 'spiritual enlightenment' might not mean much at the surface-level, but the meaning is much more profound for a spiritual guru, as the phrase references an experience, rather than an intellectual construct. Thus, our words in the English language often lose their power, as we forget their core reference, we use them in a careless manner.

Upon first learning a new word, we have the chance to recognize its essence in more depth. This can be illustrated when we examine languages other than English, for example. For instance, in German, the word 'waldeinsamkeit' refers to a feeling of aloneness and connectedness to nature. In Japanese, the word 'komorebi' refers to sunlight shining through in between tree branches. There are thousands of words in different languages that capture unique experiences which cannot be translated to English. In that sense, our language is a model for experiencing the world, but it is an incomplete model. The references we make to experiences are often superficial and limited. It is essential we recognize that language creates a sense of discursive freedom, we limit our interaction to our potential boundaries set in language. However, consciousness was never constrained to those boundaries, it might be experienced through a temporal shade, a temporal language-based expression for now, but this is not a be-all end-all expression.

The use of language is linked to the scope of our conscious experience, in so much as we identify with our language as the main method of forming connections with others. Podcaster Rich Jones made the observation that certain cultures seem to exist within particular states of consciousness, which are reinforced through their language interactions. For instance, Jones highlighted that the French dialect appears to be more sensual and free-flowing than the dialect of those living in the United Kingdom, which comes across as refined and ordered (15).

The link between language and consciousness states is also relevant in professional discourses and subcultures. Mathematicians around the world have a similar method of thinking, of assimilating the world, and of experiencing consciousness despite their regional location. Let's consider another example. Someone operating from a collective lawyer consciousness level might be more attuned to particular details of their environment consisting of legal mandates, rules, and regulations. Someone who is a chef, for instance, has a greater awareness of taste, sensual pleasure, nuance, and so forth. The discourse we use reinforces certain realities. But, again, it's important to remember that these are just temporal embodiments of consciousness. It is fine to create new languages, perceptions, and methods of experiencing the world in this manner, as long as we do not lose ourselves in them. So often, people confuse themselves for their profession, their regional or cultural association, rather than recognizing these qualities as mere temporal expressions within infinite scope of consciousness.

An individual operating from a state of ultimate freedom recognizes their potential to reinvent their scope of experience on a moment-to-moment basis. Embracing our total experience allows us to express our broad potential from within. At one moment I might be a writer, at another a painter, and at another a different embodiment of consciousness. The construct must not define the individual (discursive freedom). Rather, the individual defines the construct (ultimate freedom).

The idea of discursive freedom can be illustrated further. Let's the word 'vegetarian,' for instance. Most people find it easier to use the word 'vegetarian,' rather than having to confront the notion of murdering and eating animals. If I went out to a restaurant and asked the waiter whether there are some vegetarian options available on the menu, this would be quiet a reasonable request to make in modern times. Yet, if I asked the waiter whether any dishes are available that do not have dead animals in them, he might look at me strangely. This is quite odd, in fact, as the second statement is a clearer representation of reality than the vague generalized term 'vegetarian' used in the first statement.

Whilst on the example of food, consider linguistic labels such as 'organic.' Food should not be treated with chemicals in the first place. But, we call food that has been poisoned just 'food,' while natural food is often referred to with added terms such as 'organic food,' 'natural food,' and 'biodynamic food,' and we justify paying twice or thrice the price for something that is, in fact, just food. It is rather the chemically-treated food that should have the added labels 'genetically-modified,' or 'chemically-treated,' with niche shops and markets that charge twice the price, whilst normal untreated food ought to just be called food, and made available in local farms and markets.

Throughout various discourses we sublimate our realities in this manner quite often. Realities that are not popular in the mainstream are pushed out of conscious focus through the cunning use of particular language constructs that diminish their power. As such, our range of consciousness in this world tends to be limited to the predominant constructs that reign. Alternative experiences are sublimated. Eating meat is the normal trend, eating chemically-treated food is the normal trend. There are no qualifiers attached to these experiences. I might just state that 'I am going to dinner to a restaurant,' (and it is assumed dead animals make up a standard meal) or 'I am going to the supermarket' (and it is assumed, but rarely critically examined, that I will buy poisoned food). But, when we refer to experiences outside of the mainstream, no matter how true or natural these are, we are forced, via our discursive language, to qualify them: 'I am going to a vegetarian restaurant,' 'I am going to the organic fruit shop.'

To further the example of eating animals, a number of vegetarian restaurants now make a habit of creating mock meats. These venues still present duck, chicken, fish, and other meat-like items on their menus, but these dishes are made entirely from tofu or a combination on non-animal products. This is perhaps one of the most interesting examples of how language paradigms dominate in our world. Rather than creating new experiences, we acquiesce to mainstream dominant paradigms. This is just one example. Reflect on other examples that illustrate how we acquiesce our original creative expression to predetermined concepts. There are countless examples in which we have strict rules about how we perceive the world, and the perceptions and experiences that challenge these are then wrapped into ambiguous terms that are represented as relative, rather than unique, to their more mainstream counterparts.

In science and academia, for example, new ideas, new creations, and new models, must fit into the previous theories and models that existed before them – a 'matryoshka' doll of ideas that increases a layer as the theories develop. Hence, in a number of science programs, students are taught to replicate existing methods, and then to consider making small improvements or adjustments to existing models – nothing too radical or that would challenge entire thinking paradigms. Doctors tend to standardize treatments for illness instead of exploring a broad spectrum of healing approaches. Engineers tend to develop similar plans for producing energy solutions, instead of devising innovative methods of meeting the world's power and energy needs. Likewise, this process can be observed in a number of life areas. For instance, politicians tend to develop ill-informed policies based on their ideological predispositions, rather than boundless creative solutions that serve all. Radical creative expression is, in turn, discouraged, in a world of constructs.

But, no construct can be more powerful than another, as all constructs are born from the same source: Firsthand conscious experience. It is foolish to weigh them against each other. Yet, this is the basis of how we organize, structure, and present particular ideas in our world. Indeed, we do not see things for their true nature, but rather through the dominant constructs of our time. Therefore, in the last revolution, we shall recognize that discursive freedom could never, and will never, capture the ultimate freedom of the conscious soul.

EXPLORATION: FOCAL POINT

Free will relates to our mode of perception, as much, if not more than, the mere behavioral choices we make. In perceiving the world through a certain light, we also contribute to its collective creation. As we expand our consciousness, our range of perception and experience also expands. In our world, people are taught to never take their focus out of the constructed self and its achievements, ever bolstering their own self-worth and possessions. The single-pointed focus in our world pushes people toward becoming a 'good' doctor, lawyer, businessperson, or other career-oriented outcome, with little creative diversion in this process.

A new focus gives birth to new potential realities, as we see more, rather than just through our constructed filters of perception. We become more than 'just that,' and recognize our connection to broader consciousness experiences. Therefore, learning how to focus is perhaps the most relevant and powerful technique for engaging our consciousness. At first, this might seem trivial, but indeed, the construction of the self arises from a sheer focus on building particular behaviors, habits, and attitudes and reinforcing them. Just so, we can change focus to renew our perception.

MISSION TASK 94: FREEDOM PART I

Completion Goal I:

Reflect on the connection between free will and consciousness. Is there a difference between the freedom to choose particular behaviors, and freedom in terms of range of experience? What is the experience of ultimate freedom, for you?

Completion Goal II:

Recall three examples throughout your life in which you felt a total sense of freedom. Reflect on what it was about the quality of these experiences that made them stand out in terms of the overall quality of feeling free. Did this feeling differ from traditional definitions of freedom, such as the freedom to choose between two different predetermined outcomes?

MISSION TASK 95: FREEDOM PART II

At a fundamental level, others cannot control our core experience of consciousness. It is our ever-present directive to decide to engage with other people's realities, or to reframe them with a unique perspective. A common example that we can draw upon is that of two people who speak different languages. If you visit a foreign country, and a robber walks up to you in the street and asks you for all of your money, you may not be able to even understand what the robber is saying in order to hand over your money in the first place. Of course, you may infer the implications of the situation if the robber is carrying a knife or a gun. Despite this, even in the most seemingly predetermined situations, there are opportunities to reframe these realities (such as fighting or distracting the robber, in this example).

In these sort of situations, most people do not consider free will as relevant, since their pursuit of being safe and secure exceeds their need for freedom. But, it is those of us who recognize that freedom is ultimate that have made the biggest impact upon the world. Those who fight for equal rights across genders and races have made a substantial world impact in terms of promoting universal suffrage and the essential freedom of each human being, for example.

Individuals who constrict their understanding of a conscious self to a specific race or gender, instead create a surface-level divide, and thus breed conflict. Their freedoms are limited to social paradigms, and are discursive, whilst those who transcend social paradigms recognize the ultimate freedom of each conscious soul, and make this clear to others. These individuals recognize that personal consciousness is free at a fundamental level. It is when we engage with particular discourse at a constructed level, and limit our entire conscious experience to this scope, that we begin to renegotiate our ultimate freedom for something less than it is worth.

Even so, the perceived loss of ultimate inner freedom is a temporal illusion, as consciousness is not subject to discursive restrictions. The limitations we place on freedom in our inner world arise from our own self-restrictions. At its core, inner experience cannot be limited by outer concepts. Yet, it's amazing that we do not just surrender our essential freedoms (freedom to act, think, or feel in a certain manner) in dire or immediately stressful situations, as we also surrender these freedoms on a daily basis, by acquiescing to other people's realities. We accept the scope of choice handed down to us throughout our lives, rather than creating new realities from sheer willpower, from sheer conscious creation. In each moment, in each of our interactions, we are faced with a choice: Acquiesce and surrender our ultimate freedom for someone else's constructed realities, or pave a new path.

Completion Goal:

Reflect on the differences between discursive freedom and ultimate freedom.

Side Notes:

Remember, ultimate freedom relates to the transcendence of tangible constructs, recognizing that our conscious experience exists irrespective of these temporal forms. This is the freedom of action, mind, emotion, and soul. Ultimate freedom can be contrasted with discursive freedom, which is born and dies with a given construct, a given parameter for self-expression. Discursive freedom relates to the temporal rights and freedoms that someone else constructs, the allowances and liberties that we are granted within certain legal, social, and political boundaries.

A useful approach for reflecting on freedom is to consider the source of our free will. Does an external power or authority provide certain rights or freedoms? Or, rather, is our source of freedom intrinsic, arising from our soul nature?

MISSION TASK 96: FREEDOM PART III

Completion Goal I:

Reflect on the following statement, from an intuitive stance: Is my internal emotional and spiritual state subject to the events of the external world?

Completion Goal II:

Choose five factors in life that aim to place limitations on your ultimate inner freedom and potential to express yourself. Reflect on how you either limit your free will by constraining your self-expression to these rules, or how you transcend these constructs in your self-expression.

Side Note: Some examples might include family traditions, societal etiquette, fashion trends, collegial pressures, and particular rituals or procedures. How do these five factors aim to restrict ultimate freedom in your society? In some instances, is it beneficial to live within these structures, while in other instances, is it beneficial to transcend them and express our true self irrespective of the external climate. Reflect on this further.

Completion Goal III:

Some people do not question their free will, as a number of these societal rituals are so engrained from childhood that they accept these as intrinsic elements of their world, rather than recognizing the potential to traverse these limiting factors and rediscover their ultimate creative expression. Reflect on how people's emotional and spiritual depth of experience tends to be linked to external motivators (such as fashion trends, social class, religious doctrine, social etiquette, and so forth) rather than anchored in their authentic self-experience. How does this limit their ultimate freedom? Brainstorm 10 examples based on your own life experience and discuss these cases with a close friend.

MISSION TASK 97: RE-FOCUS

In Chapter Six, we reflected on the idea of reframing, and how we tend to either take on other people's realities, or create our own narrative and instead inform their realities. Indeed, human connection is a process of mediating realities, and shaping meaning. Consider how the concepts related to reframing are also relevant to the idea of ultimate freedom. Although we might be compelled to behave in a certain way in society, because of the need to follow constructed laws, and to honor social etiquette, are we ultimately forced to accept external ideas and to integrate them into our core conscious experience?

Completion Goal I:

Practice being present with your own direct experience of consciousness. In line with the earlier meditation exercises, start this practice by 'just being,' focusing on your essential state of awareness in the here-and-now, without the constant barrage of mental commentaries, chaotic emotions, and to-do lists. Can you recognize your sovereignty over your inner space, your consciousness? Do you recognize your power to direct your core focus in a given moment?

Completion Goal II:

Reflect on how our conscious focus is shaped and directed in the external world on an ongoing basis. Do you notice how your perception in life is constantly shaped by how others draw and direct your conscious attention, your focus? Reflect on how this process of focusing is relevant to our discussion so far.

Completion Goal III:

Upon waking up tomorrow morning, set an intention of 'my focus for today.' This can be a particular goal, emotion, or state of being that you would like to cultivate tomorrow.

Side Note: Recall the one percent focus exercise from Chapter Three. Just by focusing a small percentage of our attention on a particular task, we can engage our consciousness and magnetize new perspectives and new realities that link to this task. The unconscious mind seeks out input from the external world to help us achieve these goals. The connection between focus and consciousness is quite powerful in that regard. Creating a mental intention, or focus, at the start of your day, can have quite an immense result in gravitating your life experience toward this particular focus area. Test it out and see to what extent this exercise works.

MISSION TASK 98: CONSCIOUSNESS AS AUTHORITY

There is a constant process of informing, shaping, and instilling meaning in all human interactions. From all of these interactions, we come to a seeming understanding of reality that is mediated by other people's beliefs, perceptions, laws, rules, regulations, and ideologies. But, what about your direct sacred experience of consciousness? Is your direct perception not the ultimate authority on how you should act, feel, and think? There is a certain authority, a certain ultimate power, in connecting with this unique presence of being within.

Completion Goal:

Reflect on the ideas that we considered earlier about the numerous external authorities prevalent in our world. Thousands upon thousands of authoritarian powers dictate how we should live our lives. How does our experience of consciousness, the authentic self, fit into this framework? Does our conscious experience transcend this authoritarian framework of rules altogether? Reflect on your personal experience.

MISSION TASK 99: PERCEPTION

Completion Goal I:

Events and interactions in the external world tend to capture and divert our attention, our conscious focus. Refer to the 'Focal Point' sheet in Appendix C. Focus on the dot in the middle of the page for 30 seconds, without taking your attention away from this dot. Do you notice that there is a foreground and background to how we perceive things? Your entire focus can remain on the dot, but it is still possible to perceive the objects in the room around the dot with your peripheral vision.

Side Note: If someone walks into the room and tries to get your attention during this practice, your focus might shift from the dot in order to see what they are saying. Consider whether such subtle shifts in our attention are made consciously, or whether certain objects, people, and experiences rather tend to grab our attention and divert it.

Completion Goal II:

Even while focusing on the dot, it is possible to become aware of the room and the objects in it. Hence, it is possible to focus on a given object and all the while remain conscious of other objects at the same time. Repeat the practice above, for 45 seconds, and this time notice the other objects around the room without moving your attention from the dot. You could attempt this by naming particular objects in the room around you, without moving awareness away from the dot. Notice that by naming 10 or so objects around the room in your immediate peripheral awareness (such as the monitor, the keyboard, a lamp, and so forth), your conscious awareness expands, without you necessarily having to move your focus from single point of perception.

LIVING OUTSIDE OF OURSELVES

Transcendence experiences show us that our mode of perceiving the world is just one variation of conscious experience. The nature of consciousness is fluid and amenable to unlimited experiences. But, most people lack the courage to explore their true nature, their soul essence; instead, clinging to familiar common realities and reiterating these over and over.

Throughout this book I've attempted to explore the notion that consciousness exists outside of the temporal constructs that we have conceived. In fact, consciousness exists outside the confines of our self-concept altogether. Based on this, it is possible to understand the true meaning of compassion and altruism, as these qualities do not arise within the constructed self, but are rather qualities of the transcendental soul. For example, a person can appear to be altruistic in that they donate $50 to charity every month, but that person might do this just to impress their friends, or to tune their moral compass. True compassion, on the other hand, arises outside of the self altogether, it occurs when we forget about ourselves and encompass the conscious experience of compassion.

These transcendent experiences are common in motherhood, for instance. But, mothers often later integrate these states into their self-concept, reinforcing the constructed image of being a good mother. All the while, it is never about being a good mother, or a good person, or a selfless individual, it is the conscious experience of compassion that is most important. There is no need to categorize the state of essential compassion, or to attach a particular construct to it. Direct conscious experiences with love, compassion, gratitude, and human connection, do not need to be reduced to tangible forms. These conscious experiences take us out of the constructed self and into direct connection with another conscious being, without expectation or presumption.

Instead of recognizing these transcendent qualities of consciousness, we tend to bolster the constructed self, and to look after our own personal needs. In particular, in the West, most people seem to care little about others and the broader problems of the world, instead believing that it is just their own self that is of ultimate importance. This is what happens when we disconnect from our inherent conscious experience, and bolster the constructed self. In a connected state of consciousness, we recognize that all beings are connected, and all happiness, as well as all suffering, is shared on a cosmic level. On the other hand, once we sever that connection, we see the world just through our own eyes, no-one else's experience matters from this ego-constructed vantage point. This is the real danger of forming an intellectual wall around our connection to direct conscious experience, as we lose our sense of essential compassion and essential connection with life itself.

Direct conscious experiences of compassion, love, and happiness, arise within the moment, but rather than embracing these states, we often attempt to hold on to them, to constrain them, and to encapsulate these experiences in a permanent construct. This is the reason that there is such a lack of authentic love, a lack of authentic happiness in our world. We attempt to grip so tightly to these direct conscious experiences, we do not recognize that transcendental states cannot be captured or contained in a single form. Rather than recognizing our transpersonal connection to the cosmic mind, we restrict our conscious experience to the egoic mind.

The concept of ownership is one of the best examples of attempting to form connection with another human being via a construct. The desire for ownership is not the conscious desire to love, or connect, but rather a constructed desire to control and suppress a particular individual to a certain shape, a certain image of love or connection. Marriage would indicate that we can own another person. Possessing a passport or travel visa would indicate that we have the right reside in a certain country. However, at a relational conscious level, can someone own another person? Can someone own a piece of land? As soon as we reduce these constructs of ownership to their essence, we can then recognize that all notions of ownership and control are illusions of the constructed self. Their basis is meaningless at the consciousness level.

To own something is to assume that we can somehow hold something, or someone, for an indefinite period of time. Yet, this is impossible. True freedom comes from the wisdom of learning to let go, to accept the impermanence of all things. In liberating others, we liberate ourselves. As we surrender our constructs, we recognize the essence behind them. There is a certain transcendental freedom in allowing things, and people, to be as they are, without attempting to capture or reduce them to a certain construct. It is this process of liberating our consciousness that is paramount in clearing our filters of perception, and perceiving life experience as it is, rather than through the shape of our preconceived mind.

The constructed mind tends to claim and attribute ownership to raw consciousness experiences. Certain landmarks around the world are claimed as the most beautiful places to visit in a given country. Likewise, it is possible to claim that a particular religion treats minority groups with more compassion than another religion. These claims are all contrived and compared at the construct-level, and never quite capture the direct conscious experience behind them. There are no countries in the natural world, just beautiful mountains, beaches, and forests that spread across the earth, boundless and unrestricted. There are no religious, or spiritual, or political ideologies that can claim to treat certain groups of people with more compassion than others; compassion is an experience, it is not claimable nor definable in a theoretical model.

Scientists claim ownership over consciousness theories with their neurocognitive models. Religions claim ownership over the sacred, the spiritual, the divine, and the transcendent. But, the transcendent exists outside of the construct. The sacred ineffable arises all around us, and can be perceived through the clear soul, the unadulterated mind.

As one example, consider love. Love is an experience outside of the constructed self, we can encounter it without needing to suppress or control it. Likewise, spiritual emergence, the emergence of the soul of human experience arises from this ultimate state of free expression, it can never be derived from, nor replicated in, a temporal construct.

It is in such moments that we step outside of ourselves, that we can gain a glimpse of the true nature of transcendence. The essential experience of consciousness does not stop with the cessation of one's constructed self. As we turn our magnetism from bolstering ourselves to helping others, to contributing to collective conscious growth, we take a step outside of ourselves. Individuals who have demonstrated tremendous altruism do not have some kind of special characteristic or selfless feature embedded in their self-construct, it is rather that those individuals have transcended the self altogether. These experiences of transcendence have nothing to do with integrating qualities of a caring person. Rather this is a conscious process of recognizing that the small self is just a droplet our greater collective whole.

From this frame, we step outside of ourselves not because we sacrifice ourselves for the benefit of others, but rather because we see that the constructed self is an illusion to begin with, and residing there alone has little meaning left. No true love, peace, happiness, or connection can come from it. It is when we step outside and connect with felt experience, not to validate ourselves, but rather to project our consciousness into the collective, that these felt transcendental experiences become possible: Authentic compassion, connection, and universal love. The concept of 'agape,' of universal love, as the utmost importance in life becomes clear here at the experiential level. Here, we do not lose ourselves as such, but rather we recognize our unique purpose in the world – as we contribute in this manner, so too we enrich our soul experience. No longer divided and isolated, we move into being with the world, rather than reacting to it just for the purpose of surviving and looking out for ourselves. To look past the self is to experience soul-liberation; to let go of ourselves is to rediscover ultimate freedom.

In our world we have come to a rare crossroads, in which we no longer just have to fight for survival and just to make a living. As humanitarians such as Michael Tellinger have pointed out, we now have sufficient global resources in our world to abolish outdated constructs such as having to work for 40 hours a week, the idea of paid housing, paid roads, and paid utilities such as fresh water, for example. These structures tend to now exist as a means of control, the provision of essential needs are centered on profit, rather than authentic care for our fellow beings. These bolster the self, the constructed identities of the corporation, rather than facilitating collective conscious growth for all.

Thus, we now have a rare chance to turn our energies toward cultivating our unique creative essence and figuring out our essential contribution to this world – our purpose for being here (and no, at the soul-level, our purpose is not to pay the bills). This calls for our courage to step outside of bolstering the self with its endless needs for acquisition. Rather than attempting to own our images of other people, we can thus learn to support their unique spiritual emergence. Rather than attempting to self-sustain our material lives, we can turn our attention to sustaining the collective creative, emotional, and spiritual growth of all conscious beings on the planet.

The core states of compassion and love then become our essential driving forces, as the constructed self takes a back seat. The purpose then is no longer to integrate good or wholesome qualities within one's self, but rather to transcend self altogether and to experience the encompassing nature of interconnected consciousness without border. These powerful transcendental states move us into a greater spiritual awareness, that is, once we allow ourselves cultivate them and release our attachment to the mind illusion.

EXPLORATION: CONSCIOUS PROGRESSION

The grounding that we have in our constructed sense of self provides a comfortable scope for experiencing the world. However, when we form a transpersonal connection with broader states of consciousness, we can recognize that the conscious soul is not limited to a single material construct. There appears to be a certain progression that leads people to this conclusion.

People tend to take direct life experience for granted and reduce it to limited forms, and in doing so limit other people's creative expression, as their experience is no longer a direct transpersonal connection with their higher soul aspect, but rather an experience of the constructed self that is limited in scope and potential. The freedom of the soul is unlimited and vast, it cannot be contained nor is it subject to social, legal, or cultural limitations. However, the constructed self cannot envision such a profound freedom, for it perceive the world through its own devices.

Thus, we could sum up in stating that at first, we perceive all realities through the lens of the constructed self, our personal biases and perceptions shape our experience of the world. Then, as we mature and form interpersonal relationships, we come to an understanding of the world through a more relational framework, this perspective allows more fluid perceptions, and new experiences to filter through our frame of consciousness. In later stages of development, we recognize that the human being is a contributing factor to the expansion of the collective social group in all aspects. From that stance, we recognize that the social construction of meaning and experience is mediated in each of our group interactions, as we aim to come to a consensus conscious experience, and consensus grounded understanding of the world. Hence, I believe we are all on a constant path toward broadening our self-experience, extending our consciousness, and discovering what true creative freedom implies.

Perhaps a good means of summing up our progression toward ultimate freedom can be considered in four provisional stages. First, we move from a conscious state of 1) the egoic being, perceiving the world through the prison of our internal programming, to 2) the relational being, mediating realities in our connections, but more often than not acquiescing to broader social structures such as tradition, religion, and custom. Then, as we become 3) the sovereign being, we recognize that freedom of mind is in fact more powerful than freedom of the external construct, and in the final step as 4) the transpersonal being, we recognize our co-creative potential to set the parameters of our emotional and spiritual exploration, without the once finite and rigid limits of the mind illusion, relational boundaries, and external constructs.

As transpersonal beings, we perceive that the impacts of our consciousness are not somehow isolated to our own lives, but that we can in fact participate in the conscious creation process of the world, as we help liberate others from their shackles of self and facilitate our collective progression. In order to discover our ultimate freedom then, we must step outside of the constructed self and reconnect with our original source of creative power. In this exploration, let's consider the experience of consciousness outside of our concept of self. In 'no mind' states, we can step outside of ourselves for a moment to discover alternate realities with direct conscious experience.

MISSION TASK 100: ALL-SELF

In literature about out-of-body experiences (OBEs) and astral projection, it is common to find techniques that require a high level of discipline and focus. Some authors believe that as our focus becomes more refined, we can perceive even more detail, even more subtleties, in the world around us, as well as within. In some esoteric circles, there is a technique called mental projection. This techniques can be used to project our consciousness into an external object in order to experience its core essence (16). For example, focusing our entire consciousness on a candle flame for a few minutes can allow us to embody the flame itself and experience the presence of being in union with the flame. In these instances, consciousness moves from our bodies and into the external realm for a few moments – we literally embody a part of reality that appears outside of ourselves, but a part of the collective whole nonetheless.

Completion Goal I:

Practice the perception mission from the previous exploration again, but this time focus on a living, moving conscious essence, such as a candle flame, or the blades of grass outside, or even another person (ask their permission to practice), or an animal such as a pet dog, for instance. Practice meditating on this conscious being for at least five minutes.

Side Note: There is a great line attributed to Friedrich Nietzsche that applies somewhat here: "if you gaze into the abyss, the abyss gazes also into you." The original wording referred to a sort of prudence and caution when battling our demons, as remaining in battle for too long, we find the demon's essence reflected within ourselves. However, this idea can also be applied to consciousness dynamics. After we spend a long portion of time with a particular person, or animal, or even with a monument at a particular site of significance, we begin to merge consciousness states. Thus, our consciousness is not static, it moves forth and explores the outer realm. As we magnetize our consciousness on a particular aspect of reality, we literally project it forth, a part of us embodies the once seeming external; our consciousness travels outward and expands to encompass a broader scope of experience.

Completion Goal II:

How does the above mission task fit in with your current worldview? Do you believe that your consciousness can transcend the physical body and temporarily embody other experiences, other conscious beings, and other aspects of reality? Did the above mission challenge your experience of self-consciousness? Reflect on whether practicing the mission task above had some kind of impact on how you experience the world, if at all.

MISSION TASK 101: NO-SELF

From an experiential viewpoint, it appears that consciousness is a continuum of experience, rather than a discrete, isolated sense of awareness. Each conscious being in the universe is connected at some level, and we can go even beyond empathizing with others, we can literally embody aspects of their experience and gain a glimpse into their personal shade of consciousness, their local mind-frame.

Let's consider again that there is no single self-construct that reigns over consciousness. Rather, it is from within consciousness that the determinants of self arise. Each of our socially constructed ideas, our language, our logic systems, our inner maps of the world, arise within consciousness, these concepts never exist in isolation. Therefore, from a philosophical point of view, we can consider that there is no such thing as a constructed self, or, at least, not a permanent constructed self. In unlimited variations, consciousness can move from experience to experience, each time witnessing the world in a new light. Therefore, the constructed self can be seen as a limited embodiment of conscious experience in the local mind.

Completion Goal:

Reflect on the following question: Who would I be without a constructed self to hold my identity together?

Side Note: Although we have considered similar variations of the above mission task throughout this book, it is important to ask ourselves this question at least a few times throughout life. As we unravel the determinants of the constructed self, it becomes quite clear just how flexible and mutable our conscious experience is. The fixation on the constructed self is indeed, a decision, a reflection of our free will, rather than an imposed threshold of conscious experience that is somehow dictated by an unseen external power.

MISSION TASK 102: META MIND CONNECTION

There is a prevalent belief in our world that the constructed self is self-sustaining. However, it is in fact consciousness which drives all of our experience and sustains them, not the constructed self. The constructed self externalizes its connection to the super-conscious, it turns to gods and ultimate authorities that would claim to rule over life experience. On the other hand, the awakened individual has a perpetual connection to the higher mind, a transpersonal connection that transcends the constructed self.

Completion Goal:

Reflect on the following question: 'Do I have a strong sense of connection to a higher consciousness experience beyond the personal self?'

Side Notes:

An interesting example that can extend this mission task is that of prayer. Those who surrender their connection to intuition in place of an external power such as religion, tend to believe that their single solace can be found by attending church meetings, and praying to an external God. It is interesting that when most people pray, they ask God for something, whether it is more money, more happiness, or more success in life. This is quite disempowering, and reinforces the process of surrendering our transpersonal connection to the higher cosmic mind. From a perspective of discursive freedom, people perceive God as a force outside of themselves that might decide to grant their prayers sometimes, and at other times might choose to punish them are not grant their prayers. From a perspective of ultimate freedom, we can recognize God, and all higher expressions of consciousness within ourselves, these states of higher connection were never separate from us. The cosmic mind moves in union with the local mind – our personal experience of consciousness.

There is no division, or seeming gap between the seemingly two minds (local and cosmic). The separation of God and man depicted in da Vinci's portrait is a construct that reflects the sadness we feel from this seeming disconnect between the material and the ethereal. However, it is the constructed self that disconnect us from continuous conscious experience, not God. Higher states of consciousness could never be disconnected from our material experience, as our material experiences are contained within the continuum of consciousness.

From this stance, all prayer is a call to move into alignment with our higher self, or our higher mind connection. Therefore, a good alternative prayer (to the standard process of asking God for help) would be to offer gratitude for the guidance that is ever-present in our lives, delivered via our intuitive capacities. Perhaps a better method of prayer would be to ask how we can best recognize our intuitive connection, or better yet, what we can do to enrich the world, rather than what this higher force can do for us (to serve our own ego). This approach is a much more empowering process than traditional methods of asking for help from an external force.

In this mission task, aim to come to an experiential understanding your connection to broader states of conscious experience. Reflect on how direct spiritual transcendence experiences contrast with conceptions of transcendence in religious and spiritual ideals.

MISSION TASK 103: PURE STATES

Completion Goal:

Recall five states of consciousness that you have experienced that seemed to arise outside of your sense of self. These could include a state of love, compassion, or gratitude, for instance. These states tend to stand out, in that we seem to forget about ourselves during these moments and become immersed in the conscious experience that overtakes our entire being – it is as though the overall feeling of love, compassion, or gratitude overpowers our sense of self.

MISSION TASK 104: QUINTESSENTIAL NATURE

In philosophy, there is a term called 'quiddity,' which refers to the essential nature of a given object, person, or state. If you could boil down your entire self-experience to a single feeling, or state of being, what would that feeling be? What is your essential quality of consciousness? Reflect.

Completion Goal:

Repeat the practice in mission task 100 ('All-Self'), but this time, throughout the process notice whether you can connect with the overall core energy of the people or objects that you practice with during the task. You might also like to refer back to mission task 77 ('Relational Impact') in Chapter Six, as that mission task builds up to the present task.

Side Note: In my experience of practicing the earlier task of transferring awareness from my own body to the external environment, I have found a particular spaces, objects, and individuals contain a certain core energy, an overall feeling or sense that emanates from their being – a soul essence, if you will.

MISSION TASK 105: A VEHICLE FOR CONSCIOUSNESS

The constructed self can be seen as a vehicle for consciousness. We are having the conscious experience of 'me' in this lifetime, but the consciousness itself that drives that experience is not limited to the parameters of 'me.' All planes of existence, the underlying unconscious, the imaginative super-conscious, and all dimensions in between, are accessible, once we learn to explore the depths of our experience past the constructed ego. This process shows us that we are more than just our behaviors, our emotions, our thoughts, we are the consciousness that experiences the art that is the imagined self.

In most fast-paced societies, people are preoccupied with moving from task to task, without taking a moment to stop, and just to observe life unfold. In our culture we have developed an addiction of attempting to control reality, to shape it to our personalized perception. However, there can be much wisdom in stepping back and observing our experiences and the bigger picture, recognizing that we are just a vehicle for consciousness in this lifetime.

Completion Goal:

Spend 10 minutes of time during the day tomorrow in passive observation. Instead of becoming engaged in any particular tasks, emotions, or thoughts, step back and observe how your reality unfolds in front of you when you are not perpetually engaged and preoccupied with it. Note any interesting results that you have with this mission task.

CHAPTER EIGHT

OUR HIGHER MIND POTENTIAL

The bounds of a person's inner power reach further
than the boundaries of their self-image.

Several centuries ago in a small village along the coastline, a man was born with total blindness, he could not see through either of his eyes. He had no idea what it would be like to see. However, the man did not feel as though he had lost anything, because he had no experience of what it is like to be able to see in the first place. He became accustomed to his version of reality, which visual perception was not a part of.

At dawn, one morning the man woke up, and something amazing happened. For the first time, he opened his eyes and saw the ceiling above him. He stood up and walked toward the window. He could see the ocean in the distance with 20/20 clarity. He felt astounded by all of the new objects and scenes around him, he walked outside and sat on chair on his veranda. He watched the sun rise, as it illuminated more and more of the world around him with color, tone, and texture. The world came to life for the first time, and he was there to witness it.

The process that the man underwent opened his entire reality to a new level of conscious experience. For the first time, he began to perceive the world around him with a new sense, soaking up all of the new sensory information and experiences around him. This tale is analogous with the experience of opening our connection to broader states of consciousness. There is so much more in the world than most of us can perceive. Although we have clear physical sight, we lack spiritual sight – we are blind to the subtle aspects of our reality that is all around us. The experience of spiritual awakening can be likened to discovering a new sense, realizing what we had been missing out on the entire time.

Most people's basic understanding of the physical world is grounded within a five sensory model, and most mainstream scientists believe that consciousness arises from an interplay of neural activity and perception through the five senses. However, throughout this book, I have been considering the possibility that consciousness could precede the development of the intellect, and perhaps even tangible matter. This would suggest that the material realm arises from within consciousness, and that the five senses are just one means of perceiving the world.

Exploring such a prospect is discouraged in the mainstream, as we tend to perceive the world through the five senses alone, never imagining that there could be something beyond our perception; we are taught to settle for the worldview that we have. This is fair enough, as the man in the metaphor above would not have anticipated what it was like to see, before he experienced the visual world for the first time. Likewise, people who tend to perceive the world in a logical, ordered fashion, often emphatically state that they will only begin to believe in something once they perceive it with their own eyes. This is quite a deceptive approach, as we perceive through the mental models that we have acquired throughout our lifetime.

During transcendence experiences, individuals often report encounters with the extended mind. These individuals find that abilities such as telepathic communication, out-of-body experiences (OBEs), and deep spiritual healing experiences become quite possible. In this chapter, I would like to explore the notion of extra-sensory perception (ESP); that is, perception beyond the five ordinary senses, and how this relates to transcendental states. Like in the account above, when we experience a broader spectrum of self-awareness, the limitations that we once perceived begin to vanish. In these moments of transcendence, we experience a broader world, beyond five-sense perception.

Hence, transcendence experiences illustrate that our entire reality is much vaster than we believe at the constructed intellectual level. Individuals who report the existence of a sixth sense, or extrasensory abilities such as telepathic communication, clairvoyance, and precognition, are often labelled as frauds and liars in our world; however these abilities do exist, but these experiences do not fit into our current five-sense mode of perception. These potentials are unseen, whilst we remain trapped within a finite construct of the world, with our eyes closed.

Over the previous seven chapters we have considered how transcendence experiences can help us to reconnect with a deeper part of ourselves, a part outside of the social and cultural constructs that we live in. Throughout those chapters, we explored 1) the construction of an intellectualized self, 2) how myth and symbolism reinforces certain realities, 3) the fluid, rather than fixed, nature of our personality, 4) the conscious source of our emotions, 5) the true power of the awakened individual, 6) conscious connections in relationships, and 7) the nature of ultimate freedom.

In this chapter, I would like to change track somewhat and focus on some of the higher potentials of the awakened mind. These higher mind encounters are perhaps some of the more interesting experiences we can have as human beings. Phenomena such as cosmic synchronicities, mind-over-matter interaction, and psychic encounters can be experienced firsthand once we master our connection to the broader collective mind.

Though most strict materialists deem these extended mind abilities impossible, the debate concerning the connection between the material and the non-material has long continued throughout the ages. It is a shame that most modern societies accept the materialist-reductionist perspective without even considering for a brief section, the alternative. Hence, rather than filling this book with anecdotes from individuals who have had spiritual awakening experiences, astral travel voyages into other realms of consciousness, and expressions of psychic abilities that challenge our concept of what is and is not possible, I have aimed to take a different approach throughout here.

As there are thousands of books available on these topics, I have aimed to cultivate a curiosity and interest in these topics here, so that you might have a starting point for conscious exploration after completing this chapter. So, although I will touch on a few anecdotes and case experiences in this chapter, I encourage readers to consider how these experiences relate to our consciousness potential, rather than categorizing these as rare, or near-impossible, instances. In fact, each human being is capable of awakening their higher mind potential, and we can learn how to do so.

SUBTLE MINDS: METAPHORS

During transcendence experiences, people often speak about a state of no-self. A sense of consciousness, or presence, remains; but their personality, their constructed ego, is no longer present. These accounts are quite interesting, as in meditation it is also possible to achieve a state of mind in which the constructed self is no longer present. No sense of self that remains in such states, but a distinct presence of consciousness remains and never fades.

In considering these experiences, it makes little sense to discuss consciousness as though it is something that can be created or destroyed, rather consciousness appears to fluctuate between two states – conscious and unconscious, guided by our focused awareness. In experiences of no-self, it is possible to come into contact with the super-conscious mind, or the all-mind. These meta-mind experiences illustrate that our experience of the world is just a droplet in an infinite ocean of possibilities. Before we get started with these explorations, I would like to explore two metaphors for the super-conscious mind, these will serve as a framework for some of the later ideas in this chapter. The first metaphor relates to how we tend to separate our individual conscious experience from the greater collective whole, and the second metaphor relates to how we can traverse the consciousness divide that we construct on an intellectual level.

The constructed self appears to act as a self-sustaining force, as though it is somehow separate from the remainder of the universe. People tend to believe that their consciousness is contained in an individualistic, separate mind of their own. There is a false belief prominent in our world that suggests each individual generates a separate consciousness with no direct connection to the greater collective conscious field. In fact, this separation is contrived. There is no separation when it comes to consciousness, apart from the separation that we choose to experience via a subjective lens of perception. In that sense, consciousness is continuous, not contingent upon separate minds, or separate selves that would aim to differentiate it. Mind cannot be plural, in that sense. However, the collective mind is limitless in expression, thus giving rise to limitless embodiments of experience.

Alan Watts purported that there is no such thing as self-consciousness, but rather, just consciousness. The sense of self we attach to the idea of consciousness is an illusion, a fractal of all potential possibilities, so to speak. We fall for the allure of the societal conditioning about this idea of an all-encompassing self-construct. But, we can observe that the conceptualization of the self, as a separate self-sustaining consciousness, is flawed, as it depends on social reinforcement. For instance, in a number of Eastern cultures, we can see a distinct move from an individualistic, self-based consciousness, to a more holistic awareness of the collective or societal consciousness. There is much less emphasis on a self-sustained individual in such societies. Hence, our self-construct is mediated by consciousness, it is not self-sustained as we might believe.

This emphasis on reinforcing the constructed self seems to be more pronounced in capitalist societies, in which we have formed a sort of megalomania and we praise the self as a sovereign god – the single judge of life experience. This is problematic, as we have imagined ourselves in a limited light, rather than recognizing the limitless nature of conscious experience that cannot be contained to a particular form. We can draw lines around ourselves. We can form a box. We can point to that box with great conviction and tell our neighbors that all that exists is in that box: Me, in my box of self. However, the truth is that raw conscious experience cannot be contained. We fool ourselves into thinking that consciousness can be encased, through creating rigid and limited outlines around our direct life experience. In recognizing this, we can still express ourselves through the mode of the constructed self, but we can also re-imagine this construct in a new light if we choose, we can change it and transcend it, as we recognize that we are not 'just that.'

Metaphor 1 (Circles and Lines): Imagine that I take out a blank piece of paper and pen and draw a circle right in the middle. Next, I take a ruler and draw a vertical line down the middle of the circle to split it into two parts. Then, I take the same ruler and draw a horizontal line to form four quadrants to the circle. I continue drawing lines until there are dozens of parts to the original circle. This circle represents the higher mind, or the super-conscious mind, as we might like to call it. It contains all human potential and broader possibilities. However, we segment our experience of consciousness to create a self-consciousness, which resides in one of the separate quadrants of the circle, it seems separated from the rest of the circle. This quadrant represents the constructed self. It's worth considering that we still know on some level that it is possible to blur these lines to experience the broader range of consciousness all around us. At least, we have an intuitive sense that this is possible, although most might maintain the illusion that the lines are absolute and immovable.

In this metaphor I have aimed to build on Alan Watt's ideas, not in rejecting the notion of the individual self altogether, but rather suggesting that our self-consciousness is more malleable than we might at first grant. Instead of looking within, we often get caught up in the images that other people project. We focus on establishing differences and harsh lines around conscious experience, rather than transcending those boundaries to experience raw connections at the broader mind level.

It is the constructed intellectual mind that differentiates and finds difference. At the direct consciousness level, there is no difference, there is no gradation, just continuum. This is a useful metaphor to consider when exploring how the constructed mind limits our direct conscious experience. Rigid lines that delineate the self also limit our potential for growth, expansion, and change. If we believe that the segment of the circle is all there is, then no true connection between two individuals can form, because each remains in a separate chamber and asserts their own sense of self. To become vulnerable, to blur the line, is quite a courageous feat.

Metaphor 2 (Embodiment): In the motion picture 'The Matrix,' we are introduced to the protagonist (Neo) who connects his brain to a computer after exiting the Matrix; Neo finds that he must re-learn all of the basic skills, such as walking and breathing. In connecting his brain to a computer device, he then literally downloads new skills, abilities, and insights within seconds to his local mind. He learns kung fu and other specific skills almost instantly, as the information downloads to his individual awareness within seconds. Then, we see Neo use the skills within minutes of learning them. Neo becomes the kung fu master, without taking a single kung fu class in the traditional sense of learning. This process of learning is analogous with downloading knowledge and wisdom from the super-conscious mind.

In relation to our discussion in Chapter Two, we can consider that all knowledge exists on some level, although we might not be aware of it in our present state of mind – the knowledge exists somewhere, it just does not have essence. Recall how in Chapter Six, we considered that all power arises from the individual soul. It is not the words in a book that have meaning in themselves, their power acquires essence when a conscious being interacts with the words and enriches them with meaning. Even during school and college, the learning process occurs in a mediation of minds, not on the printed text in a book or the images on a lecture slide as such. The words in themselves have no meaning. Meaning does not exist in libraries or books, but rather meaning is created through conscious interaction. It is when consciousness touches the words on a page, meaning comes to life.

There appears a paradox of learning here. Particular spiritual teachers and gurus discuss great wisdom and knowledge, without having attended a single class of school or college, for example. In the emptiness of mind, mind becomes amenable to all knowledge. It is the mind that is full that cannot learn, because it is filled with pre-existing notions that shape the new input, and in fact limit the new input altogether. Thus, this relates to the idea of conscious embodiment in this metaphor.

A few years ago, when I was writing the first draft of this book, my partner, Izabel had an interesting dream experience in which she acquired skills and expertise that she otherwise did not know. In her dream, she was a fighter pilot in the midst of World War II. During the dream she experienced advanced knowledge of military strategies, skills in flying the aircraft, and secret knowledge about how to infiltrate the enemy's base. In a temporal state, she had acquired the mind of a skilled fighter pilot. In dreams, our self-perception often blurs in a similar manner, and sometimes we can even acquire experiences or specialized knowledge that we can no longer access when we wake up, we take on new roles and possibilities that otherwise seem impossible in a regular waking state.

So, how does this relate to the notion of conscious embodiment? Before we consider this, let's reflect on the idea of the constructed self as a set of programmed behaviors, attitudes, and perceptions. In personal development circles, co-developer of Neuro-Linguistic Programming (NLP), Richard Bandler, is a well-known name. However, few people also know that Bandler had a computer science background alongside his psychology qualifications. In fact, Bandler alluded to the make-up of the individual self as analogous to a computer software package, that local mind is constructed via the acquisition of language and ideas, much like the input of ones and zeros of machine language that produce a groundwork for software programming. Bandler developed NLP in order to help people re-program their potential for greater success in life, much like someone would write a computer program to patch or fix a problem with the existing software.

For example, one might practice taking on the mind of an outstanding public speaker, or taking on the mind of an expert basketball player, to improve their performance in each of these skills (this is called modelling in NLP lingo). In that sense, by imagining that we take on the expert mind of those who have already mastered a particular skill, we are more easily able to assimilate these positive qualities into our own self-consciousness. This illustrates the process we covered in Chapter Three, on the power of reimagining ourselves in a new light. However, based on the understanding of the super-conscious mind we have been exploring, this re-imagination and re-learning process takes on a whole new powerful meaning. Doesn't it?

Modern neuroscience has advanced to such an extent that the idea of learning via direct input to the brain-mind does not seem as far-fetched as it once did. The metaphor of the local mind as a form of computer is more relevant now than ever before, as we can program and develop new applications, new filters through which to experience the world and ourselves. In his notable work, 'Prometheus Rising,' Robert Anton Wilson alluded to the following question: If we perceive the functioning of our local mind as a sort of computer software, then who is the programmer?

EXPLORATION: DREAM A NEW WORLD

MISSION TASK 106: OPEN MIND

In the dominant materialist paradigm of our world, we make a presumption that the human mind is a closed mechanism. The thoughts that we experience, we experience in solitude. The emotions that we experience, we experience in solitude, according to this idea. However, research into consciousness suggests that this is not the case. Rather than being a closed system, the local mind is in fact interconnected with a higher, or collective, mind. This notion of an open mind explains experiences of telepathic and empathic communication. And, this also relates to our discussion on relational consciousness fields, in which meaning arises when two conscious beings connect, rather than in local consciousness fields.

Completion Goal:

What is your personal experience of the first metaphor (circles and lines) in this subchapter above? Do you believe that two individuals can bridge the divide, and achieve a union of mind at some level? Have you had experiences such as this personally?

Side Note: Some experiences that might be relevant here include telepathic and empathic communication (knowing or feeling someone's experience without them having to verbalize it, and then later receiving confirmation that this is indeed what the person was thinking or feeling), recurring synchronicities, and other such experiences in which a blurring of lines (of self) occurs.

MISSION TASK 107: TRANCE-FORMED

Remember, in earlier chapters we considered that the constructed self can be quite easily hypnotized into believing that it has certain characteristics, qualities, or even tangible skills? In fact, in many ways, our self-construct is subject to mass hypnosis, the acquisition of particular traits and habits throughout life. A self-aware being is not as subject to this programming, as she recognizes that without conscious consent, no mind changes can occur.

Completion Goal I:

Have you ever had a dream in which you experienced your sense of self differently to how you experience it in everyday life? For instance, you might have had different characteristics or qualities, or you might have been an entirely different person altogether. Reflect on the significance of these experiences in the dream state.

Completion Goal II:

Is learning a process of conscious connection? Reflect. I have found that I learn best when a teacher has embodied the knowledge within their own field of consciousness, and shares their direct experience with others. Teachers who talk about subjects they have no direct firsthand experience with often fail to generate an effective learning environment. An abstract intellectual model is not as easy to understand as a conscious experience shared in an empathic environment. Reflect, to what extent is learning and understanding a process of conscious connection?

MISSION TASK 108: SUPER-CONSCIOUS EXPERIENCES

Learning can also occur in meditation and in stillness of mind. This contradicts the idea that an active, engaged mind, is required for intensive learning. In fact, some of the most profound wisdom comes about in silence, as we tune in, and eavesdrop on the collective mind.

In Zen Buddhist tradition, 'satori' experiences refer to a direct knowing. This is not the knowing of the intellectual mind that thinks it knows. It is the knowing of the soul; the direct, unambiguous, through-and-through understanding. In dreams, the consciousness threshold lowers, and we have a better connection to the super-conscious mind, where these experiences of deep-seated knowing arise. Thus, it could be said that the source of timeless wisdom and creative potential arises from within, not from the external world.

Completion Goal:

Recollect three experiences throughout your lifetime during which you have had a profound sense of wisdom or direct knowing that just seemed to rise without any direct effort on your part, a wisdom that seemed to originate from the depths of your soul.

MISSION TASK 109: COLLECTIVE POTENTIAL PART I

There are particular collective biases in our world that force us into communicating, learning, and experiencing through fixed modes of expression. Yet, within our potential to ask the 'collective miracle question' lies the power to dream a new world (17). In satori moments of wisdom the constructed wall we have built is bypassed, and we temporarily experience a broader potential for wisdom, creation, and experience via the super-conscious mind.

Completion Goal I:

Recollect 10 historical examples in which the world was experienced through a particular, finite lens of perception. For example, in a pre-Copernican world, all people believed that the earth was the center of the universe. Likewise, less than half a century ago minority groups such as people of different races, genders, and sexual preferences were considered sub-human. Even though false nature of these past perceptions might be obvious to us now, we take our current truth for granted in the present moment; this truth was not considered so obvious and plain in our historic past.

Side Note: It is more difficult to perceive some of the ways in which our present world is shaped in front of us. In part, there seems to be a self-serving bias that suggests most of the problems of the past are no longer prevalent in the present. However, in 50 years from now, we will probably look back on our society and find a number of skewed perceptions that are present in our world now. In retrospect, everything is 20/20. But, still, there are a vast aspects of our human experience that we are unaware of, even with all of our modern technologies.

Completion Goal II:

Imagine that you had a time machine and could travel 50 years into the future. What would you see there? In what ways with the world differ from our present world? Reflect on how those living in the future would perceive our present version of life. Come up with 10 potential issues with our world that we might perceive as 'normal' now, that might be perceived as strange and unusual behavior from the vantage point of a more advanced human race.

MISSION TASK 110: COLLECTIVE POTENTIAL PART II

From the perspective of the closed mind, we tend to reinforce the belief that ideas can only arise in local minds. However, some believe that each human being is connected at the collective consciousness level, as this book has been suggesting. The illusion of an isolated local mind is a persistent one, but at some level we do have, and have always had, a direct connection the collective mind. Researchers at the Global Consciousness Project, for example, found that major world events, such as 9/11, caused an impact on our collective consciousness hours before news of the explosions broke. It appears that just as birds flock together in seemingly intuitive patterns, our consciousness also moves in alignment with the collective mind.

In the previous chapter we considered the idea of selflessness, and that is not possible to permanently own anything in the material world. But, what about ideas? Can ideas be owned and claimed by seeming individual minds? There is a phenomena in science, in which the same inventions and discoveries are made by several individuals in quite a close time bracket. Different laboratories, working on different sides of the globe, all make the same discovery, within a period of months, for instance. Although some people chalk this up to plagiarism, theft of ideas, or the fact that it was just a coincidence, there appears to be something more to this.

Ideas appear to spread at a consciousness level. Ideas enter into our local consciousness field, and the greater the number of people looking into a particular facet of consciousness at a given time, the faster that particular dimension of conscious experience opens up. Our collective consciousness hits a critical mass, so to speak, and all people around the globe accept the new, sometimes revolutionary ideas, as inherent truths. Inspiration, creativity, and innovation, appears to arise from a place beyond the constructed self, it is a quality of consciousness that we cannot define or capture.

Based on this observation, it is somewhat bizarre when someone is inspired toward a particular idea, or invention, or a book, or piece of art, and then feels an urge to claim the idea as their own work alone. The selfless, unlimited source of inspiration is then attributed to a temporal self. I've always found this process a bit unusual. In our patent-driven law-obsessed world, we tend to insist that ideas and imagination arises from the constructed self, when in fact, these moments of inspiration come about when we open our minds to a broader consciousness, the super-conscious mind within which all ideas and potentialities reside.

Completion Goal I:

Recollect three experiences of synchronicity in your life. For example, you might have just been thinking about a particular person and they called you or sent you a message a moment later. Or, if you have ever had a very unique idea, have you noticed others around you also talking about a similar topic or idea that related to your thoughts? How do these experiences fit into our discussion so far?

Completion Goal II:

Reflect on the following question: Can an idea belong to a person?

Completion Goal III:

Reflect on the main ideas or worldviews that we perpetuate at the collective consciousness level in our world. Recollect five main ideas that we perpetuate about the potential of the mind, the nature of self, and the experience of human consciousness. How do people conceptualize these notions in particular social groups, religions, or societal structures?

Completion Goal IV:

Reflect on 10 ways in which this book has challenged some of the above ideas about the potential of the mind, the nature of self, and the experience of human consciousness.

MISSION TASK III: IMAGINATION AS CREATION

As a collective whole, we tend to reinforce certain realities in our world, while negating others. This is the reason that is so important to cultivate the archetypes of the artist, the hermit, the creative revolutionary in our world. When we move as a flock, we tend to only follow the ideas that the authorities in place dictate – governments, religions, lawmakers, and so forth. But, to deviate from the flock, is to perceive the world in a new light, and to reinvent the world, in fact. But, this process is not about bolstering the constructed self through one's inventions or unique achievements, it is the process of conscious creation for its own sake. It is a process of recognizing that as a collective, there are infinite possibilities that we can create.

Completion Goal:

Is there a particular hobby, or task that you are involved in, where you can express your creative energy without boundaries? If so, remind yourself of the importance of cultivating this inner space of creative expression. If not, consider finding an outlet, a quiet place, or an activity, in which you can express and explore your creativity.

Side Note: In our society, introspective and creative pursuits are often discouraged, as from schooling we are taught that group-work is much more important than individual exploration. However, this reinforces more linear ways of perceiving the world, and discourages more abstract, creative approaches. Therefore, although these pursuits are often looked down upon in our world, it is worthwhile to remind ourselves of the true value of inner creative exploration. Likewise, if you do not have a particular task or activity as a creative outlet, it can be worthwhile to think back to childhood and to recall some of your creative interests back then, as most of us are inclined toward more creative pursuits earlier on in life.

EXTENDED MIND CAPABILITIES

Each fortnight, I send out a newsletter to the subscribers at my website, and I usually receive a handful of responses with some reflections, experiences, and thoughts. In response to one of my newsletters a few years ago, a woman had e-mailed me with a fascinating story of how she spontaneously developed a number of psychic abilities. The woman spoke of an experience of being electrocuted in her basement while accidently touching a metal light with her wet hand. The electricity jolted through her whole body, and for whatever reason, this seemed to open her awareness to a new level of mind potential. Since the experience, she reported that she was able to see people's auras with little effort, and had recurring clairvoyant visions of the future. From her vantage point, it was almost like a light switch had been flicked on in her mind, and she suddenly had all of these extended mind abilities open.

Potentials of the mind such as these are more common than most people believe. It is, however, easy to fall for the notion that only those born with a natural gift or exceptional saints or gurus can cultivate abilities such as these. This could not be further from the truth. In fact, I believe that we are all capable of learning how to work with extraordinary consciousness states such as these – it is a matter of mind exploration, and understanding the mind-brain connection.

The shamanic-like mind state that Jill Bolte Taylor experienced after her stroke also points to a meta-mind experience that comes about when our brain processes either slow down or become incapacitated for a brief moment (11). In her various talks, interviews, and written accounts, Taylor paints a narrative of super-conscious states of expanded awareness, universal love and connection, as pre-existing aspects of our life experience, and not the result of malfunctioning in brain chemistry. It is rather the intellectual mind that anesthetizes us from having these experiences, as well as psychic, and exceptional mind potentials. But, these potentialities exist all the while, awaiting our awareness, awaiting our recognition.

It is well known in literature that individuals who have near-death experiences (NDEs) or those who experiment with mind-altering substances, report psychical experiences such as this more often than those in the general population do. This is not surprising, as both NDEs and mind-altering substances affect the brain in such a manner that the local mind seems to become dislodged in terms of the mind-brain connection. This is what occurred in the case of the woman who e-mailed me with her account, as well as in Taylor's case. Free to roam, our consciousness is boundless. But, it is not psychic and transcendent experiences themselves that produce these exceptional phenomena, it is rather that the experiences uncover what was present all along, beneath the surface – our broader consciousness.

Those individuals who have not had transcendence experiences firsthand, and have not yet recognized the exceptional capabilities of the mind, often question my interest in these particular psychic faculties of consciousness. However, from my perspective, an interest in this area of inquiry is inevitable. Some people argue that the human experience, as it is, is enough, and pose the question: Why should we look for more? Yet, the broader conscious experience shows us that the mind is capable of so much more, both in terms of transcendent emotional and spiritual connection, and in terms of psychical abilities such as feats of mind-over-matter. These faculties reflect our true nature at a deeper level, as it is the transpersonal nature of consciousness to traverse individual minds, and at the core of it, we are conscious beings, not mere egoic minds.

After a person has recognized the power of the mind firsthand, questioning their interest in this area of investigation is pointless. Doing so is tantamount to asking a basketball player why he chooses to tie one hand behind his back and only use the other hand for the entire game. These mind capabilities are accessible to each conscious being, but most people ignore them outright, as our awareness has been enraptured by the limited constructed mind.

Rather than endeavoring toward a process of developing our mind capabilities, we might see this as more of a process uncovering, recognizing within ourselves a broader mind connection. Michael Thalbourne's idea of transliminality suggests that psychological content flows in and out of local and the broader states of consciousness. These higher potentials seep through the super-conscious mind, and into one's local conscious experience, if one is willing enough, open enough.

So, what are higher mind abilities? In his book 'The End of Materialism,' Charles Tart suggests that the five more well-documented psychic abilities include: Telepathy (mind-to-mind communication), clairvoyance (perception outside of time-space constraints), precognition (intuitive knowledge of future events), psychokinesis (mind-over-matter), and psychic healing (physical, emotional, and spiritual healing via non-physical means).

Scientists have attempted to explain these abilities by considering that these mind potentials could have something to do with subtle non-physical energy transfer. This is not a particularly new idea, as the idea of subtle energy has been alluded to in many Eastern traditions. For example, the word 'prana' (Sanskrit) and 'chi' (in traditional Chinese culture) refers to subtle energy. In the West, we tend to use the word 'psi' to refer to these energetic processes that enable mind-over-matter abilities.

As we considered in Chapter Six, the nature of consciousness itself is energetic, it is ever expansive. Therefore, I believe that a number of these exceptional experiences relate to an expansion of consciousness. It is through our consciousness that we infuse the world with certain energies and core ideas that shape our overall life experience. Although certain psychic abilities might seem bizarre or difficult to conceptualize, this is often the case because our worldview is quite limited, and most mainstream cultures tend to reject even the potential existence of alternative states of conscious experiences such as these.

Our connection to the ethereal, to the psychic dimensions, is sublimated in most modern cultures. The inherent power of the mind is rejected, in place of the power of the external object. The dreamer is often mocked in the West, as artists and dreamers are perceived as time-wasters in our fast-paced culture. Yet, it is the dreamers who shape the world. In traditional shamanic practices, psychic rituals and conscious dreaming states are revered for their immense wisdom, for their potential to illuminate the numinous, to bring to light the broader spectrum of conscious potential. For example, as Graham Hancock has pointed out in his work, our Western culture reveres intellect stimulants, while suppressing and making illegal substances that expand one's consciousness. The mind illusion is enforced, whilst generating a soul connection to consciousness is ignored.

Drugs such as coffee, alcohol, and cigarettes are so common in the modern world, and these all cause much more harm than consciousness-activating entheogens such as the ayahuasca plant and psilocybin mushrooms. The latter are outlawed, with hefty penalties of up to 25 years in state prison having been enforced for possessing them, even though these substances cause minimum harm to individuals, with a much greater benefit than stimulants that we depend on in our world (18). The core difference between stimulants and entheogens is that the former help us become more efficient workers, and that the latter assist us in opening the doors of consciousness, but serve no real benefit to the worker-society mindset, thus we seem to deem them unimportant. We live in an adrenaline culture. But, we have forgotten how to dream.

Graham Hancock often discusses his use of certain substances such as marijuana and the ayahuasca plant in order to cultivate states of human creative potential. Such substances cause certain left-brain processes to slow down, and this allows us to reconnect with the cosmic, super-conscious mind; thus, these substances cause our consciousness threshold to expand on a temporal basis. This is perhaps the reason that much of the work done by shamans and healers documented in ancient cultures involved the use of entheogens such as the ayahuasca plant. Shamans used these plants in order to cultivate a waking-dream state in which communication with one's soul aspect, our higher self, became possible. Yet, entheogen-induced spiritual experiences can often be quite temporal. David Hawkins suggested certain substances serve as a shortcut to transcendental states, but we can in fact also establish a connection to these higher thresholds of consciousness on a more permanent basis without depending on these external substances.

This psychic ability that seems so mysterious in esoteric circles, is in fact just an extension of the awakened conscious mind; these higher mind potentials are accessible to all. Based on personal practice, I have found that a number of exceptional human abilities are possible when we refine our focus and perceive things at a much more subtle level. In our world, people often behave as though they are living in overdrive, in constant stress. These stimulated states seem to tune out our connection to subtle energies, and to psychic experiences. On the other hand, when we meditate, focus, and open up our consciousness, our higher mind connection becomes more prominent. The world is no longer a distraction, and the link to the super-conscious mind becomes clearer in these states.

Let's consider the example of healing, for instance. In his work 'Be Here Now,' Ram Dass spoke about the interconnectedness of all conscious being. He offered the example of the parent who ignores his child when the child is screaming in the back seat of the car. Ram Dass then contrasted this to a parent who stops the car and gives the child his undivided attention. Just by giving others our full and complete attention and awareness, we cultivate a healing quality. This process has nothing to do with the intellectual mind, it is an intuitive healing process. Attention, compassion, and awareness have healing qualities in themselves. The power of clear perception and attention is a healing force.

Healing at the soul-level can be extended even further, however. In his book, Quantum-Touch, Richard Gordon posits that life-force energy exists all around us. Remember how we explored this idea briefly in Chapter Six, when we considered that the human consciousness field is sensitive to external energies? We can cultivate our awareness of core energies in healing and creative expression once we learn how to notice their subtle presence. There are a number of modalities that teach techniques along these lines, such as Quantum-Touch, Reiki, Qi Gong, and

Pranic Healing. As we refine our attention and tune to the presence of these subtle energies, it's possible to become aware of just how wide the applications here are.

It is pointless to debate whether these exceptional mind abilities exists or not, it is much more worthwhile to test their existence firsthand, and to form an empirical understanding. Just as in the example of hands-on healing above, mind abilities such as clairvoyance (clear seeing, or clear sight) can also be learned with practice. It's important to remember that the conscious being is unlimited in expression, but the curriculum that we are taught in our schooling is quite finite and limited to subjects that reinforce linear, left-brain thinking (note, that even at college and university, there are only a handful of higher learning institutions around the world that teach experiential parapsychology, the study of psychic phenomena).

As most people experience a discord between the conscious and unconscious mind, clairvoyance and psychic information is difficult to interpret, as our unconscious impressions at first appear ambiguous, dreamlike, and scattered. However, as we learn how to interpret data from the unconscious and super-conscious mind, we can begin to understand, at the intuitive level, how abilities such as clairvoyance function. In the 'The Happiness Hike,' J Lowet introduces a number of techniques for opening our visual perception centers to clairvoyant information, for example.

Incidentally, I based a number of my earlier workshops around Lowet's ideas on cultivating visual information from the unconscious mind. In addition, I also used some of the ideas from Elkhonon Goldberg's book, 'The Executive Brain,' which suggests that, with conscious intention, we can exercise the frontal lobes of our brain in order to enhance our executive functioning (such as enhancing abstract, conceptual, and spatial thinking abilities). Indeed, we can also place our conscious attention on different areas of physiology, in order to 'activate' them, so to speak. Neil Slade's technique of 'tickling the amygdala' to trigger states of mental bliss is another example (19). The old proverb "where attention goes, energy flows," is empirically observable, as our consciousness can in fact influence physical matter, once we learn to read and understand its subtle nuances and movements.

J Lowet's techniques in 'The Happiness Hike,' for example, illustrate that with visual experiments we can strengthen our propensity for visualization and clairvoyance. For instance, focusing on a candle flame in a dimly-lit room, and then closing one's eyes in order to perceive the afterglow of the flame can be an effective technique to stimulate one's visualization. Through visualization and image streaming practice, it is possible to, in time, perceive geometric patterns, visual impressions, and even intuitive information in our mind's eye (20). In more advanced practices, it is even possible to trick the mind into perceiving the environment around us while our eyes are shut. From a limited perspective, this might seem impossible. But, if we grant that consciousness can travel beyond the physical body, this is much more tenable.

There are other techniques that can also be used to cultivate imagery from the super-conscious mind. For example, some individuals use mirrors in order to project inward imagery and psychic insights onto a mirror in front of them. Gnostic Master Samael Aun Weor spoke of perceiving rich motion-picture like visuals on his wall as a child (see his book, 'The Three Mountains'). Researchers such as Paul Schenk have used hypnotic induction techniques to bring about 'waking dreams' in which one's consciousness travels to a different plane of mental or emotional awareness in order to facilitate a connection to higher wisdom (see Schenk's book, 'The Hypnotic Use of Waking Dreams'). It is common to connect with streams of conscious information outside of ourselves in this manner. However, most of us filter this process, and instead, just focus on our immediate experience of the constructed self.

Lucid dreaming can also be used to facilitate this process. In lucid dreams it is possible to travel to other dimensions in which esoteric and deeper knowledge is accessible to us. Most of us experience dreams as a montage of random images, environments that seem to make much sense at all. Most of the time, we are completely unconscious during dreams. However, individuals who have trained themselves to cultivate lucid dreams, have found that their experience of dreams becomes much more solid, consistent, and conscious. In a number of lucid dreams that I have experienced, I recall that the dream environment felt even more real and vivid than the normal waking state of consciousness. In this way, dreams show us that there is a much broader reality beyond what we can experience here and now. The dream realm is a world in and of itself, and not just the aggregation of images and ideas that come from the unconscious mind.

Prophetic and symbolic dreams can be foreboding of things to come, for instance (for example, dreaming of an event, and then finding that event comes to pass a few days from now). In Anthony Peake's work 'A Life of Philip K Dick,' Peake explored the notion that many of Philip K Dick's inspirations came from a direct source of information from the future. Likewise, we can reflect on da Vinci's sketches of seeming tanks and helicopters. Time is not as linear as we might believe. At a cosmic consciousness level, all information is accessible, outside of time-space constraints. Yet, we tend to devalue the meaning of our dreams, and thus our connection with the unconscious realm is often distorted, we have forgotten how to trust that deeper part of ourselves, that intuitive connection.

The common narrative that suggests these mind potentials are rare and experienced by the selected few is not particularly helpful, as our connection to this cosmic source of insight is ever-present, most of us have just lost awareness of it. Awakening to our spiritual and psychical abilities is an empowering process, and it is not a process that we should depend upon books or teachers alone in exploring. The knowledge, and insight, and mind abilities, are within us at a deeper level, and this becomes quite evident when we look past the constructed self and into our hearts, into the depths of our souls for meaning.

To sum up this subchapter, let's consider again how our perception of the world has been shaped in a particular light. Human beings are so consumed with the mechanics of their lives, that they have disconnected themselves from their intuition. Their consciousness has been sublimated in religious belief, and their access to external avenues for spiritual exploration has either been suppressed or replaced with mind-numbing drugs and engrained societal rituals. Therefore, even at a subtle level, we are disconnected from the natural world. Human beings have predetermined their scope of experience based on the mind illusion – it feeds us images of what we ought to fear, what we ought to love, and how we ought to live. This illusion has been superimposed over our essential being. At a deeper level, we have sublimated essential empathic and telepathic connection with our fellow beings for the construct of language; our centers for dreaming, for clairvoyance and imagination, have likewise been shut down.

Thus, it's essential that we re-empower ourselves and ask the important questions about our mind potential. In fact, we are not mere flesh and blood and bone interacting with a material canvas, our minds have some reign over matter and direct life experience. At the deepest level of psychological programming, we can recognize that our reality is very subtly shaped by the main cultural and social paradigms in which we were brought up in. However, it is important to recognize that these were never true reflections of our original, innate center of consciousness, but rather temporal means of interacting with the external world.

The value of cherishing one's direct experience cannot be found in the generic ability to choose between path A and path B, but it is rather found in knowing oneself and finding one's unique purpose in life. This comes down to questioning the presumptions we have been taught throughout our lives about the limits of the human mind. Thus, we must develop of fortitude of will, the recognition that our personal experience of consciousness is sovereign, it is no-one else's, and no external construct, no matter how powerful, can ever replicate or constrain it. Independence of mind (independent thought) is critical in that regard. However, the process toward ultimate empowerment is not just about achieving independent thought, it is also about having the courage to feel our personal emotions and to act on them despite external pressures: It is about discovering our own path, rather than finding a pre-set path relative to the mainstream paradigm. It is about generating new fields of collective conscious experience, rather than re-propagating our existing paradigms over and over.

EXPLORATION: THE EXTENDED MIND

Your mission is to uncover some of the hidden abilities of the human mind, and to come to an experiential understanding of how these abilities can enrich our potential in this lifetime. Can these higher mind abilities be cultivated?

MISSION TASK 112: PARAPSYCHOLOGIST FOR A DAY

Pretend that you are a parapsychologist for a day (an investigator into paranormal and psychical activity).

Completion Goal I:

Have you had any personal experiences with the following psychic mind abilities: Telepathy (mind-to-mind communication), clairvoyance, precognition (intuitive knowledge of future events), psychokinesis (mind-over-matter, such as moving an object with the power of the mind), or hands-on healing? If so, how did those experiences influence your perspective on life? Reflect.

Completion Goal II:

Ask three of your closest friends if they have ever had any personal experiences with the following psychic mind abilities: Telepathy (mind-to-mind communication), clairvoyance, precognition (intuitive knowledge of future events), psychokinesis (mind-over-matter, such as moving an object with the power of the mind), or hands-on healing. Then, ask them how those experiences influenced their perspective on life, if at all.

Completion Goal III:

Choose one of the techniques discussed in this subchapter and explore that technique in more depth by locating at least 10 articles about the approach via the world-wide-web (for example: Hands-on healing, image streaming, waking dreams, and so forth).

Side Note: Reflect on how the articles you read can be considered in terms of the main ideas presented in this subchapter – that is, the notion that we can connect with and foster these abilities with the power of conscious intention.

MISSION TASK 113: PARADIGMS

Completion Goal:

Read 'Appendix A: Double Standard Skepticism.' Reflect on how the ideas in that appendix relate to our discussion on human consciousness.

MISSION TASK 114: LIBERATED HEARTS

Completion Goal:

Read 'Appendix B: The Transpersonal Dream.' Reflect on how the ideas in that appendix relate to our discussion on human consciousness.

TRANSCENDENCE

The conscious soul is undervalued in our materialism-centered world. Its qualities of universal love, compassion, and empathic connection, are seldom explored in our cultural discourses. Instead of exploring the unique experiences of self-transcendence and soul-connection, we tend to bloat the constructed self to extremes.

In meditation, it soon becomes clear that the nuances and movements of the conscious soul can be distinguished from the mechanistic superimposed movements of the constructed self. There is a certain rhythm, a certain flow that is present in direct, human conscious experience. The mechanics of the constructed self appear robotic, repetitive, and born from fixed constructs, while the soul experience of unadulterated consciousness is ever-expansive with each new moment: Unlimited, in the ultimate sense of the word.

Yet, too often the subtle rhythms of consciousness are sublimated with our tightly-held mask of self, with its own contrived rules and self-sustaining logic. In masking our ultimate experience, we sever our connection to our emotional and spiritual centers. We live in a world governed and informed by an intellectually-driven, rather than an emotionally and spiritually-driven, focus.

What then, has come of transcendence? The notion of transcendence, of courageous spiritual exploration, has been driven to the obscure corners of religion and esoterica; it is ignored by the many, revered by some, and experienced by only the few.

Direct experiences of transcendence and reconnecting with our spiritual center, are meanwhile seldom explored from a practical perspective. It is, however, encouraging to see the growth of new fields in psychology, such as the exploration of peak and flow consciousness states in positive psychology, and the growing recognition of ideas from the field of transpersonal psychology in the mainstream. Nonetheless, the impetus to explore our consciousness remains within our hands.

> We can use mindfulness to 'wake up,' connect with ourselves, and appreciate the fullness of each moment of life. We can use it to improve our self-knowledge – to learn more about how we feel and think and react. We can use it to connect deeply and intimately with the people we care about, including ourselves. And we can use it to consciously influence our own behavior and increase our range of responses to the world we live in. It is the art of living consciously – a profound way to enhance psychological resilience and increase life satisfaction.
>
> – Russ Harris

In the above passage, Russ Harris discusses the benefits of meta-perception, of recognizing that it is a content-free conscious perception that drives the constructed self, that there is a conscious essence behind each of our thoughts, emotions, and behaviors. In cultivating more mindful states, more peak states of consciousness, we break free from the herd mindset, the indoctrinated self, and we rediscover our broader transcendent potential.

Robert Anton Wilson believed that there is an inherent quality in consciousness to expand and explore new frontiers of experience. Wilson believed that there are much better odds that our world will become more open to higher states of conscious experience in the near future, rather than descending into a dystopic prison that is so often depicted in modern post-apocalyptic motion pictures. However, the perpetual exploration of higher states cannot just be left to governments, nor religions, nor even scientists. Each one of us must go inward and discover for ourselves, the true meaning of transcendence, and the essence of our deeper-level conscious experience. We must question the confined self, and break from our preconceived boundaries. We must step from the island of 'me,' to discover it all.

There is a deep-seated authenticity, a congruence that arises from knowing ourselves at the emotional and spiritual levels of being. We no longer have to hide behind the constructed mask, for fear of what others will think of us. We recognize that the self is just an illusion, but that doesn't mean that it is inherently good or bad as a construct. Rather, our self-experience is just one shade, one reflection of light on the continuum of consciousness.

As we recognize that each of our created external constructs arise at first from within, from the conscious mind, we can then re-empower ourselves. We can once more recognize the power of our conscious focus in framing new realities, new potentialities. The experience of life itself arises from within. Life does not happen to us in a sort of chessboard game unfoldment, but rather, we are the invisible chess masters, observing and influencing the game, but never constrained to it alone. Our emotions and our thoughts do not just happen to us, even though most people have an automatic stream of emotions and thoughts that are triggered each second of their lives. In truth, at the consciousness level, we focus on the cultivation of particular mental and emotional patterns, we integrate and build particular realities, we consent to the construction of an individual self – but we were never that, or at least not just that.

Spiritual gurus who state "you are 'that'" refer to the ineffable conscious force, the indefinable, eternal essence that is consciousness itself. Yet, we take a small fragment, a miniscule representation and draw boundaries around ourselves, deciding that we are going to limit our self-consciousness in one fashion or another. But, even the limiting process comes from within. We are sovereign over our threshold of conscious experience.

To live life through the lens of the small self, whilst still having a strong connection to the cosmic mind, is perhaps the spiritual secret of life. It is through spontaneous transcendence experiences that people often first encounter the cosmic unlimited mind, but the truth is that each of us is capable of achieving union with this higher aspect of our consciousness.

During meditation, there is a certain moment that I have full and total control over the meditation practice, and the next moment it appears as though the meditation itself takes over and has control over me. The meditation draws me in, and the self becomes the follower rather than the leader. It is in moments such as these that I have found it's possible to connect with a direct conscious experience beneath the surface, beneath the individual 'I.' The construct is recognized for what it is, a temporal and limited means of encapsulating consciousness.

In these moments of transcendence, we do not become unconscious because our constructed sense of self is lost, but rather we become even more conscious, super-conscious, so to speak. Although the sense of the ego is no longer present, a prevailing connection with our soul aspect, the original Self remains. It is in these moments that we can become immersed, absorbed in life itself, without feeling a need to construct or conceptualize our experience. The experience for the sake of experience is then paramount. We feel for the sake of feeling, we connect for the sake of connecting, we share for the sake of sharing, rather than linking all of these experiences to the intricate expectations of a given construct.

Philosopher Heraclitus is known to have said that "one cannot step twice in the same river." And, indeed, conscious experience cannot be replicated. Each moment is unique. Each moment is a gift. And then, it is gone. But, so often we persist to emphatically capture the moment, to elongate it and to freeze it in frame. We instill the qualities we adore in our lovers and expect them never to change, accusing them of abandoning us if they dare to grow into a new person. We hold our idols to ideals based on their accomplishments which are now long gone. We hold God to a representation in scripture. But, in truth, no conscious experience can be held, for all conscious experiences transcend our intellectualization of them.

Each conscious moment is unique on no uncertain terms. It is rather the constructed self that would believe a moment can be repeated or somehow replicated, it is the illusion of sameness and difference that seems to persist when we live outside of the eternal present moment. From the intellectual mind's illusion, we convince ourselves that conscious experience can somehow be compared, conceptualized, differentiated. In fact, our experience of consciousness comes from engaging with the here-and-now, from opening our centers of intuition, of empathic connection; from learning the experiential value of love, of inner peace, of wisdom. These states must be experienced firsthand, there is no sense in attempting to capture them with the intellect.

All experiences that would seem to fit into a theory or a model are not true representations of their essential nature. Although in this lifetime we are bound to the material realm, this does not infer that we must lose our sense of self in it. It is possible to use our discourse, our language, and our art to express our conscious experiences, as long as we do not forget their original source and lose ourselves in the immutable structures we build. The temporal disguise we hide in is a mere shadow amid the wavering radiance of consciousness.

A deep gaze toward the sun falling behind the seascape, or the soft comforting words of someone close to us, or the interplay of light that paints a rainbow in front of us, are all experiences that draw our consciousness in, we cannot capture nor contain them, but we can fully experience them, merge with them, and feel them at the core of our being.

We have forgotten this art of experiencing and exploring consciousness in our world. The value of this deeper emotional-spiritual engagement has been lost to the revered virtues of reason. Although we were born as explorers, unbound and without border, we have become lesser forms of our now imperceptible light. It is thus our ultimate mission to broaden our conscious experience in this world, not to settle for a lesser shape of existence, no matter how vehemently others would attempt to dictate the terms of our tangible realities.

The conscious soul is in perpetual transcendence, it is transcendent by nature. But, the constructed self attempts to cling to the familiar and the definable. Thus, transcendental states create a temporal break in our sustained self-concept. Moments of transcendence wake us up. They remind us of our origins. They call us to engage with our conscious experience without boundary. They provide a new starting point from which to perceive life: A new canvas for exploration.

EXPLORATION: A NEW CANVAS

I commenced this book with the contention that consciousness is not some abstract idea found in philosophy or neuroscience, but rather that we can learn how to connect with and expand our conscious experience on a practical level. I've also aimed to illustrate how our consciousness has been sublimated and directed toward a construction of an individual 'self,' that neither represents nor contains our ultimate potential.

Thus, I've aimed to write this work not with the intention of providing clear answers, but rather with the aim of encouraging readers to explore their personal experience of self and consciousness. As such, I hope that you have expanded the boundaries of your conscious experience throughout this book, utilizing the practices and techniques here that aim to cultivate states of self-transcendence.

In this exploration, I've aimed to sum up some of the tasks introduced throughout the book, as well as encouraging readers to adopt a more intuitive connection with their emotional and spiritual centers. If this book has challenged your experience of self-consciousness, then it has accomplished its purpose. Thus, in this exploration, I would like for you to reflect on some of the main aspects of this book that you found challenged or enriched your life experience, if at all.

MISSION TASK 115: SOURCE OF MIND

Completion Goal:

Reflect on how (if at all) your self-experience has altered throughout this book. List up to five changes that have occurred which have influenced your understanding of consciousness and self.

MISSION TASK 116: ORIGIN OF POWER

Completion Goal:

Reflect on the following question: How does my sense of power and control within particular constructs contrast with the ultimate power of my conscious soul?

MISSION TASK 117: CONSCIOUSNESS LEVELS

In Spiral Dynamics theory, there is a notion that consciousness unfolds at a natural progressive pace. Therefore, when ideas and concepts from one country are impressed upon another country, the residents living there might be unable to understand or integrate them (for instance, imposing our school system on a country where ways of perceiving and integrating world experiences differ). Likewise, concepts from particular disciplines may not cross over to other disciplines well (for instance, a lawyer attempting to explain legal concepts to a doctor might struggle, and vice versa, as the discourses, as well as the consciousness levels, of each of these professions are too different).

Completion Goal:

Reflect on the unfoldment of human consciousness. Are certain people that you know more in-tune with their emotional and spiritual development? Do others operate from a more intellectual mode of processing the world?

Side Note: Perhaps our ultimate mission as human beings is to become conscious of the human experience, however this process of unfoldment is unique to each individual.

MISSION TASK 118: OUR CREATIVE INHERITANCE

Completion Goal:

Meditate on the barriers that exist within yourself that prevent a clear connection with your source of creative power. Note any intuitive impressions that you encounter, and consider re-practicing some of the mission tasks in Chapter Three and Chapter Four on cultivating imagination and raw states of experience.

MISSION TASK 119: REFLECTIONS

Completion Goal I:

Reflect on one subchapter or exploration in this book that you found most useful and develop your own creative approach to how you could incorporate the core ideas and techniques in that section to further your personal and spiritual development.

Completion Goal II:

Reflect on five individual mission goals or tasks that you found particularly interesting or useful in this book. How could you adapt or creatively improve upon these tasks to gain even more benefit from them?

Alexander De Foe

Completion Goal III:

Share your experiences with the mission tasks or goals that you decided to focus on above. You might like to do this via the direct website feedback form for this book, or via social media channels, to share and discuss your experiences with others.

MISSION TASK 120: BEGIN

Rather than developing a central theory throughout this book, I have aimed to cultivate a unique perspective in the reader. I have aimed to encourage conscious emotional and spiritual exploration as unique modes of experiencing life: A new set of approaches for engaging with our consciousness.

All paintings have a border. All artworks fade and whither in time. But consciousness is borderless light. It is boundless in expression that never fades. Thus, rather than remaining slaves to our once revered creations, it's important to once again recognize our potential to imagine and explore new realities, new experiences, and new potentials.

Completion Goal:

In each new endeavor that you undertake, engage your intention, and consider how you will cultivate your greater creative potential in life.

APPENDICES

APPENDIX A: DOUBLE STANDARD SKEPTICISM

I would like to draw your attention to one of the most important letters written in the previous decade. The letter was drafted by Etzel Cardeña, a professor of Psychology at Lund University in Sweden, and it was addressed to the highly-regarded scientific journal, 'Frontiers in Human Neuroscience.' Titled, 'A call for an open, informed study of all aspects of consciousness,' the short letter called scientists to consider all aspects of consciousness with a greater degree of seriousness. It was undersigned by dozens of distinguished scientists working on the broader aspects of human consciousness and exceptional human potential.

As part of the call for an open investigation into consciousness, Cardeña noted that more than 20 Nobel Prize winners and numerous eminent scientists have, throughout their careers, endorsed investigation into phenomena that we might call anomalous or paranormal. If we look to the historical documents, eminent scientists such as Nikola Tesla, William James, and Albert Einstein have all alluded to personal encounters with the mystical, spiritual, and transcendent dimensions of consciousness. Each of these brilliant minds also worked toward understanding how the transpersonal aspects of consciousness could be applied in our world. Tesla's famous quote "the day science begins to study non-physical phenomena, it will make more progress in one decade than in all the previous centuries of its existence" captures the critical importance of exploring conscious experience beyond our experience of the material world.

In our dominant materialistic paradigm, people tend to believe that the human mind is limited to the constraints of the physical environment, the brain, and the physical body. However, parapsychologists involved in researching psi have spent well over a century exploring an alternative hypothesis, that the mind in fact has the potential to influence and transcend matter. If this is true, then what limitations, if any, can be placed on the conscious, awakened mind?

The psi hypothesis proposes that telepathic communication between minds, clairvoyance, precognition, psychokinesis, absent healing, and other mind-over-matter phenomena are possible. Since the foundation of the 'Society for Psychical Research' in 1882, parapsychologists have demonstrated these super-human capabilities of the mind in countless rigorous laboratory experiments. Further, millions of people around the world report these exceptional potentials of consciousness. But, in the mainstream, we tend to ignore these accounts, and instead focus on reinforcing a limited, constructed idea of the self that is restricted to a temporal material existence.

These research studies often go discounted as the threat of any notion that suggests we are more than flesh and blood seems too dramatic for mainstream debate. There thus seems to be a double standard in both scientific and media representations of research into psi abilities – we refuse to examine them with seriousness, despite the growing evidence for the transcendent nature of consciousness.

In a book chapter, 'Is Anti-Science not-Science?,' researchers Trevor Pinch and Harry Collins postulated that scientific ideas should never prejudiced based solely on social ideology (see the book 'Counter-Movements in the Sciences' by Helga Nowotny and Hilary Rose). Pinch and Collins argued that although the quality of research conducted by a research team is subject to critique, the original thought and ideas must not be subject to prejudice on their own merit, until tested, no matter how outlandish or difficult to fathom an initial idea might be on first glance. However, this is often not the case in how other scientists perceive parapsychology (an area of investigation concerned with psi, or exceptional mind abilities), as research into exceptional mind potential is seldom given a chance from the outset.

This is quite interesting, as it is not the quality of research that tends to undermine parapsychology's voice in the conventional sciences (as a vast majority of research in the field of parapsychology meets the strict scientific standards required of any other sub-discipline of psychology), but rather parapsychology tends to be discriminated against because its predominant ideas are not compatible with prevalent theories in other disciplines. Thus, at the heart of the psi debate is not an issue of lacking evidence (which parapsychology has provided amply) or poor research methodologies (which are often as rigorous, if not more rigorous, than the methodologies used in other sciences), but rather an issue of incompatibility between psi theories and more widely accepted notions in mainstream science.

Parapsychology has, at times, been guilty of putting the carriage before the horse, depending on data and observation, and insufficiently developing sound theories to explain and contextualize positive psi findings more broadly. We have a broad range of data, and empirical accounts of mind-over-matter phenomena, but is this enough to meet the burden of science? In many ways, yes. But, in some ways, no.

The repeated observation and demonstration of certain phenomena represents just one aspect intrinsic to the scientific method, however empirical observations, without supporting theory, are not sufficient. This is the reason that approaches such as acupuncture and hypnotherapy are often not considered evidence-based therapies. It is not enough to show that a particular technique works, it must also be explained how it works.

Despite this, the high volume of public reports claiming experience with extra-sensory perception (ESP) and psi phenomena divide researchers, and force them to ask: Can all of these reports be accounted for by instances of fraud or by purely psychological explanations (such as hallucinations)? And, are genuine instances of psi in fact reported amongst at least some of these accounts? It is pre-emptive of scholars to discount all cases as fraud or hallucination, especially in light of recent evidence regarding the existence of psi phenomena.

In 2010, Lance Storm and his colleagues presented evidence of psi (based on meta-analyses across a broad number of studies) in the high-impact journal, Psychological Bulletin. Daryl Bem also recently conducted a group of experiments involving more than 1,000 participants which indicated strong evidence for precognitive ability demonstrated in laboratory conditions; the findings were published in the leading psychological journal, Personality and Social Psychology. Although other researchers have failed to replicate the positive psi findings, the methodological debate continues.

But, consider this. Methodological debates exist in many scientific fields, and just because scientists disagree about a particular group of results, this does not infer that the research is bad science. In fact, disagreement and debate is a critical part of scientific process. Hence, why is research into psi treated differently, then? There is a difference here between skepticism and intolerance in that regard. Likewise, there is a difference between critiquing research and dismissing it outright before even exploring it. The issue then is not that parapsychologists have lost the debate about these exceptional mind abilities, it is that there was no real debate to begin with, at least not one on a broader scientific scale. There is an excellent article by Nancy Zingrone which was published on the 'Skeptical Investigations' website titled 'Failing to Go the Distance' that canvasses this lack of scientific collaboration well.

Since the Age of Reason, which brought a reductionist approach to making sense of the world, we have been consumed with segmenting our understanding of reality into the smallest possible fragments of information – this can be observed in all of the scientific disciplines, such as physics, chemistry, or biology, for instance, in which processes are considered in isolation, rather than as part of an encompassing ubiquitous whole. Therefore, we have learned how to think about the world, and how to experience the world, at this micro-level. The emotional-spiritual modes of

293

experiencing life are hence often considered nonsensical and useless in our world, as these do not lead to a reductionist understanding.

However, when we approach certain scientific processes, social processes, and even human processes as part of a greater whole, new approaches for engaging with the world can be gleaned. For example, there are a number of alternative medical approaches that promote healing with more effective results than mainstream medicine offers, but these are often not based on reductionist approaches, and rather consider the human being as a whole person, encompassing their emotional and spiritual dimensions of health.

Likewise, it appears that psi phenomena works on a holistic, quantum level, and cannot be reduced to atoms, elements, or DNA like we have gone about doing in other scientific areas. There appear to be greater processes at work with psi; however, just because we cannot understand these processes within our modern materialistic framework, we should not have the hubris to rule them out of existence altogether.

It's important we consider our own biases, how our grounding in the world has been shaped via external influences, and how we take certain ideas for granted without questioning them. In this appendix, I'd like to consider how the mainstream media shapes people's reluctance about psi phenomena, and, I'd like to offer some considerations about the importance of examining consciousness from a more open-minded perspective, both in scientific and social forums.

The mainstream media is well-known for misinterpreting scientific research and shading it with their own biases and ideologies. This could not be truer when it comes to psi research. To illustrate this, let's consider a few examples: 1) The case of Susan Blackmore, 2) the case of National Geographic, and 3) the case of Rupert Sheldrake.

First of all, let's consider Susan Blackmore's work. Susan Blackmore was a prominent parapsychologist who later become an advocate for the skepticism movement. In fact, after more than 20 years of researching psi, Blackmore announced that throughout her research career conducting experiments into anomalous phenomena, none of her findings indicated the existence of psi. Blackmore even published an article on her website entitled 'Why I have given up,' claiming that no evidence for psi phenomena exists. Interestingly, in 1989, Rick Berger conducted a follow-up analysis of Blackmore's experiments and found a number of methodological flaws throughout Blackmore's studies into psi (Berger's analysis can be found in volume 89 of The Journal of the American Society for Psychical Research). More interesting is the fact that after correcting the methodological errors and replicating Blackmore's experiments, Berger found evidence of psi in Blackmore's data.

To date, skeptics tend to refer to Blackmore's work in support of the null hypothesis (that is, psi does not exist), without considering Berger's follow-up work. Blackmore's null findings fit the acceptable social and scientific paradigm, that psi could never exist. However, it is problematic to cite Blackmore's work as evidence for the null hypothesis without considering more recent evidence (such as Berger's research), and furthermore, whilst there are much broader studies available. If hard data is available, then this ought to trump expert opinion. Yet, skeptical researchers continue to use Blackmore's case as evidence that the existence of psi could never be possible.

Let's examine another example: The misrepresentation of Piers Howe's and Margaret E Webb's research on change perception that was published in the Public Library of Science (One), entitled 'Detecting Unidentified Changes.' These authors found that participants could identify a minor (almost undetectable to the human eye) change in visual stimuli, but were not able to localize the nature of the change; this suggests that unconscious processes had a role in participants recognizing slight changes in their visual perspective, without being able to stipulate the specific changes. Although these authors did not use the terms 'psi,' 'ESP,' 'sixth sense,' or related vernacular in the research, on January 21 (8 days after the study was published), National Geographic Daily News printed an article entitled 'ESP Is Put to the Test – Can You Foretell the Results? It's just hokum, say researchers, who offer a new experiment as proof.'

A barrage of other media outlets followed suit and published similar interpretations of the research within a week of the results being published (including The Guardian and the Huffington Post). The original data had no relation to psi research whatsoever, yet media outlets used the results to allegedly prove that there exists a lack of evidence for psi. None of the major media articles covering the research have since been redacted, despite their inaccurate representation of the research. Indeed, it appears most people don't give it a second thought and assume that the media knows what they are talking about in cases such as this; it's interesting to consider the proportion of the mainstream public who looked deeper and examined the source of the research, which, in this case, had nothing at all to do with ESP. A reluctance to fact-check and maintain an open mind on the part of the mainstream public means that media misinterpretations tend to shape mass perspectives on psi research.

A final example: The widespread public and academic opinion regarding Rupert Sheldrake's TED Talk as a 'dissent' against science. Rupert Sheldrake is a biologist with a distinguished career researching ESP and mind potential. Sheldrake's TED Talk, 'The Science Delusion,' was originally broadcast on February 13th, 2013 (it is now censored).

Now, before we get started, let's consider that TED Talks is a media platform which broadcasts a series of international conferences via a number of popular outlets (including YouTube). In his TED Talk, Sheldrake discussed some of the limitations in scientific discourse that prevent psi research from being considered in the mainstream. The program was later removed and censored from further media publication after a scientific panel deemed Sheldrake's work unscientific and not suitable for the public (note, this occurred about one month after the talk was broadcast and made accessible to the public via the TED platform).

It should be noted that within the previous decade, TED Talks has broadcast programs which have broadly spanned ideas from speakers such as Edward Snowden, to innovators such as Steve Jobs, for instance, thus I should emphasize here that TED is not a scientific discussion platform, it represents 'Ideas worth spreading,' which is TED's slogan. These 'ideas worth spreading' are often presented by inspirational and entertaining speakers, and are not limited to ideas in the domain of science.

Yet, the TED Talks Panel argued that Sheldrake's work misrepresented scientific principles and thus decided on censoring the program from the main TED Talks website. But, as several people have pointed out, the program was not removed due to poor methodological design or a lack of ethical practices in Sheldrake's research, but rather because Sheldrake's viewpoint challenged the current scientific paradigm, as Sheldrake is a proponent of psi phenomena. The official panel notes (explaining their reasoning for censoring the talk) stipulated that the program did not meet the appropriate standard for scientific discussion. However, no documentation was offered regarding particular methodological concerns that the panel had, despite Sheldrake having published his research in numerous refereed scientific journals (in addition to presenting sound reasoning during the program). The events surrounding the Sheldrake talk provide us with an example in which ideas are discriminated against based on their content, rather than on the standard of scientific investigation.

These three examples are interesting to consider in terms of how our social perceptions shape and limit our understanding of our greater mind potential. I have also experienced some of the above attitudes firsthand in the interviews and discussions that I have had about psi in the public sphere. Although some people are open-minded, a number of mainstream media outlets seem to be quite ignorant about the entire debate altogether. This is problematic, as the mainstream media informs most people's attitudes in our world, and we leave it up to these sources to decide what is accurate, what is credible, and what is true (of course, except for those of us who think critically about these topics).

Those readers who have a particular interest in this field might have found the same experiences in their personal interactions. In the mainstream, people tend to equate these psi abilities with mediaeval ideas and rituals, most seem to have little tolerance to even consider that their mind could in fact be more powerful than their three-pound brain. This is understandable, as it requires them to let go of a number of cultural presumptions, as well as their dependence on the external structures they have invested so much into.

Bloggers who aim to explain this resistance to investigating psi, such as Craig Weiler, believe that these limited perspectives are tantamount to bigotry, however it appears that this is more a case of ignorance and 'psi denialism' in the public – an attitude of 'I don't believe it, so I won't bother looking into it.' This is the double standard skepticism of individuals who weigh evidence based on the scale of popularity, rather than investigating our world at a deeper level. The idea of psi is thus almost taboo in most Western cultures; even with the most rigorous research and testing, results are ignored, suppressed, and misinterpreted in the mainstream.

However, I will admit that although social factors construct psi research in a negative light, there are still technical (scientific) issues to work through. For example, earlier on I stated that a good scientific model is lacking to explain psi accounts and experiences of exceptional human abilities. Often, psi researchers do not doubt the existence of these mind-over-matter phenomena, however this does not necessarily mean that it is possible to easily and scientifically explain the presence of psi. This is perhaps the major scientific dilemma that parapsychology faces as a scientific field.

Some of the research areas in parapsychology that were prevalent in the past have now been explained by more traditional science and have been accepted as truth. For example, lucid dreaming and out-of-body experiences (OBEs) are topics that are now taught in most psychological science programs at major universities. In spite of this, many other psi abilities (such as telepathic communication and mind-over-matter capabilities) cannot be explained within the boundaries of mainstream science (at least, not presently).

Therefore, it is important that we continue asking questions and keep exploring, rather than giving up. I have included this appendix here so that readers can consider some of the benefits of delving deeper into these controversial topics. More importantly, I believe it is worth exploring, intuitively, the broader potential of these encompassing mind states. I believe it is important is to ask the difficult questions about our world, the final frontiers we've yet to fathom.

Hence, although it is important to inform people's attitudes from a scientific standpoint, it is also vital to recognize consciousness (rather than the constructed self) as the driver of all human experience. And, that experience is broad. It encompasses our emotional and spiritual dimensions of being, not just the rational mind. The psi effects that we observe could indeed arise within a certain field of consciousness that cannot be grasped nor contained in scientific procedures (or at least, not by our present day procedures).

Let's consider this a bit further. In this book I have suggested that all constructs arise from a process of conscious creation first and foremost. This would suggest that even the scientific method, as a constructed method of scientific investigation, arose from direct conscious experience. Although many people in our world believe that one day everything we experience will be explained by science, I am not comfortable with this position, in light of the experiences that I have shared throughout this book. How can everything be explained by a tool that we ourselves have devised? It seems that we are chasing our tails somewhat, aiming to create a model that would explain the conscious beings that have, in fact, created the model.

In light of this, I believe that we need a different approach here altogether, rather than a purely scientific method of investigating consciousness and mind potential. Indeed, consciousness must be experienced firsthand, it must be felt, connected with, shared, and expanded. There are vast, countless realms of consciousness to explore, but perhaps we should also look outside of reductionist intellectual science, and to draw upon all of our experiences and modes of understanding (intellectual, emotional, and spiritual) in this pursuit.

As with all of the sections and chapters in this book, I have aimed to stir particular questions and curiosities within readers, rather than claiming to have the answers about these topics. I believe we have a long way to go before we even touch the surface of exploring the final frontier: Consciousness. First, we must recognize that we are not just the constructed self, that the frontiers of the mind are much vaster than our seeming conceptions of them. Thus, I encourage you to begin asking some of the critical questions about the nature of consciousness and mind, not just from an intellectual frame, but also from the point of view of emotional and spiritual exploration, of deeper inner engagement and perception (I have also uploaded this appendix, as well as the appendices that follow, publically on my website, and I encourage you to share these ideas with others to continue this exploration).

APPENDIX B: THE TRANSPERSONAL DREAM

The process of conscious awakening begins when we recognize that the external world acts as a mirror for our internal experience. Unless we delve deeper into our conscious experience, we project forth our assumptions and expectations onto the outer canvas. We perceive our unconscious inhibitions, the parts of ourselves that we refuse to face, in the external world. To break free through this wall of perception is to engage our consciousness, to connect with life in the here-and-now and to understand ourselves at a deeper level. Rather than living through the mirror of the self, we must step outside of ourselves and discover what lies on the other side.

A number of books dealing with the topics of personal and spiritual development have misinterpreted this simple truth. These works suggest that we must abolish the constructed ego and abstain from indulging in it. But, there are few works that explore the other aspect of this process. What comes next, after we recognize the constructed self for what it is and transcend its limitations?

There is a certain emptiness, a meaningless world among us that becomes apparent once we question and critique all of the projections that we put forth. As we surrender all social constructs, then what remains? This book aimed to cultivate an interest in this question from readers. In a number of spiritual and religious groups, there is a lack of dreaming, a lack of vision toward a transpersonal self, and too much time spent on battling with the ego and attempting to shape ourselves to some impossible virtue or ideal. Instead of battling with ourselves, it's more important to pursue a broader exploration of consciousness, to cultivate deeper emotional and spiritual states.

Instead of just battling the self, aiming to suppress its illusions, we ought to strive for something greater – for experiences that touch our soul and connect us with our true center of being – our inner heart. Although when I write about the inner heart, and connecting with our experiences at the heart-level, I am referring to the conscious heart, not the physical heart. That being said, we might note that neuroscientists have found that the physical heart does in fact have an open line of communication with the brain. Professor Mohamed Salem's work, entitled 'The Heart, Mind and Spirit' (published at The Royal College of Psychiatrists website), for instance, presented a good summary of noteworthy findings relevant here, suggesting that "… following several years of research, it was observed that, the heart communicates with the brain in ways that significantly affect how we perceive and react to the world."

Further, Salem noted that the heart is capable of "… sending meaningful messages to the brain that it not only understood, but also obeyed." There is something worthwhile to be gained from these research findings. However, as I am not a neurologist, and my expertise in this research area is limited, I won't remark on this too much, instead I'll focus on the spiritual, or inner, heart. I believe that the process of activating the connection with our hearts holds the secret to discovering our true power within. As we connect to our consciousness in this most intimate manner, we recognize that the core of our being is not just made up of the intellect, but something far greater.

Gregg Braden suggested that the magnetic field of the heart is about 5,000 stronger than that of the brain. This is not surprising, as that which we feel in our hearts can be much more powerful than particular thoughts or beliefs that we have about the world. Barbara Brennan, in her book 'Hands of Light' posited that the boundaries of the human energy field, or aura, extend much further than the physical body and can even encompass the space several meters outside of one's physical body. Both Braden and Brennan paint a miraculous portrait of the power of the human heart. Their vision embodies the true power of connecting with one's sacred inner experience, one's inner heart. It is the heart's power that infuses new realities with emotion, with feeling, and with 'realness.'

The heartfelt experience transcends the intellectualized experience. In dream realms, for example, a strong emotional connection or experience can transform entire realities, as the canvas of our dream world becomes imbued with this emotional-spiritual connection. This process also occurs in waking life, but we are less aware of it. It is difficult to engage with our emotional and spiritual nature if we live in a closed constructed mind. Instead, we are called to engage with our consciousness – to discover our center of self and live from it.

However, such a broad number of people still anchor themselves in their contrived constructs, rather than finding an authentic emotional and spiritual center within. This is perhaps the reason that individuals who embark on an intensive spiritual pilgrimage often find themselves out of balance for a time; in questioning their constructed self, they lose themselves for a moment. There is a periodic step between losing ourselves and finding our true selves once more.

Recall that throughout this book I asked the question 'who are you?' on multiple occasions. The question now becomes one of whether we choose to anchor ourselves in temporal constructs, or in a deeper Self-experience. In that sense, it is paramount we discover our transpersonal nature, that we awaken to the broader self.

Although most personal development books aim to help people achieve more happiness and more success in life, in this book I have aimed to illustrate that these authentic experiences cannot arise within the boundaries of our constructs – these experiences must be felt with the heart. Further, I do not believe that the pursuit of personal development should be individualistic, but rather that we ought to encourage each other toward open emotional and spiritual exploration. It is here that we can dream and create a new world in which authentic self-expression is valued to a higher degree than is material wealth, social status, or the thousands of other superficial constructs that we hide ourselves in.

The transpersonal dream is a vision of a new threshold of conscious experience, a constant strive toward self-actualizing and deepening our understanding of what it means to be alive and conscious. In the transpersonal dream, each being in our world would feel safe enough to express their emotional and spiritual truth without a need to blanket their experiences in contrived constructs of cultural routines, politics, religions, or fixed affiliations. There is something magical and transformative about connecting with our hearts and expressing our truth to others in this manner. It wakes us up, it engages us in the eternal present, and reconnect us with our true being.

It is in these experiences that boundaries between people are traversed. To find ourselves we must first step outside of ourselves, to recognize our nature as transcendent conscious beings. From this experience, we no longer consider consciousness as a mere faculty of the brain. Rather, we 'are' consciousness. From a state of consciousness engagement, we engage with the depth of liveliness of our emotional-spiritual experience.

It is in these states of conscious engagement that we are capable of traversing impossible limitations and rediscovering limitless worlds. It is here that we encounter the true meaning of spiritual awakening and self-understanding. It is in these self-transcendent states that the true meaning of flow, mindfulness, and meditation becomes known, as these become tools for deepening our essential experience. Then, rather than looking to teachings or books, we become the guides of our own internal experience and unfoldment – the inner realms, the final frontiers of exploration, at our fingertips.

APPENDIX C: TOOLKIT

HIERARCHICAL MODEL OF PRINCIPLES

Initial idea	Intellectual response (external associations)	Heart response (internal meaning)	Personal core principle	Rank

Note: A PDF version of this book is available at http://alexdefoe.com/. This handout and other pages can be printed from the PDF version. These handouts are free to use and distribute, with no restrictions as long as the source is acknowledged.

HIERARCHICAL MODEL OF PRINCIPLES SAMPLE

Initial idea	Intellectual response (external associations)	Heart response (internal meaning)	Personal core principle	Rank
I cannot make mistakes in life.	Striving to do one's best, remembering the consequences of failing	Knowing that things are OK, trust	Faith in myself	1
I need a lot of money in order to be happy.	Expensive cars, holidays, houses	Prosperity, abundance, feeling secure	A sense of fulfilment	3
My children have to listen to me.	Discipline is important	Connection with children	Mutual understanding	5
My boss has to like me.	Having to work hard, making a good impression	Respect, acknowledgment, a deeper sense of acceptance	Core confidence in myself and my abilities	2
I want a relationship that is fun.	Sex, partying, expensive vacations	Freedom, fun, being spontaneous	Expression of a deeper connection	4
...				
...				
...				
...				
...				

Note: The above are intended as examples and potential interpretations, there is no single correct or incorrect approach for completing this worksheet.

BELIEF VS EXPERIENCE

Beliefs	Knowledge
Beliefs that I hold about the world, myself, and others; personal beliefs rather than general knowledge.	Knowledge that I know to be accurate about the world, myself, or other people.
Truths	**Direct Experiences**
That which I know to be 100% true for certain without a shred of doubt.	That which I have experienced and felt to be true on a personal and direct level (beliefs, knowledge, and truth validated by direct personal experience).

BELIEF VS EXPERIENCE SAMPLE

Beliefs	Knowledge
Being tall is an attractive quality.	The world is round.
It is difficult to become successful in life.	There are 24 hours in a day.
I must be a good Christian to get into heaven.	The letter 'k' in the word 'knowledge' is silent.
Truths	**Direct Experiences**
1 + 1 = 2	True love is real.
The laws of logical deduction are universal.	God exists.
All matter is made up of atoms.	Most people have good intentions.

Note: The above are intended as examples and potential interpretations, there is no single correct or incorrect approach for completing this worksheet.

LIFE SCRIBING

1. Jot down an affirmation, or goal-statement.

2. Pick a few core principle words that relate to this statement (i.e., what is the greater purpose here? For example: truth, freedom, love, happiness etc.).

3. Create a miracle image that represents the goal-state when achieved and allows the affirmation to become realized. Notice which emotions and feelings arise during this process.

4. Re-write the original statement and ensure that it is now present-focused and positive-focused. Remove all negative or limiting conditional words (such as never, not, can't, if, when etc.). Also ensure to personalize and internalize the affirmation instead of making it about others. Incorporate your core principle words where possible.

LIFE SCRIBING SAMPLE

1. Jot down an affirmation, or goal-statement.

   I want others to stop picking on me and to stop putting me down.

2. Pick a few core principle words that relate to this statement (i.e., what is the greater purpose here? For example: truth, freedom, love, happiness etc.).

   Acceptance, tolerance, compassion, peace.

3. Create a miracle image that represents the goal-state when achieved and allows the affirmation to become realized. Notice which emotions and feelings arise during this process.

   How do I see myself when I have achieved the goal state? I walk into my workplace in the morning and find that everyone has a friendly and inviting demeanor about them. I find that it is easy to speak with them and I find that they are all accepting of me. This makes me feel at ease, secure and comfortable. *(Continue the process, imagining in detail what it would be like throughout the day, interacting with others and finding that instead of them putting you down, they accept you and enjoy connecting with you.)*

4. Re-write the original statement and ensure that it is now present-focused and positive-focused. Remove all negative or limiting conditional words (such as never, not, can't, if, when etc.). Also ensure to personalize and internalize the affirmation instead of making it about others. Incorporate your core principle words where possible.

   I allow myself to open to acceptance and love whenever I interact with others and whenever I am in my own presence alone.

The new statement is present-focused, focused toward a positive outcome rather than being about avoiding a negative outcome, incorporates core principle words and not conditioned on the actions of others.

Note: The above are intended as examples and potential interpretations, there is no single correct or incorrect approach for completing this worksheet.

EMPOWEREMENT SCALE

⟶

Disempowered   Empowered

EMPOWEREMENT SCALE SAMPLE

———————————————————————————————————→

Disempowered   Empowered

External   Internal

Reactive   Proactive

Reasons   Results

What can others do?   What can I do?

Failures   Opportunities for improvement

EMPOWEREMENT SCALE EXAMPLES

→

Disempowered   Empowered

Police, authorities, and rule makers must be   I feel safe within.
maximized to make me feel secure at home.

The economy is bad, that's the real reason I   How can I creatively make more money?
am not making much money.

If I buy these new shoes I will feel much   I am confident with who I am.
more confident.

I am a good person because I follow my   I am a good person because I live congruently.
religion.

My IQ test score is higher than yours! Hah!   Intelligence can be learned.

Note: The above are intended as examples and potential interpretations, there is no single correct or incorrect approach for completing this worksheet.

OVERLAPPED CONSCIOUSNESS I

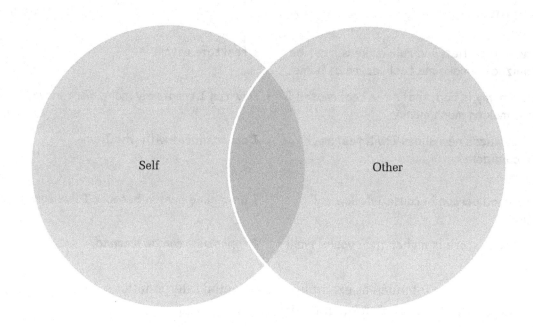

OVERLAPPED CONSCIOUSNESS II

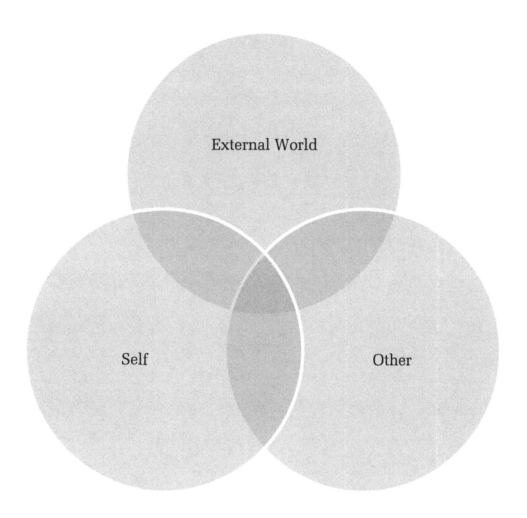

Alexander De Foe

FOCAL POINT

FOCAL POINT

APPENDIX D: NOTES

1) Russ Harris offers a generous amount of free worksheets and techniques for utilizing ACT to de-fuse from our mental commentaries. These exercises bring us into the present moment in order to consciously engage with life as-it-is, rather than fusing with our strict filters and limited perceptions of the world. You can find these resources under the 'Free Resources' section at Harris' website: http://actmindfully.com.au.

2) The Lucidity Institute website (http:// lucidity.com/) features several useful articles and tutorials on learning how to lucid dream. You can utilize these techniques in order to delve deeper into the dream realms and to recognize that our dream experience can contain much insight and wisdom.

3) Material from Hillary Raimo, Thomas Murasso, and other authors have I interviewed which are referred to throughout this book can be accessed via the archives at http://alexdefoe.com/. The entire collection of interviews are available for listening online.

4) Charlie Morley presented on Ted Talks in 2011 to discuss the topic 'Lucid Dreaming, Embracing Nightmares.' Charlie's brilliant talk highlighted the nature of emotional and spiritual truth. Often, in dream states we can perceive a big frightening monster that seems as real as real can be, yet when we engage with these negative images on an emotional level, the images transform and show their true face. Readers might at first note that this is just applicable in the dream realm, but, in fact, the closer we look, the more evident this process becomes even in waking life.

5) I'm not a big fan of personality tests, as people too often assume that their personality is immutable, and identify with the results of a certain test as their 'true self.' These tests cannot highlight the true self. These offer a mere glimpse into how we construct our personality-level expression in life. Thus, for the purposes of this exercise, I have encouraged readers to take a few personality quizzes in order to attempt breaking through their predefined personality characteristics to experience a broader self-potential. However, first, prior to doing this, it can be a good idea to evaluate which personality characteristics are most pronounced at the constructed-self level. You can do this by taking a number of free quizzes online such as the 'Myers Briggs Type Indicator' or the 'Five Factor Model' tests.

6) You can access all of the interviews that I have conducted with Chris and Sheree Geo on the 'Truth Frequency Radio' website at http://truthfrequencyradio.com.

7) Paul McKenna's hypnotic audio discs demonstrate a number of NLP and hypnosis techniques such as submodalities. The CDs are not training materials as such, but they offer a good experience of what it's like to be in hypnosis, you will be able to get an idea of some of the language patterns I've discussed here and how language has a powerful impact on conscious experience. Using language in unique ways can help us see that our words do not refer to fixed constructs in the outer world, but rather tangential ideas about our subjective experience of the world. See http://paulmckenna.com/ to order these CDs. You might like to search for a printable list of hypnotic language patterns and see if you can notice them during the CD session (as a fun experiment). Other CDs such as those by Steve G Jones or Anthony Robbins are also good, but I've found McKenna uses the biggest range of language patterns in a single session, and he makes their use quite explicit for those who are new to hypnotic scripts.

8) In the modern world we often value the surface-level expression while negating the emotion that drives the content. Yet, there is a vast emotional interplay that often determines the outcomes of relationship, business, and overall life decisions to a great degree. It's valuable to become acquainted with some of these consciousness dynamics at the emotional level and just how much these influence life events. A good introduction to this topic can be found in transactional analysis theory. For readers who are interested in learning more, a good starting book is Eric Berne's 'Games People Play: The Psychology of Human Relationships.'

9) See Franz Bardon's work 'Initiation into Hermetics' (2013, Merkur Publishing).

10) See Melita Giummarra's work at Monash University. Giummarra reported that those empathic to other people's pain tend to experience "a blurring of the boundary between self and other, with heightened empathy, acquired somatic contagion involves reduced empathic concern for others, but increased personal distress."

11) Jill Bolte Taylor's TED Talk, 'My stroke of insight,' was broadcast in 2008, and her book of the same title was published in 2009 (Plume) – in both, Taylor discusses her experience in depth.

12) Neil Kramer's work, 'The Unfoldment,' (2012, New Page Books) is well worth reading.

13) In power dynamics, an entire group of people's reality can be overwhelmed by the notion that there is a supreme godlike leader whose power is absolute and unquestionable. In ancient times, gods were thought to control forces such as lightening and major weather events. Yet, in modern times, we believe that political leaders have supreme power over our reality-experience. This shaping of power occurs as we project our own ultimate power onto an external force (whether an imaginary god, or a real person such as Hitler or Stalin, whose power is sustained through our mutual acquiescence).

14) Parapsychologists who have documented psi abilities such as telepathic communication or being able to move a physical object with one's mind power, have enlisted their participants in rigorous testing which was conducted by qualified skeptics. Interestingly, a well-known phenomenon often occurs in these cases, in which the psi agent's abilities seem to mysteriously disappear. Skeptics often use this argument to discount psi-claims, suggesting that it's 'convenient' that psi abilities only seem to work outside of rigorous testing conditions. I believe there's more to this, however, as skeptics create their own 'skeptical relational field,' just as psi proponents tend to share a collective 'psi relational field' in which these abilities become possible. J. E. Kennedy's paper 'Why is Psi so Elusive?' (Published in volume 65 of the Journal of Parapsychology in 2001) points out that just because psi phenomena might not conform to standard scientific testing protocol, this does not discount its existence.

15) Differing levels of consciousness based on cultural and social factors are explored in more depth on Rich Jones' radio show 'Thinking with Somebody Else's Head' at http://somebodyelseshead.blogspot.com.au/.

16) Some accessible techniques on mental projection and phasing can be found in a series of concise discussion forum posts by author Frank Keppel, at https://dl.dropboxusercontent.com/u/39504726/FranksPosts.pdf.

17) In 2008, a YouTube video was broadcast with a proposition as to what would happen if we asked the miracle question on a global scale. Consider the possibilities. 'What would the world look like if a miracle occurred tomorrow and a perfect world was to be seen right before us? What would people be doing? What would life feel like?' I applaud the video author for their creative approach here. It is only when we begin thinking in such terms that we recognize the true power our imagination holds to create either the darkest dystopia or the ultimate utopia here on earth. Refer to the video here: http://youtube.com/watch?v=tz4-Dj6sguw.

18) It is abundantly clear, to anyone who has spent even a few hours researching drug legalization, that the perceived benefits of criminalization are almost never based on scientific and medical evidence, and almost always based on political ideology. Professor David Nutt's work toward legalizing psilocybin mushrooms for the treatment of mental health issues such as depression, is one excellent example of this. Substances such as psilocybin and LSD have been widely reported to treat a number of 'mind' disorders (this should come as no surprise, as our minds are so overstimulated, that psychedelics allow us to slow down and cultivate the dreaming, soul-element of ourselves; to reconnect with the deeper realms of our consciousness). Yet, deep political propaganda campaigns have caused these so-called 'drugs' to be made illegal in most parts of the world.

19) Neil Slade's basic technique for 'tickling the amygdala' can be found at his website: http://neilslade.com/.

20) Image streaming is a technique to cultivate imagery from an unconscious and super-conscious mind connection. By closing your eyes and practicing image streaming, it is possible to connect with various impressions, images, and streams of information from the broader mind. There are plenty of resources and articles available on the world-wide-web that canvas this technique in depth.